John D. Balls • A. Douglas Eury
Jane C. King

Rethink, Rebuild, Rebound:

A Framework for Shared Responsibility and Accountability in Education

Second Edition

Cover Art: Courtesy of Photodisc/Getty Images

Copyright © 2011 by Pearson Learning Solutions
All rights reserved.

Permission in writing must be obtained from the publisher before any part of this work may be reproduced or transmitted in any form or by any means, electronic or mechanical, including photocopying and recording, or by any information storage or retrieval system.

All trademarks, service marks, registered trademarks, and registered service marks are the property of their respective owners and are used herein for identification purposes only.

Pearson Learning Solutions, 501 Boylston Street, Suite 900,
Boston, MA 02116
A Pearson Education Company
www.pearsoned.com

Printed in the United States of America

2 3 4 5 6 7 8 9 10 V202 16 15 14 13 12

000200010271266309

MT

ISBN 10: 1-256-41556-1
ISBN 13: 978-1-256-41556-5

Table of Contents

Acknowledgments	v
Foreword	vii
Prologue	xii
Introduction	xiii
Section I: Finding and (Re) Igniting Passion/ Disposition	**1**
Chapter 1: Passion for Learning	3
Chapter 2: Understanding Teacher Education "Dispositions"	13
Section II: Changing Learning Cultures with Value-Added Experiences	**21**
Chapter 3: Relationships Between Learning Cultures and Outcomes	23
Chapter 4: Learning Cultures	37
Chapter 5: Teacher Efficacy	43
Chapter 6: Empowerment through Organizational Structures	53
Chapter 7: Professional Learning	59
Chapter 8: Learning Communities as Professional Experience	73
Chapter 9: Dispositions and Passion to Perform	79
Chapter 10: Leadership Training and Assessment	85
Chapter 11: Value-Added Theory	97
Chapter 12: Personal Assessment	101
Chapter 13: Sustainability	113

Section III: 21st Century Skills — 119

Chapter 14: Who Are the Teachers in the 21st Century? — 121

Chapter 15: Who Are the 21st Century Learners and What is the Teaching-Learning Environment? — 135

Chapter 16: Critical Attributes of 21st Century Schools Curriculum and Instruction — 147

Chapter 17: How Do We Teach? — 161

Chapter 18: Are Students Learning? — 173

Chapter 19: How Do We Improve? — 181

Section IV: Successful School Models — 193

Chapter 20: The Challenges — 195

Chapter 21: Responses/Actions Taken — 209

Chapter 22: Results/Impact of Initiatives — 217

Chapter 23: Common Denominators among Successful Schools — 223

Chapter 24: Keys to Success — 229

Chapter 25: Next Steps/Recommendations (Short Term) — 239

Chapter 26: Next Steps/Recommendations (Longer Term) — 249

Epilogue — 269

Endnotes — 271

Index — 289

Acknowledgments

Without the support of many people from various backgrounds who have dedicated their lives to education this book would not have made it to press. The enthusiasm and commitment to purpose of all those who contributed during the research phase of the book was incredible. We are grateful to the many contributors for their time and insights in helping to make this book relevant to the critical national dialogue on education reform. We thank them all for their encouragement and invaluable assistance.

We especially want to thank several people who offered their assistance and support to make this book a reality. First and foremost, we want to thank our spouses, Greta, Janet, and Jerry who picked up the slack on the home front when we were researching and writing the book. Their support and countless words of encouragement were instrumental in making this book a reality.

A special thank you to the excellent faculty at Stanly Early College in Albemarle, North Carolina who have demonstrated that a passion for excellence, a willingness to take risks and a commitment to continuous improvement leads to academic excellence by the students they so ably educate. They serve as an inspiration for all of us.

We want to recognize the North Carolina New Schools Project (NSP) for the pioneering work they have done in education reform. As authors we have benefited from the leadership, guidance and "can do" spirit exhibited by the NSP professionals.

We are grateful for all the contributions and feedback we received from the graduate level students at Gardner-Webb University most especially the following doctoral students; Bethany Bevins, Susan Borgman, Amanda Bridges, Jennifer Condrey, Karen Henderson, Susan Miles, Daniel Wydo, Donna Howell, Aaron Slutsky, Heather Hartsell, Cristi Bostic, Scott Bowens, Lorinda Brusie, Quinetta Hall, Andrew Hooker, Tanya Hudson, Jessica Mellon, Jessica Stout, Timothy Ward, Rosanna Whisnant, La'Ronda Whiteside and Rebecca Wilson. Their insight and reflections on their experiences in education were most helpful.

Finally, we owe a debt of gratitude to the "can do" team at Pearson who demonstrated time and again their commitment to excellence and customer satisfaction. We want to thank Michlene Daoud Healy, Bill Clements and Meg Tiedemann for their patience, responsiveness and their overall outstanding support.

Foreword

There is no question that the perception of the quality of education in the United States is a troubled one, where voices from across the political and economic spectrum seem united in their concern for what they think is a lack of accountability for the educational outcomes the country so desperately needs in troubled times. The specter of disappointing achievement comparisons with other developed countries dogs those of us in the business of preparing those who will teach and lead the children of the 21st Century. Aren't you pretty sick and tired of hearing about how good Finland is compared to us, or how we're losing out to educational systems in India, China, Japan, South Korea, and Singapore? I know I am. We are further beset by reports about declining SAT scores, as well as about widespread failure to meet the AYP standards articulated in the No Child Left Behind legislation. Critics question the quality and ability of the nation's teachers, principals, superintendents, and others deeply involved in the educational enterprise. That there are many valid questions regarding the bases of these reports seems to only have merit within the educational enterprise; the critics seem not to care much about questions of research methodology, assumptions, or alternative conclusions. However good we in the enterprise might think we are, or how much alternative information we provide, those who shape and make educational policy persist in their declining opinion of the quality of "our" work.

What John Balls, Doug Eury, and Jane King offer us, ALL of us, is a clearheaded and pragmatic set of thoughts and practices to address the very criticisms that seem to bombard us. In this second edition of their book, Rethink,

Rebuild, and Rebound: A Framework for Shared Responsibility and Accountability in Education, what the authors provide is a well-researched and down-to-earth way of understanding and grasping the nexus of public concerns so that we can make the tweaks, adjustments and even systemic changes that will help bring respect and respectability back to the educational enterprise that is the single most important factor in differentiating the quality of life within the United States as well as the rest of the world. What they give us in this framework is a cogent and articulate process for sustainable change. I particularly liked their foundational premise of the importance of passion in a framework for accepting greater responsibility and accountability for outcomes. While there are certainly strategies and techniques for managing change and increasing accountability, to be successful, people who are to be influenced by change have to possess a set of beliefs that the change is important and that they will commit to it. Managing technique is easy when compared to winning hearts and minds. This book makes a strong case for understanding the importance of passion in building followership.

The authors also establish an additional foundational support by focusing their thinking on increasing responsibility and a sense of personal, professional, and organizational accountability. There cannot be any doubt that creating and communicating a greater sense of accountability and greater attention to achieving the outcomes schools need to achieve is a fundamental change to turn critics of education into advocates for education. However flawed and inappropriate we in the educational establishment might regard the application of business thinking to education, the truth is that business operates in an outcomes-based environment, where failure to meet performance targets and/or expectations can have significant consequences to their continued existence. This sense of accountability (or lack thereof) is the basis for contemporary political movements (e.g. Tea Party; Wall Street demonstrators, etc.), perceptions of effectiveness (e.g., approval ratings of political leaders), and even goes a long way to explaining what has transpired in a number of countries in the Middle East. In education, our failure to accept responsibility for NOT closing achievement gaps, reducing drop-outs, or increasing graduation rates is cut from the same cloth of expectation for needed performance outcomes. In many states, accountability frameworks will be changed, guided by Common Core Standards promulgated by the National Governors' Association (NGA) and the Council of Chief State School Officers (CCSSO). The framework presented in this book is spot on in helping educational organizations make these transitions in sustainable ways.

I was quite taken by the substantial attention the authors paid to embedding their thinking in 21st Century terms. What they teach us about change, accountability, and particularly rebounding is that we have to think about what we are doing, not just for the second decade of the 21st Century, but for the last half of the 21st Century. The high school class of 2012 will reach their 40th birthday by 2034, a time when most of us made major changes in our family structures, career paths, and life styles. Those entering Kindergarten this coming fall of 2012 will reach their 40th birthday in 2057. These are the educators, public servants, business leaders, lawyers, physicians and other health professionals, artists, professional athletes, and public safety officers who will shape the remainder of the 21st Century and whose children will inherit the 22nd Century. We in education have a responsibility to think in exactly those terms, instead of allowing our thinking to be a captive of short term thinking such as annual test score reports.

Almost all who become members of those professions, as well as the countless millions who will serve and support the infrastructure of our country and society, will find their life and work success emerging from the quality of our teaching and their learning.

There is a feature in this book I found particularly appealing. After each chapter, the authors have provided what they call "Takeaways." These takeaways are lists or sets of concepts, ideas, or especially provocations intended to be a chapter summary (perhaps), a discussion guide (probably), or the author's thinly veiled effort to promote critical thinking, which is, after all, a 21st Century skill. For example, at the end of a chapter entitled "Who Are the Teachers in the 21st Century?" the authors pose this statement in the takeaway for this chapter: "Classrooms will no longer be a place of four walls and a ceiling and floor. Classrooms will be international, online and organized in new ways of learning for students and teachers (#3, p. 134)." What a rich classroom conversation that could create with a knowledgeable and skillful facilitator. The book is filled with these kinds of value-added learning opportunities.

This book has power; it exudes pragmatism; it is both research-based and grounded in articulating best practices. The authors have captured a most elusive topic and given it both coherence and direction. One important *caveat*, if I may. Doing what the authors advocate you do will require courage and lots of it. This level of change is certainly not for the faint hearted. To any teacher educator preparing instructional plans for teacher wannabees, I would recommend using this book for provocative ideas about the teacher's role and responsibilities for 21st Century learning. For those responsible for professional learning in schools and school districts, I would recommend using this book for faculty study groups followed by shared conversations. For any in the educational enterprise, I would recommend a thorough reading to help re-discover why they came into the educational enterprise in the first place.

Respectfully,

Kenneth D. Jenkins, Ed. D
Professor of Educational Leadership (ret.)
Appalachian State University
Former Executive Director of North Carolina Principal Executive Program

Prologue

It has been said that education is simply the soul of a society as it passes from one generation to another. Stated another way, education has often been referred to as the "seed corn" for a society. Planted and nurtured properly, it will reap benefits in the form of nourishing the intellect. Furthermore, it is the only way to break the vicious cycle of dreadful poverty. The United States has been both the world leader and the beacon for innovation since the early 1900's. U.S. based businesses have led the world in patents and inventions that have significantly changed our way of life. From life saving medicines to information at your finger tips this country has been the envy of the world. Our colleges and universities are top notch. Students from all over the world seek to gain admission into these 1st rate institutions. As a country, we have set our sights on bold and audacious goals (for example, landing a person on the moon) despite the risks involved and have succeeded. With that history, no challenge is insurmountable for us and there is no more important one than re-establishing our K-12 education system as the best in the world. We owe it to our children and all generations to come. Now is the time for action.

We, as authors, have had the distinct privilege to serve as educators and as administrators focused on creating a learning environment for our students to excel. The culmination of our diverse backgrounds, our educational experiences and our passion to enhance the educational experience for students is embedded in this book. We hope it will stimulate discussion and debate, challenge the status quo and inspire the reader, in their own way, to promote change in pursuit of reinventing K-12 education in this great country.

Introduction

"We cannot solve our problems with the same thinking we used when we created them."
----Albert Einstein

"The definition of insanity is doing the same thing over and over again and expecting different results."
----Albert Einstein

Much has been written about the inevitable decline of our public education system in the United States. From devastatingly high dropout rates to widening student achievement gaps the concerns are real. In light of budget constraints and larger class sizes coupled with a flurry of new initiatives focused on the issue of the moment or quick fixes the way forward appears murky at best. Despite voluminous studies on causes, effect and potential solutions little advancement has been achieved.

This book takes the approach that we, as a nation, need to **rethink** what needs to be done, **rebuild** the "institution" before we will be able to **rebound**.

The book serves as a framework for developing shared responsibility and accountability. Beginning with a dialogue on motivation and passion the book explores what ignites or re-ignites a student's passion to achieve. It looks at self determination theory and its impact on student learning.

Evaluating teacher performance has been a topic of much discussion and debate of late. Determining teacher efficacy has been inconsistent and not reflective of student and school performance. The authors examine value-added theory and its integral role in changing the learning cultures. The discussion involves how professional development can be a prime mover in laying the foundation for the implementation of a comprehensive assessment of teacher effectiveness. The focus is on the need for new thinking and a linkage between student achievement and teacher performance.

The next section of the book addresses 21st Century Skills. From identifying the skills necessary to be an effective 21st Century teacher to assessing student learning and improving student achievement the authors explore the critical attributes which will determine success from a student, teacher and school perspective. It addresses the question of what should professional development look like in order to prepare teachers to meet successfully the challenges of the 21st century.

The final section provides a brief history on public education reform. It explores the challenges, responses and the results. The authors identify keys to successful reform initiatives and the common denominators among successful schools. The book concludes with suggested next steps with respect to short and longer term initiatives focused on improving student achievement.

At the end of each chapter we have provided a summary in the form of "Takeaways" capturing the key points from that chapter. Additionally, for many of the chapters, following 'Takeaways", we have included suggested activities, referred to as "Application", providing the reader an opportunity to put into practice the concept(s) addressed in the chapter.

Section I: Finding and (Re) Igniting Passion/Disposition

Chapter 1

Passion for Learning

"Our passions are the winds that propel our vessel. Our reason is the pilot that steers her. Without winds the vessel would not move and without a pilot she would be lost."
----*Author Unknown*

"Passion is the genesis of genius."
----*Anthony Robbins*

Defining passion is a difficult task. No words can adequately describe the feeling or what it looks like from another's perspective. However, you know it when you observe it. It is the fire in the belly, the sparkle in the eyes and spring in the step that are all telling signs. Much has been written about passion and its impact on student achievement. In the book, The Element, Dr. Ken Robinson speaks of passion in terms of one "taking a deep delight and pleasure in what they do".[1] Passion has been tied to enhanced productivity, increased focus and a willingness to take risks. All these are qualities that contribute to being a successful individual whether that person is a teacher, administrator or a student.

This chapter will explore passion and its impact on student learning as well as motivation and self determination theory. Passion and motivation is the fuel that propels the human spirit and this is at the core of student achievement. For that matter, it also is at the core of employee performance. In the educational setting, administrators and teachers are all too familiar with the student who is there in body only. A high school teacher recounted an experience she had with a student who was a voracious reader and a captivating conversationist but struggled in all his classes. He seldom volunteered information and when called on was unresponsive. This, unfortunately, happens too often in our classrooms. Working with this student the teacher was able to develop, through a series of conversations, that this student thoroughly enjoyed reading books on history and biographies. That was his passion and it led to his motivation to read books on this subject. The teacher "broke through" to this student by capitalizing on his passion for reading and making relevant in the context of history her course material.

Motivation is the driving force by which each of us achieves our goals. These goals can be personal or professional, short or long term. Motivation comes in two distinct "flavors". It can be extrinsic which comes from outside the individual. Examples of extrinsic motivation are money, time off, grades, or just public or private recognition. Studies on extrinsic motivation indicate that it has less staying power than intrinsic motivation. With extrinsic motivation with each "accomplishment", that is, good grades, winning the spelling bee, the rewards need to be increased to have the same effect as the first achievement or else the performance falls off. Intrinsic motivation comes from within the individual. It is driven by the interest and/or enjoyment in the task. It feeds on itself and generates positive energy which propels the individual to higher and higher levels of performance. In an article on student motivations and attitudes by the Science Education Resource Center at Carleton College it was stated that "students who are very grade-oriented are extrinsically motivated, whereas students who seem to truly embrace their work and take a genuine interest in it are intrinsically motivated".[2]

Intrinsically motivated students seem to retain information and concepts more readily. They are less likely to need remedial courses and/or reviews. Furthermore, intrinsically motivated students are more likely to be lifelong learners. They often times continue to seek learning outside of the classroom setting and do it for personal gratification versus some external reward such as grades or a formal recognition. It should be noted here that some educators may use the term disposition instead of passion or motivation. This will be addressed in the next chapter.

There are several theories or concepts on or related to motivation. Perhaps the most widely quoted theories/concepts are the theory of attribution, self-determination theory and the concept of self-efficacy. We will explore here the essence of each and how it relates to motivation. It is the linkage between (student) motivation and (student) achievement that we are most interested in. Understanding the complexities of what motivates someone to achieve a goal provides the foundation for connecting with that student by the teacher.

Dr. Fritz Heider, a renowned Austrian psychologist, wrote extensively on the psychology of interpersonal relations. His published work entitled The Psychology of Interpersonal Relationships contains many influential ideas/concepts that are as relevant today as they were in the late 1950's. He explored the notion of how people see the causes of behavior and the explanations they make which he refers to as "attributions". This led him to the development of his Attribution theory which is perhaps his most noted work in this area. Attribution theory describes how one explains the behavior of others and themselves. The theory postulates that behavior is attributed to a disposition, whether that be an attitude or a motive, or it can be attributed to situations such as peer pressure.[3]

The concept of self efficacy has received much attention in studying individual motivation. According to Dr. Albert Bandura's theory of self-efficacy, an individual's "abilities, attitudes and cognitive skills comprise what is known as the self-system. Badura described these beliefs as determinants of how people think, behave, and feel".[4] Bandura along with his contemporaries discovered that self-efficacy is a major determinant in "how goals, tasks and challenges are approached".[5] In subsequent chapters on value-added experiences and education reform more will be explored and developed with respect to self-efficacy.

The other related theory on motivation which deserves highlighting here is the work of Drs. Deci and Ryan on Self-Determination theory (SDT) in the 1980's. This theory was based on research from intrinsic motivation studies. At the core of SDT is the belief that "people have innate psychological needs that are the basis for self-motivation and personality integration".[6] SDT singles out three innate needs that provide for optimal function and growth, if satisfied. They are 1) competence, 2) relatedness, and 3) autonomy. These attributes play a dominant role in motivation. Throughout this text, whether the topic is learning cultures and value-added experiences or 21st century skills or keys to successful education reforms these attributes in one shade or another come into play. It is not surprising that so much attention has been paid to SDT in recent years. While the primary focus in this text is the educational environment there is definite applicability to the business environment as well.

There is one more "force" which serves as a catalyst in igniting the passion which generates the motivation to achieve a goal. This force is empowerment. Empowerment has been called the supercharger for passion in action. Empowerment is essentially the idea that you can gain control over matters thereby increasing the power one can exert in one's life simply by the way you think, feel and behave.[7] Free will provides you the ability to create any experience you want. To experience true empowerment you must act on that ability. Empowering yourself to seek whatever means (legally of course) to achieve your goals fuels the passion in each of us. Empowering can come from others. For example, your teacher can empower you to make a decision whether you want to take the final exam or write a term paper. You have the choice and you can make that decision. This type of empowerment is transference of power from the teacher to the student. It has the same effect as self-empowerment that is the recipient, let's say the student in the example above, can either do the paper or take the exam. That is the student's decision to make. However there is a major difference and it has to do with where the power originated. If it is "self originated" it has a direct impact (that is, increases) on one's disposition.

Managers, school administrators and teachers are frequently confronted with situations where the employee or student is reluctant to take a position or take action. Often times they are simply suppressing their free will and squelching their motivation which becomes habit forming. The environment plays a major role in shaping this behavior. A caring, stimulating and encouraging environment produces "positive vibrations" which in turn powers individual motivation. In a school setting this translates into a classroom which is conducive to high student achievement. "High motivation and engagement in learning have consistently been linked to reduced dropout rates and increased levels of student success".[8]

Below are some of the most typical and frequent comments made by teachers, administrators and employers regarding student or employee motivation (or lack thereof):

"Students constantly implore the teacher to 'just tell us what will be on the test and we'll study that'."

"Students ask 'why do we have to know all this? I will never use this information'."

"Students have an aversion to reading. They want the condensed version."

"My employees are always seeking the short cut to completing their tasks."

"I wish I could instill in my organization the work ethic necessary to meet the challenges we face as a business".

"Going above and beyond is so foreign to my associates that it is hopeless to have a conversation about what it takes to be successful."

"Where are the over-achievers anymore?"

These comments are only the start of a lengthy discussion on what it takes to bring out the best in students, employees, and for that matter, teachers, administrators and managers. The precipitous decline over the years in the individual work ethic is cause for alarm. This decline is most pronounced in the early years, that is, middle and high school students. Without "redirection", it only worsens as the time passes. The business community is constantly seeking strategies to "ignite" that work ethic in their employee population as it is a competitive imperative for them to do so. Likewise, many teachers and administrators have taken on the challenge as well. Working the relationship part in a meaningful and sincere way with each and every student and ensuring their lesson plans are relevant and rigorous, many have "turned the tide" in creating an environment conducive to student motivation.

According to Barbara Gross Davis, "research has shown that good everyday teaching practices can do more to counter student apathy than special efforts to attack motivation directly".[9]

Ms. Davis in her book, Tools for Teaching, offers many salient, practical tips on creating that environment conducive to student motivation. She provides useful instructional strategies de-emphasizing grades and promoting learning for learning's sake. Listed below are some of those strategies:[10]

- Give frequent, early positive feedback that support students' beliefs that they can do well.
- Ensure opportunities for students' by assigning tasks that are neither too easy nor too difficult.
- Help students find personal meaning and value in the material.
- Create an atmosphere that is open and positive.
- Help students feel that they are valued members of a learning community.

In addition to the above strategies there are a few others to add to the list. They are:

- Foster collaboration among students. Seek an environment of "coopetition". The teacher should emphasize first and foremost the need and value of cooperating with one another in the learning process. Stress competition in the spirit of competing against oneself in striving to do better each time around (for example, doing better on the next test, report, oral presentation).
- Recognize developmental differences.
- Make real world connections for the students and use technologies that they are familiar with and likely proficient in.

- Engage students in setting measurable, relevant and achievable (with stretch) learning goals.

These same strategies can be applied to the workplace and used by managers. They are, in that sense, universal tenets in creating an environment where students and employees can and will do their best and reach their potential. In Stephen Covey's book, <u>The Seven Habits of Highly Effective People</u>, his first habit and, perhaps the most critical one, is to be proactive. He uses the word proactive to encompass a comprehensive set of behaviors. He speaks of taking responsibility for your actions, adopting a "can do" attitude, initiating and promoting ideas and taking action.[11] How appropriate to lead with being proactive as the 1st habit. It sets the pace for the ones to follow. Being proactive is the essence of wanting to make a difference in all we do and "making it happen". More importantly, it is the positive momentum that drives all other behaviors. For that reason, the authors chose to begin this book with a discussion on passion and motivation.

Takeaways

1. *Motivation is the central driving force by which each of us achieves our goals whether they are personal or professional, formal or informal, short or long term.*
2. *Two major types of motivation are extrinsic and intrinsic. Extrinsic motivation is more short term. It is driven by external incentives such as recognition, grades, and/or awards. Intrinsic motivation is longer lasting and the incentives come from within the person. It feeds on itself. Intrinsic motivation serves to breed lifelong learners.*
3. *Key theories/concept with respect to motivation are the Theory of Attribution, Self-Determination Theory and the concept of Self-Efficacy. Each provides an understanding of motivation from a different perspective.*
4. *Empowerment is the supercharger for passion. It is the act of gaining control over matters and exerting one's free will.*
5. *There are several concrete strategies/tips that can be employed in the classroom setting or the workplace to create an environment conducive to self motivation.*

Application

You are asked by your superintendent to speak to a group of 1st year teachers on student motivation.

Draft an outline of your presentation addressing; 1) how to create a climate conducive to student-driven motivation, 2) discuss the linkage between passion and student motivation.

Chapter 2

Understanding Teacher Education "Dispositions"

"A courage which looks easy and yet is rare; the courage of a teacher repeating day after day the same lessons—the least rewarded of all forms of courage."
----Honore de Balzac

"Wise teachers create an environment that encourages students to teach themselves."
----Leonard Roy Frank

Many studies supported by reams of research papers have been done on what makes for an <u>effective</u> teacher. What are the qualities/traits? Is it a "right brain/left brain" phenomenon? Are the requisite skills and traits teachable or is it that you either have it or you don't like a gift. These questions and many more have been studied over the years. Not surprisingly, the studies have concluded that it takes more than just being a subject matter expert or an efficient planner to be an effective teacher. There is a lot more to it. In recent years many of the studies have focused on teacher dispositions. Dispositions are beliefs or one's value system. They are a compendium of qualities such as professional conduct, attitudes, beliefs, and work ethic which are on display in and out of the classroom setting. Teachers are role models and their students emulate their behavior. Students know and can sense when teachers are in it for them, the students. There is an ageless expression that captures this awareness, "students don't care what you know until they know you care". Students can be quick to challenge teachers on what they say or how they act and this exposes the teachers' dispositions. It was once commented on that teaching was 15% subject matter mastery, 15% preparation, 15% delivery and 55% dispositions. It should be noted here that dispositions also apply to students, parents, employees, managers, etc. However, this chapter will focus on teacher education dispositions and the research done in this area.

An article on Mansfield University's teacher education program lists 11 dispositions that teachers should be assessed on and education majors at Mansfield University are exposed to in the classroom and in their student teaching.[12] If truly embraced, dispositions should lead to actions and patterns of behavior consistent with the pre-scribed professional conduct of a teacher.

According to the article, Mansfield University's Education Department has identified eleven dispositions that form the core for their framework for preparing prospective teachers.

These dispositions are listed below;[13]

- **Reflection** – Teachers should recognize that professional reflection combined with experience leads to professional growth. Teachers should be thoughtful about their teaching, critically examine their teaching practices, and strive for ongoing professional improvement.

- **Professional conduct** – Teachers should exercise sound judgment and ethical professional behavior. Teachers should represent positive role models for their students and be supportive colleagues with other professionals and paraprofessionals.

- **Respect for diversity** – Teachers should be sensitive to individual differences among students and promote understanding of students' varied cultural traditions and learning strengths and needs.

- **High expectations** – Teachers should believe that their students can learn and should set high, yet realistic goals for student success. Teachers should communicate those high expectations to their students in positive ways.

- **Respect for others** – Teachers should develop and maintain classroom communities marked by student respect for other students and free from bullying and belittling behaviors. Teachers should interact with their students, fellow teachers, administrators, parents, and other community members with courtesy and civility. Respect is also demonstrated by pre-service teachers in the professionally appropriate ways in which they address fellow students, staff, faculty members, and administrators.

- **Compassion** – Teachers should demonstrate professional friendliness, warmth, and genuine caring in their relationships with students. Teachers should attempt to establish student-teacher relationships characterized by respect and rapport.

- **Advocacy** – Teachers should work to promote positive changes in schools and communities that benefit the welfare of their students. Teachers should work to assure that their students are afforded the services they need.

- **Curiosity** – Teachers should promote and support curiosity in their students and encourage active inquiry. Teachers should be professionally active lifelong learners and seek opportunities for professional development.

- **Dedication** – Teachers should be committed to the profession of teaching and to the betterment of their schools, communities, and students. Dedication is also demonstrated by pre-service teachers by class attendance, participation, completion of outside readings and assignments, and overall performance in teacher education courses.

- **Honesty** – Teachers should model personal and academic integrity by their actions. Teachers should be forthright in their interactions with others and uphold high standards of trust, character, and academic integrity.

- **Fairness** – Teachers should promote social justice, treat students equitably, maintain appropriate standards of confidentiality, and exercise fairness in academic assessment. Teachers should promote fairness in students' interactions with others.

The article states that "because teaching dispositions encompass both beliefs and actions, Mansfield University has developed a pair of essays written in required teacher education courses and observational assessments in required field experiences in schools. In keeping with established assessment principles and practices, the assessments are varied, multiple, and spread throughout the teacher education program".[14]

Many of the colleges/schools of education (COE) within the universities and colleges in the U.S. are incorporating similar frameworks emphasizing the need to take a holistic approach to preparing teachers for the 21st Century. This will be addressed in much more detail in later chapters in the book.

The National Council for Accreditation of Teacher Education (NCATE, 2002) requires COEs to address these characteristics in their programs. There is a direct linkage between high student achievement and positive dispositions. That said, NCATE's Executive Board has clarified its definition of professional dispositions. It encourages COEs to work with students, parents and communities to develop a framework consistent with the teaching profession standards and beliefs.[15] Jane Leibbrand, vice president of communications for NCATE states that "professional dispositions are integral to our standards".[16] She goes on to say that NCATE "expects schools of education to assess their candidates on: fairness, and the belief that all students can learn".[17] In that same article, Mark Wasicsko, director of the National Network for the Study of Educator Dispositions (NNSED), believes effective teacher dispositions can be organized into four measurable and discrete domains as outlined below:[18]

- **The most effective teachers perceive themselves as effective.**
  "These teachers are self-confident and optimistic," says Wasicsko.
  "They can identify with a broad and diverse range of people."

- **They believe that all students can learn.**

- **They have a broad frame of reference and see a larger purpose for what they do.** "Yes, their job is to teach a foreign language, or whatever subject they teach," says Wasicsko. "But it is also to teach a disposition for learning."

- **They look at the people element.** "We are all emotional learners," says Wasicsko. "What really good teachers know is that it is all about people. You can get magnificent learning to happen when you know that."

Some educators refer to dispositions, which can be negative or positive, as soft skills or characteristics. Some would argue that because they are based on beliefs and attitude that they are difficult to assess at least objectively. There has been much research done on assessing teacher dispositions some by the various State education departments. There are various constructs for assessing teacher dispositions. Some include surveys/feedback forms provided to students, faculty members, administrators and, in the case of primary and secondary teachers, to the students' parents. For teacher candidates in COEs the faculty advisor takes the lead in gaining feedback with respect to the teacher's dispositions. The assessment of teacher dispositions is very much work in progress. With pay for performance initiatives under study and in a few cases in the process of being implemented teacher evaluations/assessments will be front and center. Specific criteria including exemplars with respect to dispositions will need to be incorporated into the teacher overall assessment. Again, there are many models to choose from each with perhaps a slightly different emphasis. Before one adopts a model for assessing dispositions at the state or school district level spade work needs to be done to ensure its fairness with an emphasis on being an objective oriented process to the extent possible. Communications is the key here.

Research is only the first step. While a very important first step it still has to be immediately followed by actions. The COEs need to adopt a model that has as its foundation these four "domains" guided by the overarching principles of fairness and the belief that all students can learn. Yes, there is more to teaching than what meets the eye and dispositions play a crucial role in determining the efficacy of the teachers. This will be explored in more detail in subsequent chapters in this book.

Takeaways

1. Teacher dispositions (whether positive or negative) have a profound impact on student achievement, student academic growth and overall student success.
2. Teacher dispositions are one's beliefs and one's value system. They are professional conduct, attitudes, beliefs, work ethic, etc.
3. According to Mansfield University's College of Education (COE) there are eleven dispositions; reflection, professional conduct, respect for diversity, high expectations, respect for others, compassion, advocacy, curiosity, dedication, honesty and fairness.
4. The National Council for Accreditation of Teacher Education (NCATE, 2002) stipulates that schools of education assess their candidates on fairness and the belief that all students can learn.
5. The National Network for the Study of Educator Dispositions (NNSED) director believes that effective teacher dispositions can be organized into four measurable and discrete domains;
    a) The most effective teachers perceive themselves as effective,
    b) They believe that all students can learn,
    c) They have a broad frame of reference and see a larger purpose for what they do,
    d) They look at the people element
6. There are a variety of model constructs in measuring teacher dispositions. Much research has been done already with some of the models in use today in a number of COEs.
7. With teacher pay for performance plans on the horizon the criticality of state and local school districts

coalescing around a framework for identifying the key teacher dispositions to be assessed and how they will be assessed including how they will be weighted in terms of the overall teacher evaluation is essential.

Application

You are teaching a college course to undergraduate students in the school of education on teacher dispositions. A student asks you why dispositions are relevant to student achievement. How would you respond to the student and the class?

Section II: Changing Learning Cultures with Value-Added Experiences

Chapter 3

Relationships Between Learning Cultures and Outcomes

"Effective professional development for teachers is collaborative because it emphasizes both active and interactive learning experiences, often through participation in learning communities"

----*J. Hunzicker*[1]

"Leaders develop sustainability by committing to and protecting deep learning in their schools; by trying to ensure that improvements last over time, especially after they have gone; by distributing leadership and responsibility to others; by sustaining themselves so that they can persist with their schools and communities around them; by sustaining themselves so that they can persist with their vision and avoid burning out; by promoting and perpetuating diverse approaches to reform rather than standardized prescriptions for teaching and learning; and by engaging actively in their environments"

----*Hargreaves & Fink*[2]

Value-added models of student achievement have received widespread attention in light of the current test-based accountability movement. These models use longitudinal growth modeling techniques to identify effective schools or teachers based upon the results of changes in student achievement test scores or on the achievement of predictive results calculated on prior performance. This focus is leading to a change in teacher assessment, student assessment, and even differentiated pay scales. Consistent with most educational reform models is the weakness of providing immediate measurable results as well as the inconsistency in creating sustainable reform initiatives. Most reform initiatives center on working harder to achieve these predicted pre determined student scores. While there is some value in this approach, long-term sustainable teacher performance is more closely tied to creating a learning culture that sustains itself. This chapter will examine the approach of changing the outcomes voiced in this text not with "cookbook" recipes for reform, but rather through the implementation of a model that facilitates the evolvement of a learning culture through research-based experiences supported by various theories of change and sustained learning. Well understood in the educational community is the fact that student progress depends on the ability and instructional delivery skills of the teacher facilitating student learning. While there are abundant data, mostly summative in nature, they are more closely related to student skill demonstrations in validated student scores. There are too few opportunities for teachers to share practices and strengthen the profession with experiences aimed at impacting individual self-efficacy and collective efficacy within the structures of the arranged school setting. This model suggests new ways of gaining insight into teachers' practices, new ways of examining their strengths and weaknesses, and new ways to develop teacher capacity in individual and collective considerations. A goal of this model is to provide information that will ultimately improve teacher effectiveness with a system of shared experiences and knowledge consistent with a true learning community. This model in no way suggests that educational leaders should ignore student gains, but rather they should create value in reflection and experience that will enhance the ability to impact those desired gains.

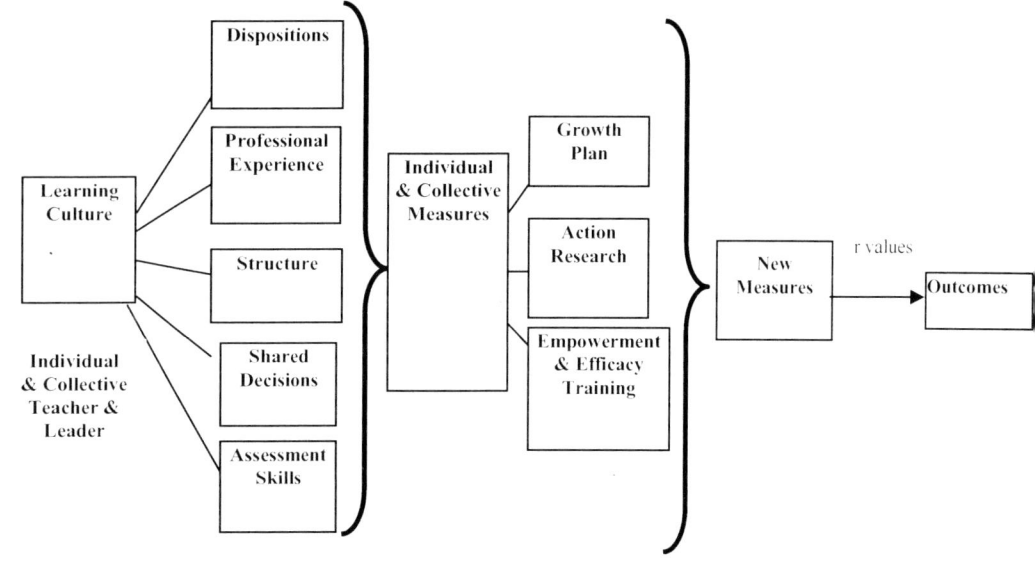

Figure: Value-added assessment model created by Doug Eury

Value-Added Experience Model

The model above is a value-added assessment with accompanying plan for cultural transformation aimed at enhanced organizational performance. Through the transformational opportunity, it is anticipated that multiple student outcomes will be impacted: graduation rate, student promotional rate, student proficiency rate, and postsecondary indicators. Facilitated adequately, the model suggests using research techniques to complete a thorough needs assessment and match those needs to proven strategies that will address individual and organizational growth, especially in the areas of individual self-efficacy and collective efficacy. Consistent with the philosophy of the National Race to the Top initiative,[3] the efforts focus on leadership development at all levels.

The depicted graphic above demonstrates the continuum for this program. Under the direction of a qualified facilitator and with the collaboration of the school system, a measure could be calculated by individual and by organization through the implementation of an instrument that provides measures in five domains (indicated in the second column). The instrument would yield an individual metric and a collective organizational metric for baseline considerations. Instrument domain one would provide data that indicate the disposition for performance by individual and collective individuals based on the theory of the impact of one's inherent value system on performance and commitment to organizational goals. Instrument domain two would measure and provide an assessment of individual professional experiences that are proven to impact one's ability through organized activities and personal habits. Instrument domain three would examine the organizational structure that each individual and collective group experience on a routine basis. The focus is to examine the degree of the professional learning community that may or may not be present. The fourth domain would measure the degree of shared decision-making opportunities to contribute to the development of productive interactions, routines, and common language for learning. Research indicates that interactions, routines, and the language of learning are the key factors to cultural health. The final domain measured would be a determination of the level of skill of individuals in the necessary theory of assessment and evaluation. The focus of this measure will be the planning, implementation and evaluation phases of formative assessment.

As indicated in the graphic, the domain measurement will yield a metric for each individual and a collective index for each organizational entity. At this point, a regression analysis could be conducted to examine the significance of each domain on the individual and cumulative metrics. This statistical measure will allow specific improvement plans for each organization as well as provide insight into the most significant domain for the individual organization.

The next phase in the plan would facilitate three experiences indicated in the fourth column. A growth or improvement plan will be developed for each individual and school population. This plan would serve as the framework for action for each school. A second experience would be to involve staff in multiple action research projects that target identified needs in previous assessments. The final experience is to implement training in the areas of empowerment and efficacy. Following these experiences, new indexes will be computed to determine impact of the activities. The new indexes will then be subject to correlational calculations with indexes relating to climate survey data, student proficiency levels, and student perceptions of presence of learning culture. The decision as to what outcome measure should be used for correlation depends on the goals of the organization. This could result in a combination of outcome measures such as student predicted growth attainment and teacher summative scores. An organization might use student perception of learning culture and teacher summative scores. The key to this model is to examine for increased correlational values following the prescribed experiences. There is emphasis throughout some states to consider the degree of attainment of predicted growth. These measures may be housed in system data bases or state-wide scores.

In addition to the planned activities in the model, principles that support cultural building will also be incorporated. For example, Schools to Watch[4] criteria identify the following four key areas for school success: academic excellence, developmental responsiveness, social equity, and organizational structures. The expectations of the value-added experiences would be to adhere to these proven principles in assisting the transformational efforts. Any measure of learning culture development based on some level of teacher and organizational effectiveness should support the continued growth of teachers indicating a need to reflect upon the concepts presented in these criteria as a support for continued and sustained growth. Support again appears to revolve around interactions, routines, and language. It also brings to mind Stephen Covey's 7 *Habits of Highly Effective People* in that to be a more effective teacher, one must become a more effective person. Thus the routine and language are reinforced in the effectiveness (efficacy) of the individuals and the collective group. Listed below is a summary of the Schools to Watch criteria with a listing of specific descriptors by criteria (Schools to Watch).[4] This is pertinent to the discussion on organizational cultures as it provides additional reflective information for self-assessment.

Academic Excellence

High-performing schools are academically excellent. They challenge all students to use their minds well.

1. All students are expected to meet high academic standards. Teachers supply students with exemplars of high quality work that meet the performance standard. Students revise their work based on feedback until they meet or exceed the performance standard.

2. Curriculum, instruction, and assessment are aligned with high standards. They provide a coherent vision for what students should know and be able to do. The curriculum is rigorous and nonrepetitive; it moves forward substantially as students progress through the middle grades.

3. The curriculum emphasizes deep understanding of important concepts, development of essential skills, and the ability to apply what one has learned to real-world problems. By making connections across the disciplines, the curriculum helps reinforce important concepts.

4. Instructional strategies include a variety of challenging and engaging activities that are clearly related to the concepts and skills being taught.

5. Teachers use a variety of methods to assess student performance (e.g., exhibitions, projects, performance tasks) and maintain a collection of student work. Students learn how to assess their own and others' work against the performance standards.

6. The school provides students time to meet rigorous academic standards. Flexible scheduling enables students to engage in extended projects, hands-on experiences, and inquiry-based learning. Most class time is devoted to learning and applying knowledge or skills rather than classroom management and discipline.

7. Students have the supports they need to meet rigorous academic standards. They have multiple opportunities to succeed and extra help as needed.

8. The adults in the school have opportunities to plan, select, and engage in professional development aligned with nationally recognized standards. They have regular opportunities to work with their colleagues to deepen their knowledge and improve their practice. They collaborate in making decisions about rigorous curriculum and effective instructional methods. They discuss student work as a means of enhancing their own practice.

Developmental Responsiveness

High-performing schools are sensitive to the unique developmental challenges of early adolescence.

1. The school creates a personalized environment that supports each student's intellectual, ethical, social, and physical development. The school groups adults and students in small learning communities characterized by stable, close, and mutually respectful relationships.

2. The school provides access to comprehensive services to foster healthy physical, social, emotional, and intellectual development.

3. Teachers use a wide variety of instructional strategies to foster curiosity, exploration, creativity, and the development of social skills.

4. The curriculum is both socially significant and relevant to the personal interests of young adolescents.

5. Teachers make connections across disciplines to help reinforce important concepts and address real-world problems.

6. The school provides multiple opportunities for students to explore a rich variety of topics and interests in order to develop their identity, discover and demonstrate their own competence, and plan for their future.

7. Students have opportunities to have their voice heard through posing questions, reflecting on experiences, developing rubrics, and participating in decisions.

8. The school develops alliances with families to enhance and support the well-being of their children. It involves families as partners in their children's education, keeping them informed, involving them in their children's learning, and assuring participation in decision-making.

9. The school provides students with opportunities to develop citizenship skills, uses the community as a classroom, and engages the community in providing resources and support.

10. The school provides age-appropriate co-curricular activities.

Social Equity

High-performing schools are socially equitable, democratic, and fair. They provide every student with high-quality teachers, resources, learning opportunities, and supports. They keep positive options open for all students.

1. Faculty and administrators expect high-quality work from all students and are committed to helping each student produce it. Evidence of this commitment includes tutoring, mentoring, special adaptations, and other supports.

2. Students may use many and varied approaches to achieve and demonstrate competence and mastery of standards.

3. The school continually adapts curriculum, instruction, assessment, and scheduling to meet its students' diverse and changing needs.

4. All students have equal access to valued knowledge in all school classes and activities.

5. Students have ongoing opportunities to learn about and appreciate their own and others' cultures. The school values knowledge from the diverse cultures represented in the school and our nation.

6. Each child's voice is heard, acknowledged, and respected.

7. The school welcomes and encourages the active participation of all its families.

8. The school's reward system demonstrates that it values diversity, civility, service, and democratic citizenship.

9. The faculty is culturally and linguistically diverse.

10. The school's suspension rate is low and in proportion to the student population.

Organizational Structures and Processes

High-performing schools are learning organizations that establish norms, structures, and organizational arrangements to support and sustain their trajectory toward excellence.

1. A shared vision of what a high-performing school is and does drives every facet of school change. Shared and sustained leadership propels the school forward and preserves its institutional memory and purpose.

2. Someone in the school has the responsibility and authority to hold the school-improvement enterprise together, including day-to-day know-how, coordination, strategic planning, and communication.

3. The school is a community of practice in which learning, experimentation, and reflection are the norm. Expectations of continuous improvement permeate the school. The school devotes resources to ensure that teachers have time and opportunity to reflect on their classroom practice and learn from one another. At school everyone's job is to learn.

4. The school devotes resources to content-rich professional development, which is connected to reaching and sustaining the school vision. Professional development is intensive, of high quality, and ongoing.

5. The school is not an island unto itself. It draws upon others' experiences, research, and wisdom; it enters into relationships such as networks and community partnerships that benefit students' and teachers' development and learning.

6. The school holds itself accountable for its students' successes rather than blaming others for its shortcomings. The school collects, analyzes, and uses data as a basis for making decisions. The school grapples with school-generated evaluation data to identify areas for more extensive and intensive improvement. It delineates benchmarks, and insists upon evidence and results. The school intentionally and explicitly

reconsiders its vision and practices when data call them into question.

7. Key people possess and cultivate the collective will to persevere and overcome barriers, believing it is their business to produce increased achievement and enhanced development for all students.

8. The school works with colleges and universities to recruit, prepare, and mentor novice and experienced teachers. It insists on having teachers who promote young adolescents' intellectual, social, emotional, physical, and ethical growth. It recruits a faculty that is culturally and linguistically diverse.

9. The school includes families and community members in setting and supporting the school's trajectory toward high performance. The school informs families and community members about its goals for students and the students' responsibility for meeting them. It engages all stakeholders in ongoing and reflective conversation, consensus building, and decision making about governance to promote school improvement.

This information, as included on the Schools to Watch website, is an excellent tool for descriptors for cultural analysis. While qualitative in nature, the indicators of successful characteristics are starting points for any consideration of the relationship between collective efficacy and desired cultures.

Takeaways

1. Changing student learning is most effectively impacted by changing the learning culture, not by providing additional inputs.
2. A model that focuses on healthy interactions, sustainable routines, and a reinforcing common language will produce measurable results in demonstrated learning.
3. Self-efficacy and collective efficacy are most likely impacted by the behaviors of the leader of the organization.
4. Impacting the learning culture is more sustainable than raising test scores.
5. Organizational structures establish healthy relationships, consistent routines and a common language of learning.
6. 21st Century leadership standards and teaching standards support the need for a value-added reform model.
7. The key to a value added-model is built on the concept that trust empowers others supported by mutual benefit.

Applications

1. Create an instrument for measuring each of the domains: dispositions, professional experience, structure, shared decisions, and assessment skills. Justify the intended data that may be generated.
2. Create a graphic representation or Venn diagram to show relationship of the value-added model to Schools to Watch criterion.

3. Create and justify a metric for measuring levels of the five domains. You may use the instruments created in application one.

Chapter 4

Learning Cultures

"Culture is the process by which a person becomes all that they were created capable of being."
----*Thomas Carlyle*

While learning might be most commonly associated with student demonstrations of cognitive gains, a more contributive approach, as indicated in this value-added model, is the level of adult gains in the context of learning. What is significant is the consideration of gaining and sharing knowledge as opposed to the distribution of information. Shared knowledge is best facilitated through conversations, interdisciplinary interactions, and sharing other practices that authenticate the information. The degree of learning is a function of various characteristics or variables including learning as a transfer of knowledge, affective responses to performance recognition, degree of creativity in one's search for efficacy, acceptance of the principles of change theory, collaboration as a norm, and connected practices. Learning as a transfer of knowledge validates the available information leading to a perpetual action of accumulated knowledge, thus empowering individuals to create learning experiences that reward learner and facilitator. Additionally, a transfer of learning supports sustainable learning as it provides additional relevance to the experience as well as problem-solving skills. Performance recognition is vital, but varies with the level of expected or needed reward by different individuals. This indicates a highly social component of a learning community challenging leadership to nurture interpersonal relationships. The implications to this conversation are that organizational leaders must be sensitive to the varying degrees of needed recognition as well as have an understanding of meaningful recognition. Judging affective responses includes open visual reactions and the reactions that are protected by some, whether positive or negative. Creativity is not random experiments that are judged for impact, but rather connected to one's alignment of goals and desired outcomes, but with the flexibility to alter practices at a level acceptable to the environment. In searching for optimum self-efficacy, creativity is desired as a state of constant assessment of impact as well as a vehicle for sharing models of impact with members of the learning culture. Creativity is significant to the development of self-efficacy in that it takes the individual beyond outcome measures that are static to outcome measures that are aligned with developing needs. Change theory comes into play as the organization must be open to individual and group critiques which may be uncomfortable or at least unsettling. Operating in an environment of a learning culture involves fundamental changes in the management techniques as well as noticeable differences in the roles and responsibilities of all individuals in the learning community, including employees, parents, and students. Too many individuals think of change theory as a component of year-to-year needs, not the implications of change theory to the day-to-day operations of the organization. This brings to question such components of change as role clarification, leadership skills, and accountability. Since accountability may be an overused concept, the concept of responsibility in the change theory consideration may be more applicable. Collaboration seen as a norm is measured by the degree of shared practices and the drive for continued improvement achieved only by positive interactions. The level of collaboration is supported by the level of expectations resulting from customs, clarified values, and various rules. Connected practices eliminate chance and provide the opportunity for significant action with degrees of predictability. A combination of ideas from past experiences leads to the development of a checklist of indicators or pre requisites for organizational learning:

- A vision for the organization is understood and supported. This vision must address the concept of a learning culture. Most visions may use the rhetoric of learning culture, but contain verbiage of being better than current conditions. A viable vision for learning culture should include the rationale and the explanation of what entails a learning culture.

- Employees have ownership in the mission and are committed to the mission. Mission statements for an organization are best developed with role clarification. As individuals in the organization identify their roles in personal life and in the organization, they can then begin to consider how they want to be perceived in those roles. That perception directs the meaning of the mission for the organization through common identified characteristics.

- Continuous improvement is part of the language of the organization. Care should be taken to clarify continuous improvement as more than an increase in outputs. While the outputs are important, continuous improvement in the context of learning culture is a continuous improvement of learning by all in the organization, learners and facilitators.

- Leaders are continually being developed. Leadership development in the learning culture should align with the vision and mission. Developing leaders of the old paradigm does more than create more of the same. Care is needed in setting the leadership training that measures outcomes in line with self-efficacy and collective efficacy.

- Change is preceded by an analysis of the possible benefits. Educators are notorious at creating and implementing change based on subjective opinion or the attractiveness of others. Change should follow a thorough needs assessment with alignment of research-based solutions to deal with the identified needs.

- Adequacy of resources is a constant driving force. This includes human and non-human resources. While the organization may not have full control over the personnel, the quality of personnel can be addressed with adequate experiences for the individual.

- Controlling boards should monitor organizational performance. The controlling boards need to be a part of the development of the learning culture vision. Those boards have the most impact through policy and resource allocation and distribution.

- Assessment is accepted and practiced. It is stressed that assessment goes beyond measurement and is a continuation of an evaluation process. All too often, educators and leaders use the measurements to drive decisions. Assessment more correctly aligns measures with meaning and implications. Evaluation makes use of the assessments as it pertains to individual and unit improvement.

- Organizational planning reflects the evaluation results. Of the three phases of action that include planning, implementing and assessment, the planning is the most crucial. When overlooked in a reactive environment, planning should be based on the full assessment and evaluation by incremental divisions and as full organizational units.

Takeaways

1. *Organizational learning occurs as a transfer of knowledge is shared among the members of the organization.*
2. *Educational organizations cannot depend solely on information for developing improvement plans. The information must be validated, thus becoming knowledge that can drive reform.*
3. *Leadership development throughout the organization is key to building collective efficacy.*

Applications

1. Create a list of indicators that you feel best defines a learning culture.
2. Create a workable plan for developing continuous leadership development. Include possible resources.

Chapter 5

Teacher Efficacy

"People who believe they have the power to exercise some measure of control over their lives are healthier, more effective and more successful than those who lack faith in their ability to effect changes in their lives."

----*Albert Bandura*

Current trends for accountability in education mandate that educators leave no child behind; educators are challenged to redesign teaching around sophisticated models to close performance gaps among groups and increase the students' academic achievement levels. Many studies since 1980 directed educators' attention to the importance of teacher efficacy in improving student achievement.[5] Teacher efficacy is defined as "teachers' beliefs about their capability to impact students' motivation and achievement".[6] The increased focus on teacher efficacy has been substantiated from over 500,000 studies whose authors have attempted to assess the most contributing factors that influence student achievement. Hattie's[7] evaluation of these studies found teachers' responses made up 30% of the variance of determining what influenced learning the most. All other school variables were three to six times less influential on student learning than that of teacher effectiveness.[8] This finding heightened the importance for educators to focus on school organizational variables that may empower teachers' self-efficacy to improve student learning. The concept of the value added model isolates the five key variables: dispositions, professional experiences, organizational structures, degree of shared decision-making, and performance assessment skills. The ultimate goal is to produce high quality teachers. High quality teachers do have a large impact on student achievement.[9] Darling-Hammond defined high quality teachers as those who have content knowledge, the ability to engage students for knowledge transfer, and are dedicated to the enhancement of effectiveness and improvement at the school level. Improving the level of perceived teacher empowerment is one way of facilitating greater teacher quality. Lightfoot[10] described empowerment as an opportunity one has in making choices associated with his job. Schmoker[11] noted teachers who participate in collaborative decision making to plan, assess the curriculum, and design instructional strategies generate greater student learning and achievement. Bandura[12] identified four primary sources of information people utilize while constructing their beliefs, or self-efficacy: "enactive mastery…vicarious experiences…verbal persuasion…and physiological" forms of information. In general, these sources provide incentive, or disincentive, cognitive information people use to develop their belief in their capacity to perform successfully with a task. The information from the sources influences the degree of their engagement and persistence with a task. As they encounter a potential task they will reflect on previous mastery experiences to predict the potential for success. They will also draw upon their internal physiological and affective cues, such as their effort reserve, and external feedback from observing others in similar tasks. The social influence from others through words, gestures or subtle cues will impact the efficacy belief as people assess their confidence level. Personal mastery is more authentic than other sources of efficacy in helping individuals measure their capability. It represents their actual performance rather than what others indicate through the social persuasion on one's inferred capacity. The more difficulty people attribute to the accomplishment of a task, the greater positive impact it has on their self-efficacy beliefs. An individual's most recent mastery experiences will be more highly weighted and integrated into his/her appraisal of self-efficacy because they are the easiest to recall, and are the most current affirmation of performance ability.[13]

An individual who is successful with tasks perceived as very challenging, and requiring high levels of sustained effort, will receive a greater sense of self-efficacy from the recalled experience. Conversely, an individual's recall of redundant and simple tasks will have minimal impact in one's calculation of self-efficacy.[14] Social systems that recognize valued accomplishments, and give opportunities for personal advancement within the context of the profession, are more likely to reinforce mastery's impact on self-efficacy than systems where individuals work in redundant isolation.[15]

Examples of mastery come in various forms. Obviously, mastery begins with subject or content expertise. For one to enact mastery, the knowledge of contextual and theoretical information is essential. Assessment of the level of content is a continuous process of reviewing and updating principles promoted by experts in the field. Continuously sharing and embracing dialogue with peers combined with possible action research inquiries for validation of content knowledge would contribute to a growing knowledge base. As indicated in Lawler's[16] work on effectiveness, authenticating information is the best method for creating knowledge leading to an empowered individual.

Equally important in mastery consideration are the skills necessary to deliver a learning experience that transmits the knowledge into action demonstrating value to one's ability to use the information or continue to add to the ability to build on the concepts included in the content. Mastering the delivery or facilitation requires continuous formative assessment of one's practices and behaviors, not necessarily the formative assessment of student learning demonstrations. Such student demonstrations would be part of the self-assessment, but only as a source of the overall assessment with identified adjustments.

In addition to content mastery and instructional delivery mastery, there is a vital need to master the ability to create interactions that support these components of mastery. If it is assumed that cultures are built on interactions, routines and common language, mastering the ability to develop peer interactions and student interactions are as crucial as content and delivery mastery.

The second source of information for determining self-efficacy is vicarious experience. Information from vicarious experience is also used by people in determining their capacity to successfully complete a task. Vicarious experiences refer to the performance behaviors one observes from people in their surroundings who are attempting similar tasks being considered by the observer. The information observers draw from vicarious experiences is a comparative analysis of the effectiveness of the modeled behavior to their own capability as it relates to their perceived judgment of the capabilities of those modeling the behavior. Vicarious experience also provides the opportunity for an individual to learn effective steps in completing a task that were absent from the individual's previous mastery experiences.[17]

Individuals will place more emphasis on the use of successfully modeled behavior from others if they have uncertainty about their own capability to perform a task, have less mastery experience to recall, or if those effectively modeling the behavior are judged to have less, or similar efficacy, to their appraisal of self-efficacy. Bandura[18] noted that vicarious experience may also override people's direct inefficacious experiences (personal mastery) if individuals believe their capacity is equal to, or greater than, the person modeling the behavior. If the "assumed similarity" between the models and the observer is high, then the observers will place greater credence on "the models' successes and failures" when predicting their own capability for performance.[19]

It is possible for individuals to observe successful modeled behavior from a person who is judged to be more efficacious and use the experience to raise their self-efficacy beliefs if the modeled behavior reveals the "effective means" for completing a task.[20] Social cognitive theory supports the need for social systems to provide a vicarious framework in their design of operations and communication to "mobilize attentional, representational, production and motivational" opportunities for individuals to enhance their self-efficacy.[21]

It is important for educational leaders to recognize that vicarious experiences are best facilitated with structures and organizational arrangements that allow reoccurring interactions to develop. Another key contributor is the leader's ability to create opportunities that enhance the sense of empowerment and collaborative learning that can develop in designated role clarification and accountability.

The third source people draw from in determining self-efficacy beliefs is verbal persuasion. Verbal persuasion is sometimes referred to as social persuasion because one often infers information from others by means of nonverbal persuasions (i.e., expressions, recruitment of one's input, etc.). Bandura[22] emphasized the significance of social persuasion by the statement "it is easier to sustain a sense of efficacy, especially when struggling with difficulties, if significant others express faith in one's capabilities than if they convey doubts". The encouragement from social persuasion must be authentic and realistic. Social persuasion that unrealistically boosts self-efficacy beliefs will result in unrealized outcomes and discredit the trust one has for future reliance on those offering the social persuasion.

Unrealistic social persuasion will ultimately diminish people's belief in their capacity to perform successfully and minimize their use of the empowering, or enabling, potential of social persuasion.[23] Negative social persuasion infuses doubt into people's belief of their ability, or reinforces their low efficacy state, and will lessen their motivation and level of activity.[24] The understanding of social persuasion, as defined in self-efficacy theory, heightens the significance for social systems to establish a supportive communication network respectful of positive and realistic reinforcement.

Verbal persuasion is not aggressive action by educational leaders, but rather an effort to practice those leadership behaviors that clearly portray expectations, accountability, and responsibility. As indicated in the work of Jim Collins,[25] effective leaders are not leaders that deliver directives or demands, but rather leaders that can ask the best questions. This indicates questioning techniques that initiate reflection, thus providing verbal persuasion with continuous agreement in shared values and objectives.

The final source of information used in self-efficacy appraisal includes the physiological and affective states people encounter as they are determining their self-efficacy for a particular task. The physiological and affective contributors to a judgment of self-efficacy are the "somatic and emotional states" an individual interprets during self-efficacy appraisal as either supportive or inhibitive forces that will impact performance. The intensity of the physiological and affective sensations is not as important as the way the individual "perceives and interprets" these feelings. If people have a high sense of self-efficacy they will "interpret their state of affective arousal as an energizing facilitator of performance" therefore capitalizing on their feelings by channeling them as motivation for sustained effort. People with low efficacy are likely to respond to heightened affective states conversely and choose not to engage in a task or approach it with hesitancy, anxiety, and lower expectancy for reaching outcomes.[26]

Affective contributions to the level of self-efficacy are impacted by the previous three sources of processed information: mastery, vicarious experiences, and persuasion. As the three become more incorporated into one's routines, behaviors will reflect a change in the consequences of those experiences on the individual. Thus, a perpetual cycle begins which builds interactively on the contributors to self-efficacy. An educational leader must learn to assess the affective impact as well as contributors to affective growth.

Growth to productive affective reactions occurs in structured and non-structured experiences, thus contributing to the learning culture.[26a]

Takeaways

1. *Collective self-efficacy focuses on individual and group contributions to the sustained learning experience supported by principles of empowerment and accountability.*
2. *High quality teachers are those who have content knowledge, the ability to engage students, and are dedicated to the improvement of the organization.*
3. *Collective efficacy and necessary behaviors for learning success encourage autonomy and inter-dependency throughout the organization.*
4. *Leaders should examine social systems that include opportunities for vicarious experiences enhanced with modeling and collective interactions.*

Applications

1. Create and justify a checklist of vicarious experiences that might enhance professional growth.
2. List and critique various social systems found in your work environment.

Chapter 6

Empowerment through Organizational Structures

"Virtually every company will be going out and empowering their workers with a certain set of tools, and the big difference in how much value is received from that will be how much the company steps back and really thinks through their business processes…thinking through how their business can change, how their project management, their customer feedback, their planning cycles can be quite different than they ever were before."

----Bill Gates

Structures guide a school through day-to-day operations. Structures can include how students and teachers are grouped, teacher leadership, and student relationships. Schools must recognize that all students are not the same and therefore structures must meet their learning needs for optimal success. Every component of the structure should be geared toward the improvement of student achievement and anchored in the mission, vision, and culture of the school. Dialogue will occur later in this book that discusses possible models for organizational effectiveness.

Grouping students for learning is an age old concept for dealing with effective structures. Ansalone[27] found hundreds of studies that showed a positive correlation between students' social classes, grades, standardized test scores, attendance, and track placements. Many biases have been found when tracking students on the basis of race, gender and social class. Less-advantaged students seem to be the most frequently placed in lower track curriculum. Students in low ability groups often suffer from a lack of intellectual stimulation. Tracking has been found to restrict the achievement potential and opportunities of less-advantaged students by hindering their affective development, exposing them to negative teacher expectations for their performance, and causing a negative self-concept among these students. With this said, consideration for empowerment through student grouping takes on multiple meanings. Empowerment indicates a building of responsibility for learning so grouping, good or bad, must include value judgments aligned with individual and organizational goals and objectives. Building responsibility for learning should take precedence over ability grouping. It is a point of not questioning the grouping, but rather the outcome of the grouping as it relates to dispositions to learn, relevant learning experiences, and the understanding of one's responsibility.

Teacher structures to support learning tend to draw more attention in considering empowerment principles. This attention may be ill conceived as it sets empowerment as an event or action when in the most effective environment, it is more of an attitude. Thus, the importance of the domain of dispositions as it relates to self-efficacy is reinforced in this thinking. Translated, this implies that dispositions must assess the individual's and group's efforts at restructuring the paradigm of what it means to be empowered. The paradigm is not one of actions, but more correctly one of attitude. Physical requirements for teacher teaming looks at the physical space of the building allowing teacher teams to be close in proximity. Scheduling requires common time for teams to meet, receive common training, as well as teacher autonomy over their practice. Positive attributes to teacher teaming include feeling of effectiveness, sense of collegiality, more teacher interaction, opportunities for in-depth discussions, more support to try new ways of teaching, reflective teaching, shared lessons, and better student relationships. School-wide relationships, vision, and effectiveness were the major negatives for teacher teaming. Other negatives were team isolation, unhealthy competition between teams and jealousy between teams. The greatest possible impact of teacher teaming is that it may have an effect on a school culture resulting in better student achievement. Within the implications of this research is a reinforcement of the physical nature of empowerment. It is not correctly on the attitudinal needs for the paradigm shift needed. Changes in attitudes to support the strength of empowerment include the need for awareness, acceptance of the concept, and adequate monitoring of the culture of empowerment.

Empowerment structures do have a place in creating effective cultures. Professional learning communities are structures that may contribute to enhanced student learning, but not just in organization only. The learning community must have its own attitude similar to and aligned with the individual's attitude. Much like teacher teaming, professional learning communities require internal school structures consistent with common planning time and collaboration. Within that common time, practices should include the opportunity to share experiences that impact attitudes and understanding of roles and responsibilities. Negative reactions to learning communities include an inequitable distribution of work as well as an unwillingness to change mindsets towards teaching.

Studies on teacher empowerment have revealed the importance of establishing operational models in schools that allow teachers more control in making decisions to influence what and how they teach. An ex-post facto study of 3,366 K-12 career and technical education teachers revealed that teachers' perceived empowerment was consistent among males and females: the need for teachers to make meaningful decisions regarding the teaching and learning processes in their school necessary for school improvement.[28] A rationale for implementing empowerment structures in school operations is to promote greater achievement through granting authority to those who know content and students well—the teachers. Easily seen is the identified need for a focus on teacher empowerment in improving teacher effectiveness, but care must be taken to ensure that teachers understand that empowerment is more than voting or reaching a consensus. The study of teacher empowerment has resulted in many contradicting viewpoints, interpretations, and conclusions on how empowerment affects teaching and learning.

Teacher leadership

Fostering teacher leadership proves to have a positive impact on the educational climate of the school provided that individuals in the organization understand the significance of individual leadership. This concept is closely aligned with the value-added domains of shared decision making and dispositions. Within the individual, teacher leadership creates trust and caring for others, a strong sense of contribution, and a more effective alignment with the mission of the school provided. The culture of the school tends to move towards a more inclusive and collaborative one as opposed to being authoritative, linear, and mechanical. Teacher leaders should be encouraged to be assertive, take risks, assume greater organizational responsibility, and discover new purpose in themselves and the organization. Administrators assume the role of being more collaborative, nurturing, facilitators, and community builders aligned with the needs of the teacher leaders. Teacher leadership brings multiple skills to the environment enabling the organization to deal with issues and a mission in a more effective manner. Experience indicates that teachers do not see themselves as leaders, but more as directed participants. Various reasons come to mind for this phenomenon that may include a fear of accountability and responsibility. Again, the domain of disposition comes into play as the leader deals with building teacher leadership that may impact the school culture.

Takeaway

1. *The continued development of production capability requires that mutual benefit be aligned with core values of the organization.*
2. *Action research contributes to a value-added model by enhancing reflective skills aimed at assessment and evaluation, formative skills, and timely implementation of learning experiences.*
3. *Leaders must understand that empowerment is an attitude, not an activity.*
4. *Fostering teacher leadership begins with individuals in the organization understanding the significance of individual leadership.*

Application

1. Compare and contrast: structures that drive empowerment versus empowerment that drives structures.

Chapter 7

Professional Learning

"The teachers who get "burned out" are not the ones who are constantly learning, which can be exhilarating, but those who feel they must stay in control and ahead of the students at all times."

----Frank Smith

As a desired outcome, professional learning activities are expected to enhance the learning of students in the classroom. Traditional professional learning has included time spent in listening to experts' shared knowledge with attempts at motivating individuals to change habits or patterns. Isolation is often a key characteristic of this mindset leaving little opportunity for follow-up and adjustments that impact the behaviors of the participants. A more effective form of professional development would be one of constant exposure to models of success and theoretical significance. Replacing professional development training with readings, seminars, cultural experiences, and exposure to environmental relationships may prove more productive. This is where the value-added model promotes action research as a means of professional learning that becomes internalized in the individual and the organization.

It is highly possible to tie effective professional learning opportunities with creating effective learning communities. Within this experience, there are major components that support and sustain professional learning. Those components are shared leadership supporting the mission, vision, and language of the school, and there is more likely to be an environment of trust, collaboration, accountability and willingness to take risks.

Student Relationships and Structures

State and national studies have found that instructionally effective public schools most often operate outside local state guidelines related to structures. Such schools operate through a) internal, shared governance; b) locally planned professional development and staffing; c) school selected educational programs, materials and curriculum; d) self-determined vision, expectations, and assessments of student learning; e) shared partnerships with parents, communities and the business sector; and f) school determined control of site-based resources and school-based budgeting."[29] As stated, the general consensus today is that shared decision making leads to quality performance. Unfortunately, the most misused practice in the shared decision making process is empowerment. Empowerment is defined as the opportunities an individual has for autonomy, choice, responsibility, and participation in decision making in organizations. Lightfoot[30] states, "to empower others is to give a stakeholder share in the movement of and direction of the enterprise". The assumption is made that staff members who are able to initiate and carry out new ideas by involvement in decision making will create enhanced opportunities for students. Experience in working with teaching staffs helps to identify the forms considered in the effort to empower school participants:

1. provide teachers with a significant role in school decision making, thereby developing a sense of shared governance;
2. provide teachers with control over their work environment and work conditions; and

3. provide teachers with opportunities to contribute to the school in a range of professional roles: teacher, administrator, curriculum developer, mentor, and learner.

The construct of empowerment can be defined and assessed for relatedness to teacher efficacy. The operational definition of organizational empowerment is stated as the enabling capacity for an organization to support the development of self-efficacy. McGraw[31] related organizational empowerment in terms of greater teacher autonomy in decision making. McGraw believed that the way to increase teacher autonomy and empowerment was to remove time-consuming approval processes of bureaucratic leadership. This study was based on Kanter's theory of structural power viewed as an operational process in schools that gives teachers greater autonomy in decision making and access to resources, information, support and personal advancement. These liberating qualities provide teachers the power to mobilize resources and information for action.[32] An operational design in schools is important where teachers may address and resolve conflicts without delay. Teachers who have the legitimate power to control their job behavior demonstrate higher levels of efficacy than those who have diminished power to control their job behavior.[33] Empowerment is best promoted by letting teachers have control of resources and problem-solving opportunities associated with teaching. Though no specific research has been found to directly link the presence of teacher empowerment to the fostering of teacher efficacy, it still may be implied that an operational design of shared decision making over issues influencing job performance may provide an environment for the activation of the sources of efficacy defined by Bandura's social cognitive theory and the exercise of control.[34] The theoretical assumption is that the level of perceived teacher empowerment may indicate the degree to which the organizational nature of the school influences teacher self-efficacy through the provision, or inhibition, of the sources of self-efficacy. The consistent articulation of empowerment to levels of efficacy generally implies the importance for schools to value and address the nature of organizational properties. The establishment of a supportive, positive, and interactive climate which is focused on the unified purpose of advancing student achievement should receive considerable attention. In examining a number of school cultures, it is noted that if the changes in educational leadership and management processes are to be successful, it is imperative to understand the degree to which teachers perceive themselves to be empowered by the context of their school's decision making process. Once that level of perception is determined, it becomes necessary to validate such perceptions before determining relationships to such concepts as attendance, classroom management issues, and overall morale.

Certainly, every principal wants an instructionally effective school, and struggles with what it means to empower staff members and have them share in the organizational direction. The beginning of creating a team where members will give their "stakeholder share" starts with developing a sense of belonging in team members.

The feeling of the school belonging to the decision makers means more than being a member of an enriched social environment. It is the principal's responsibility to build that group of people into a team that shares the same vision for the school and is committed to do the work of the school to make the vision a reality.[35] In other words, the team is committed to the mission of the school because it is based on shared values. That commitment means that individual needs will sometimes take second place to group needs.

"Team above self" is a coaching maxim that principals have to preach and model if they are going to have an effective school improvement team, or any kind of team. Of course, if the team too often calls on self-sacrifice without realizing success in the goals the team has established, members will start to drift away and rethink their commitment to the team.

The first challenge for any principal leading a school improvement team is that some or all of the team participants may come to the task knowing little about shared decision making. They may have served on teams where the senior or the most insistent member was allowed to make the decisions and the rest of the team members simply complied. They may not be aware that effective decision making processes occur when:

(a) decisions are made by the individuals most influenced by the decisions;
(b) appropriate information is available to those making the decisions;
(c) decision makers are adequately prepared to make data-driven decisions;
(d) decisions makers hold conversations about the data and decisions;
(e) decision makers create action plans to implement decisions based on data; and
(f) decision makers are expected to be accountable for the consequences of their decisions.

The effective school principal will lead the team through these realizations while establishing and growing an atmosphere of trust where team members feel safe voicing opinions that may be in contrast to "group think".

The individuals most influenced by the decisions make decisions:

There is a marked contrast between the theory of staff empowerment and the reality of it. While educational literature and state law support the philosophy of increased localized control of school processes, the accepted practice has been to allow elected school boards and appointed superintendents to deliver controlling decisions. School communities have assumed that the prevailing operational method for schools is a system of mandated policy, mandated organization, and mandated processes for delivering instruction. Public schools typically have accepted the mandates and responded by protecting the *status quo* in terms of how decisions are made and delivered. In reality, there has been little effort by local boards and superintendents to encourage independent decisions at the local school site. Rather, local school boards tend to expect local schools to concentrate on trying to maintain regulations, guidelines, and expectations as set forth in policies and mandates. Principals also find it difficult to truly share power with their staff. After all, it is the principal, superintendent, and school board who stand in the spotlight when things go wrong. Individuals that may have shared in a decision can disappear under the guise of a team decision. The results have been that often the school improvement decisions and consequent plans become generic and simply a paper exercise that must be turned in by a certain date with a stamp of approval from a majority of the school personnel. The principal who wants to unleash the decision making power of a team needs to think through this basic inconsistency and decide just how far he/she is willing to let a school improvement team go in making decisions. He/she also needs to remember that the only legal function of the school improvement team is to create the school improvement plan. School improvement teams were not designed as sounding boards for employee concerns for hygiene factors of job satisfaction, but as leadership teams to make instructional decisions that would lead the school toward higher achievement.

Appropriate information is available to those making the decisions:

A dominant aspect missing from the site-based management movement has been the availability of appropriate and adequate data to guide and support site-based decisions. Data provided to school systems from the state typically have followed a format of district comparisons or state comparisons. Individual schools in turn receive site-specific data following a format of standardized testing results and available demographic information. More significantly, when appropriate data are provided, the skill of interpretation and the training to use the data in strategy development are severely deficient or missing completely. Schools are in need of individuals who can aggregate and disaggregate data in such a way that teams can get an insightful picture of what is happening in the school.

The argument for appropriate information is strengthened in Lawler's[36] work with organizational management. He developed a model to view the potential effectiveness of any participative decision making. The model indicates that effectiveness of participative decision making is a product of information, knowledge, power, and rewards (Lawler).[37] From an educational organization's perspective, substitute "empowerment" for "power" to facilitate the formula working for effective school teams. Important in this consideration is that if any one of the components of the model is absent or weak, the potential for effectiveness is lessened. To paraphrase Lawler, empowerment without knowledge, information, and rewards is likely to lead to poor decisions. Below is an adaption of the Lawler theory with some replacement concepts. Instead of power, this graphic uses empowerment. Notice that the implication is that information, knowledge, empowerment, and rewards all contribute to effectiveness. There is reason to consider the reciprocal relationship of information and knowledge, knowledge and empowerment, as well as empowerment and rewards. Several conclusions are presented in this graphic representation. Leaders build knowledge and efficacy with information, but we can only empower with knowledge, not just information. We cannot connect information directly to empowerment. Collective efficacy certainly benefits from this consideration as one's efficacy is based on the strength of the knowledge gained from the information, not the amount of information provided.

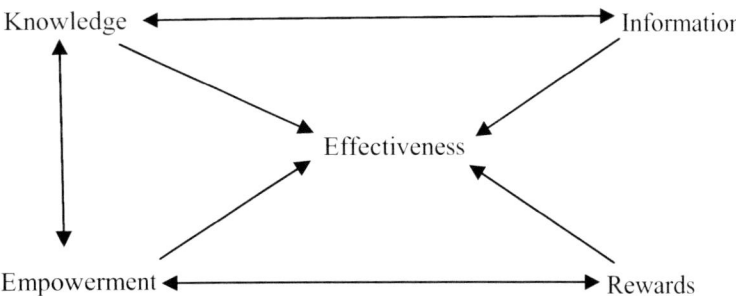

More significant to the issue of appropriate data is the distinction between information and knowledge. Information is often no more than the results of standardized tests that allow the ranking of students, classes, schools, systems, and even states. Knowledge occurs from understanding the indicators of success and from the assessment of targeted weaknesses. A school improvement team might look at standardized test results, grades at determined intervals, subgroup performances, numbers and demographics of students, instructional placement of students and teachers, attendance and tardy data, to name a few data points. The question arises: how do these artifacts of information become sources of knowledge? The first step in the process is to authenticate the information. Failing to authenticate information prevents the development of a working knowledge base. Secondly, the decision makers must assess the information as to its relevance and meaning. Data should be analyzed for trends rather than in isolation. Empowering teams to make decisions without providing them continued and growing knowledge is a formula for failure. Applying Lawler's standards for evaluating participatory processes forces educators to recognize that most data school improvement teams examine is not authenticated but is simply accepted at face value. Consider how many times in recent history test results have been altered or completely discounted because of political decisions. School improvement teams, led by the principal, should assess the information they examine and determine if it really tells them what they need to know about school performance. Needless to say, the authentication process could be difficult and time consuming. That is not to suggest that authenticating and considering such information is not a worthy use of time. Sowell advanced the theory of knowledge-based decision making by stating that as the quantity of knowledge increases, the decision makers develop expertise, and as the level of expertise expands, the decision makers are capable of developing "ideals".[38] Ideals are a way to focus back on the mission of the school and remind the team where their vision is leading them.

Decision makers are adequately prepared to make data-driven decisions:

Where does the training exist that facilitates the development of a knowledge base founded on appropriate information? The "system" of educational evaluation, in terms of instructional performance, addresses the skills of lesson preparation, behavioral management, and objective attainment. While these skills are a necessity to instructional success, little or no training is done in the skills of data analysis, identification of students' individual strengths and weaknesses, and the development of strategic plans that address continuous improvement of individuals or cohorts. The mere educational organizational structure hampers the ability to create any vertical alignment or vertical articulation of knowledge that enables school improvement teams to look long range. Unfortunately, decisions in the educational setting are made through consensus building or voting that may be based on biases that ignore a longitudinal analysis of performance. Until professional development and staff development of teachers and administrators address the skills of data analysis and data-driven decisions, schools will continue to operate as usual. Their team decisions may or may not be beneficial to improving the school.

Decision makers hold conversations about the data and decisions:

Sowell[39] addressed the issue of effectiveness as knowledge is transmitted and used in decision making. He felt that this effectiveness is dependent upon the characteristics of the specific processes incorporated in making the decision. Ultimately, the knowledge transmitting capacity of schools must be judged not only by how much information is conveyed, but how that information is used to build knowledge for decision making. Again, the professional development of educational leaders addresses communications, but little time is allotted to the skill of conveying relevant data to staff members. In addition to a lack of adequate training, structural barriers limit conversations among crucial parties in the process of developing effectiveness. There is little time for teams to talk across grade levels or departments to talk across the school. Arguably, extended days and extended school years would provide much needed time for conversations, analyses, planning, and shared decision making. But politics and popular opinion reach various ranges throughout many states limiting these extended days. Principals must make opportunities for these conversations to take place. Only when this kind of analysis becomes a priority will the school improvement team or any other leadership team be able to craft strategies that clearly move the school toward their vision.

Decision makers create action plans to implement decisions based on appropriate data:

Any school improvement team will justify its school improvement plan by saying that it is based on data. What must be asked is, are the data primarily standardized test results of a cohort of students that has moved to the next grade level or next course? While that form of standardized data has relevance, it does not consider the assessment of the most current customer. Are the plan architects looking at ongoing, formative assessment, or are they simply waiting until a school year has ended and then planning the next year based on the last? Have they chosen curricula that provide benchmark results so that end-of-year results are accurately predicted? Have they established measurable outcomes that can keep the strategic plans focused so that efforts are not simply random acts of improvement? Have they, as the primary planners for the school, chosen multiple data sources to evaluate the success of the school? Are they looking at parent, staff, and student satisfaction surveys? Are they evaluating the curricula they have chosen for effectiveness? Are they basing school improvement on something other than information that is handed to them from the chain of command? If school improvement teams take the time to brainstorm all the data sources that are available, they may find that their improvement efforts have been too narrowly defined.

Decision makers are expected to be held accountable for the outcomes of their decisions:

North Carolina has been in the accountability game longer than most states. As far back as 1989, teachers and principals were making decisions based on the requirements of The School Improvement and Accountability Act, or Senate Bill 2, as it was also called. Since 1995, some form of the ABCs of Public Education has directed many of the decisions made by school improvement teams and principals. The question becomes, who should set the standards of accountability? Should they be set by government entities, professional organizations, or, if the C of the ABCs does stand for local control, should each school set its own accountability standards? Gaines and Cornett[40] suggest that each school should set its own standards because the individual school is closest to its clientele. The political reality of media coverage and government overseeing makes it obvious that the move is toward centralization of accountability, not away from it. Under the No Child Left Behind law that went into effect in 2003-2004, Title I schools are the only ones currently sanctioned, but all schools must amend their school improvement plans to indicate how they will improve, and all schools must meet the "Highly Qualified" teacher standards, reporting their success toward Adequate Yearly Progress to parents and the public. Certainly, the school as a whole, the school improvement team, and the principal expect to be held accountable for their decisions. However, the principal is the only one who can clearly lose his or her job at a specific school because of these decisions.

Takeaways

1. *Organizational empowerment leading to professional growth and increased organizational capacity is supported by the development of self-efficacy.*
2. *Action research as part of the professional growth program contributes to a value-added model by enhancing reflective skills aimed at assessment and evaluation, formative skills, and timely implementation of learning experiences.*
3. *The quality of conversations held by decision makers determine the impact of the decisions.*
4. *Action plans created by decision makers should include professional opportunities based on sound and appropriate data.*
5. *Members of the organization must recognize the similarities and differences in accountability and responsibility.*

Applications

1. Create and support an instrument to measure effective shared-decision making processes.
2. Create a graphic to display the value of action research.
3. Create a graphic that displays similarities and differences in accountability and responsibility.
4. Create an alternative effective model to the Lawler model.

Chapter 8

Learning Communities as Professional Experience

"We need to create programs that bring us together structurally in some cases, intellectually and emotionally in others.... Learning communities are one way that we may build the commonalities and connections so essential to our education and our society."[40a]
 ----*From Learning Communities: Creating Connections Among Students, Faculty, and Disciplines*

A professional learning community may be a more accurate assessment of a school's capacity to engage teachers in a psychosocial process focused on a unified mission for the improvement of teaching and learning.[41] This implication is supported by Bandura's[42] proposal of the bidirectional quality between self-efficacy and collective efficacy. If the social-cognitive support, as assessed by the degree of use of the professional learning community concept in a school, is linked to proportionate increases in collective teacher efficacy, then researchers inferred that the organizational design of a school has the potential to empower teachers with self-efficacy through the mechanism of collective efficacy.

Professional experience can be defined as the past personal experiences of each community member as a learner, teacher, team member, and leader. Collective professional experiences of the organization as a unit can be defined as the past experiences of the organization as a whole unit.

Current research supports the trend that the collective professional experience and knowledge of the group is more beneficial to the overall learning process and promotes a more positive learning culture than individual experience. Research also supports the importance that professional colleagues, mentors, and workplace leaders have on each learner's personal experience which is perhaps the most influential factor in determining how experience affects change in practice to the benefit of student learning. Research and personal experience lead to a common set of understandings about building organizational knowledge:

   a. formal individual knowledge is developed based on each individual's formal training;
   b. experiential individual knowledge is developed based on experiences, mental models, and skills that are not formalized or conscious to the individual;
   c. formal organizational knowledge is developed based on routines, habits, and methods that are explicit and open to every individual in the group; and
   d. informal organizational knowledge is developed based on collective habits and patterns that are not formalized, which can be called the learning culture.

What is gleaned from this list of organizational or professional experience is individual increased efficacy which leads to increased collective efficacy. Thus, formal and informal experiences lead to organizational effectiveness. This supports the contention to incorporate professional experience into the value-added model.

The National Center for the Study of Adult Learning and Literacy published a research brief entitled: How Teachers Change: A Study of Professional Development in Adult Education.[43] Qualitative data was collected through questionnaires and interviews provided to a sample of one hundred and six teachers in three northern American states. The study investigated how adult education teachers changed after increasing professional experience after participating in one of three different professional development models: multisession workshops, mentor-teacher groups, or practitioner research groups. The purpose of the study was to assist school leaders in the development of meaningful professional development in order to change teacher experience and influence classroom learning. The basic theory of the study is that there are three basic factors that influence the type and amount of change teachers experience as a result of professional development. First of all, individual factors, such as their experience, background, and motivation are key to the experience. Secondly, professional development factors such as the quality and amount of professional development attended had immediate and lasting impact. Lastly, program and system factors such as the structure and support as well as the working conditions factored into the professional development experience. The authors also point out in the research brief that in order for a positive change to occur in everyday teacher practice, several factors came into play including teachers' motivation to attend professional development, years of professional experience in the field, the level of formal education, and the venue of first teaching experience. The most important factor was noted not to be past experience, but the quality and quantity of professional development experienced.

In exploring how professional individual versus group experience affects the learning culture of an organization, it can be concluded that both are important but collective group experiences have more of a positive effect on student learning. Collective professional experiences that are deliberately planned are more beneficial to the learning organization as a whole. This group experience is most beneficial when offered in a real world application setting, with its effectiveness determined by the quality, quantity, and the direct support of the supervising educational or workplace leader. Individual experiences offered in the preservice setting are highly impacted by the school placement, mentor teacher, and overall collective experience of the learning organization.

Professional Development as Professional Experience

Professional Development can be seen more adequately as guided organized action. Such a conceptual definition indicates the need for planning the events around legitimate objectives measured by valid outcome measures. Effective change is therefore dependent on any changes in the shared values that might guide organization transformation. Consistent and restrictive to the value-added model, the guided action centers on dispositions, self-efficacy, shared decision making and performance assessment skills. This particular model also establishes opportunities to personalize development based on measured indexes integrated with well-defined action research principles. The suggestion indicated here is that opposed to committing resources to programs that may not survive, professional development efforts would focus on experiences that are part of the day-to-day routines and structures supported by developing interactions and a common learning language. Not to rule out opportunities to attend professional activities, there still should be careful consideration for the alignment of training with shared values and elements of self-efficacy.

Takeaways

1. *Professional learning communities are more than teams that meet and more than team activities. A true learning community is an organism that evolves and grows with all experiences.*
2. *Sustainable practice is key to the value-added model as it promotes the ability for the organization to flourish based on assuming responsibility.*
3. *The organization's mental model of a learning community drives its existence and its function.*
4. *Professional development should include awareness and conceptualization of a learning community.*

Applications

1. Administer a PLC instrument and assess the findings.
2. Create a graphic that supports professional experience as a means of professional development.

Chapter 9

Dispositions and Passion to Perform

"No man can be a good teacher unless he has feelings of warm affection toward his pupils and a genuine desire to impart to them what he himself believes to be of value."
----*Bertrand Russell*

To be effective, there needs to be a transformation of prevailing organizational mindsets and political patterns. As individuals collectively consider their passion to excel, a new system of beliefs and practice will develop leading to a more productive level of social development. The social reality facilitates an expected norm of behavior instead of an exception to that norm. This is an extremely key point in building efficacy. Dispositions indicate a passion and desire to perform as opposed to response to reoccurring mandates to perform. As the individuals in the organization examine and reflect on their passion to excel, the overlying emphasis is on continuous examining of the impact of that passion on the performance of others, peers, and learners alike. Just as formative assessment enhances student learning, examining one's disposition leads to an organization that has shared values, shared beliefs, shared meanings, shared understanding and shared sense making. The construction of such a reality allows teachers and administrators to see and understand events, actions, objects, utterances, or situations in distinctive ways that may be used to impact overall school performance.

Teacher dispositions have become increasingly more a part of the conversation pertaining to school cultures and performance. Dispositions can be defined as the values, commitments, and professional ethics that influence behaviors towards students, families, colleagues, and communities which ultimately affect student learning, motivation, and development as well as the educator's own professional growth. Dispositions are guided by beliefs and attitudes related to the values such as caring, fairness, honesty, responsibility, and social justice. The value-added model suggests that dispositions of educators can have an effect on self-esteem, performance, and the organization as a whole. The value-added model supports teacher dispositions as predictors of enhanced teacher performance leading to increasing student outcomes. As with five prescribed domains in the value-added model, a baseline metric will provide direction for experiences that will contribute to a developing disposition.

According to Carroll Helm[44] teacher disposition affects self–esteem and student performance. This article states that students who come from advantaged households have better opportunities than students from economically disadvantaged home environments. This study focuses on how teacher disposition can affect student performance and the student's self-esteem towards school. This concept is supported in Effective School research built on writings of Jere Brophy and Thomas Goode.[45] A self-fulfilling prophecy is perpetuated by the actions and behaviors of the adults that are in contact with the learner. Thus, one's disposition impacts behaviors which in turn contribute to the outcome variable of student achievement.

According to Cole[46] wealth and social status are determining factors in who learns in our schools. However, he goes on to state that they are not the only factors that allow children to be successful. Dedication and the right teacher disposition can at times allow students to be reached by educators who would normally not have the ability to impact students of poverty. Harme and Pinanta[47] conducted a study that followed 179 students in a small school district from kindergarten through the eighth grade. The students entered the school district at the same time and remained in the district through their eighth grade year. The study addressed various aspects such as gender, ethnicity, cognitive ability, and behavior ratings of children. The student's relationship still indicated aspects of school success being predicted by teacher relationships. Woolfolk[48] goes on to state that there are six indicators of excellent teaching: 1) love for children, 2) respect all children and parents in all circumstances, 3) see potential in all children, 4) motivate children to reach their highest potential, 5) be a spontaneous and creative educator who is able to see teachable moments and seizes them and 6) have a sense of humor. Davies and Brember[49] found that feelings of worth could affect reading and mathematics and potentially self-image.

Wayda and Lund[50] produced a study using teachers from teacher education programs to find what dispositions were needed to address the student's sustainability for the teaching profession. They produced rubrics displaying specific dispositions of students such as, "caring, kindness, integrity, initiative, and skill development". Wakefield[51] produced a study showing, "A strong relationship between learning style and teacher disposition". Helm states that teachers in teacher education programs must make students aware and model key dispositions. These dispositions should be modeled for the entire duration of the program. Students must observe dispositions through field experiences.

In an article by Jung and Rhodes,[52] research on disposition assessment in teacher education was expanded to clarify several issues. One issue dealt with whether competence-related dispositions should be examined more thoroughly and in conjunction with character-related dispositions. Also, the authors assessed how the consistency of disposition assessment may have produced results with conflicting information. In addition, the rapid societal changes has made technology disposition essential. A close look at these issues in various teacher education programs in the United States is the focal point of this review.

The challenges of assessing dispositions lie in what is measured and how the results are used. Jung and Rhodes[53] proclaim that a problem encountered was the validity of measurement related to teacher dispositions. Competence-related disposition indicators measure teacher effectiveness as it relates to the behavior of the teacher. The validity is questioned as to the degree of impact on student performance and justification of the term "effectiveness".

The entire discussion on dispositions becomes complicated with the influx of technological skills needed for teaching and for developing student skills. It has become crucial that schools and specifically teachers acquire the 21st-century skills and concepts needed to effectively enhance teaching and learning. Teachers who are competent in technology demonstrate a willingness to embrace the technological changes found in society. Schools looking to hire teachers will be looking for strong technology dispositions. Jung and Rhoades[54] list the following as propositions for measuring technology dispositions: 1) willingness and intention to embrace change, 2) beliefs in the values of technology with positive attitudes regarding its use, 3) intention to increase capability to use technology, 4) a sense of confidence and controllability in using technology, and 5) use of technology skills in an educational context. The implications here are that baseline disposition measures and benchmark disposition measures must not only include philosophical indexes, but also technological attitudes and skills. By broadening the teacher disposition focus to include competence-related dispositions and technology dispositions along with the traditional character-related disposition, a model of prescribed training and experiences could contribute to a more competent and effective teacher, thus improving the efficacy of the individual and ultimately the organizational group.

Having a positive attitude is one essential disposition that a teacher must possess before he or she can begin to work with students. If teachers look for strengths and the potential of students instead of any deficits, they may gain trust and have positive interactions with the families as well as the children. Having a negative attitude, the teacher may have issues creating a nurturing environment. Many people make the assumptions that all teachers are natural nurturers. While this may be the case for some, there are teachers who may demonstrate dispositions that interfere with their ability to connect with students. A solution and challenge for organizational transformation programs is the ability to prepare teachers by helping them develop a disposition that directly impacts outcomes. Deploying an empowerment disposition is complex. It takes commitment and time to implement strategies to allow empowering relationships to occur. Empowerment is inserted in this discussion as the interaction of the domains of the value-added model. This discussion operates on the concept that improving the individual and collective disposition results in a self-sustaining level of continuous refinement of the collective ability of the group.

Takeaways

1. *Mindsets and political patterns act to create dispositions that impact the performance of the organization. Political patterns are demonstrated in the daily behaviors of the leadership at various levels.*
2. *Collective dispositions understandably have the greatest impact on self-efficacy because of the role of self-fulfilling theory.*
3. *Without a passion to perform, individuals revert to minimal standards for self-assessment.*
4. *Since relationships are vital to cultural development, dispositions should be addressed early in any transformation effort.*

Application

1. List and discuss political patterns that have impact on dispositions. Distinguish the levels of impact.

Chapter 10

Leadership Training and Assessment

"Leadership is all about enabling followers to attain meaningful goals, especially goals that are bigger than any single individual could accomplish alone. The best and most mature leadership is about selfless service, not about gaining power and control over people."

----David Antonioni

Research indicates that leadership is the key factor in transforming organizational performance. Typical research includes the North Carolina Turnaround[55] project which is a concentrated series of assessments and improvement plans with the emphasis on leadership and learning cultures. According to the North Carolina Turnaround Project Web Site:[56]

In 2005, North Carolina embarked on a high school turnaround initiative to reculture or restructure a group of persistently low performing high schools. In 2006, additional high schools and middle schools were added to this effort, creating a group of 66 high schools and 37 middle schools to be "turned around." High-quality professional development on research-based best practices to create school teams to reculture schools, coupled with intensive, targeted, and sustained coaching for successful implementation of reculturing strategies learned during the professional development, yielded significant change in leadership and instructional practice which, in most cases, resulted in significant student achievement gains.

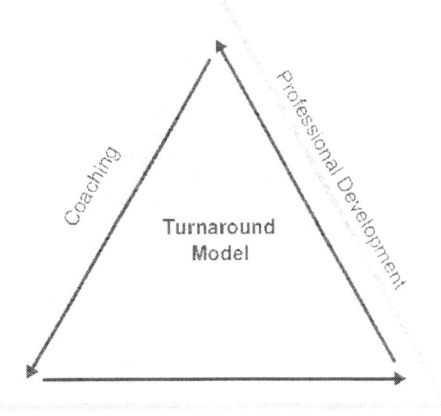

Best Practices of Effective Schools

Experience with the coaching component of the model revealed insights to the impact of leadership behaviors and the measurable outcomes associated with goals of the Turnaround Project. Included in lessons learned by this writer is that there is a definite link between leadership behaviors and organizational cultures that are academically effective or productive. This is an important lesson in the value-added model as it pertains to the self-efficacy of the leadership and the collective efficacy of the administrative team. It is imperative that leaders in education recognize the significance of protecting and supporting the self-efficacy of their teachers. Leaders must realize their role and responsibility to value opportunities to help teachers realize and reflect on mastery experiences. Educational leaders should create shared opportunities for the positive vicarious and persuasive activities surrounding teaching and learning. Finally, leaders must be cognizant of the constraints and barriers perceived by the teachers and collaboratively participate in the removal of the limiting conditions. Such support would decrease the level of task difficulty a teacher considers when appraising their self-efficacy for successfully accomplishing a task.[57] Training with school leaders to recognize the empowering quality of a school to support self-efficacy are keys to this theoretical construct. Following are categorical questions that principals may address to assess potential leadership effectiveness across the domains of leadership, general organization, curriculum and instruction, professional development, general management, and stakeholder involvement. This material is attributed to the Leadership Group of the Carolinas[58]. It is logical that these prompts would provide valuable data in the analysis of leadership efficacy—individually and collectively. Most significantly, the data would provide direction and assessment of the cultural condition of the organization.

Leadership

KEY QUESTION: *Does the leadership in the school reflect both a deep understanding of contemporary practices—including distributed leadership involving faculty and other stakeholders—as well as a total commitment to success at the highest levels for all students?*

- Is the principal's leader behavior inclusive? Is it facilitative? Is it effective?

- Do the principal and all assistants spend effective time daily monitoring instruction? Is there a written plan for so doing?

- Does the school leadership ensure the use of evidence-based practices and arrangements in every classroom?

- Is the principal's decision-making model inclusive, and is it effective?

- Is the faculty widely involved in the leadership of the school? Do they participate in real decisions regarding teaching/learning, finance, scheduling, etc.?

- Are faculty selection and assignment based on student learning needs rather than individual preferences? Who's involved in these decisions?

- Does the principal demonstrate strong commitment to developing faculty leadership, and is there a written plan for so doing? Is there an active and meaningful faculty council, a well-developed teacher-leader training effort, etc.?

- What is the level of student leadership in the school? Is the principal committed to developing student leaders who play an active role in the life of the school? Is there evidence of it?

- To what extent do the faculty and community demonstrate ownership of decisions which the school and principal make?

General Organization

KEY QUESTION: *Is the school organized in such a manner as to assure a rigorous and relevant education for all students, with a curriculum that assures equity for all students?*

- Are high academic standards the rule for all students?

- Is there tight alignment between curriculum, instruction, assessment and interventions—with high standards?

- What guidance provisions are in place to assure effecttive planning for success for all students, focusing on preparation for a rigorous high school experience?

- Is there a "house" or other advisory structure which supports positive relationships with adults in the school? Are efforts to create smaller learning communities evident?

- How is the master schedule developed? Who's involved, and how?

- Does the master schedule allow needed time to meet rigorous standards?

- Is prescriptive scheduling for success evident? What provisions are there for acceleration and remediation?

- Is flexibility to meet both teachers' and students' needs the rule?

- Is priority given to common/team planning teachers?

Curriculum and Instruction

KEY QUESTION: *Does the overall curriculum mirror contemporary organization in a way that focuses on high levels of success for all students, and does the instructional program mirror best practices in middle grades education?*

- Are the school's core curricular offerings tightly aligned with a prescribed Standard Course of Study?

- Is a well articulated and relevant curriculum, designed to prepare every student for high levels of success, in place?

- Are pacing guides evident, up-to-date, and appropriately used?

- Is the curriculum organized to raise expectations for all students, or is "sorting and selecting" evident?

- Is formative assessment a key facet of instruction? How are data being used to inform curricular decisions and to guide instructional practices?

- Do faculty demonstrate a deep understanding of key concepts and skills?

- Are a variety of appropriate and related instructional practices evident?

- Is student predictive data in use? Are principals and teachers fluent?

- What relationships are evident between the structure of curriculum/program of studies and guidance patterns of elementary schools which feed the school?

- Is strong teaching evident across the curriculum?

- Are overall teacher-student relationships positive? Mutually respectful?

Professional Development and Staff Utilization

KEY QUESTION: *Is there an effective process of teacher recruitment, successful means of teacher retention, and a comprehensive program of professional development? Are all integrated into the culture of the school? Is work towards a PLC evident?*

- Is there an effective (written) faculty recruitment plan?

- Are teachers utilized effectively—that is, to serve identified student needs within their own demonstrated skill areas?

- Are teacher assignments made equitably? Is the faculty leadership included in assignment decisions?

- Is there an imbedded high quality professional development plan which focuses on both instructional goals and organizational goals, aligned with individual teacher needs, and readily accessible to all?

- Does the professional development plan include provisions for maximizing instructional time, differenttiating instruction, teaching diverse learners, pacing for success, and similar contemporary school needs?

- Are daily instructional monitoring, formative observation, and a systematic feedback system evident? Is there a written plan?

- Is the principal clearly attuned to curriculum and instruction, and does he or she have the skill needed to assure a laser-like focus on successful teaching practices across the curriculum?

- Where is the school with regards to developing a PLC?

General Management

KEY QUESTION: *Is the school organized and managed in an effective manner which reflects a total commitment to supporting teachers, serving student needs, and using best practices from both the academic and business sectors? And do all of the policies and procedures of the schools support the goal of a superior middle school where success for all students is the rule?*

- Is the school organized and managed in a safe and effective manner?

- Are academic practices clearly intended to support high achievement for all students? (Illustrative issues: course selection procedures, grading practices, promotion practices, make-up credit procedures, acceleration provisions, etc.)

- Are appropriate interventions for inappropriate behaviors evident?

- Do all management functions—finance, organization, staffing, food services, custodial services, transportation, etc.—reflect commitment to student success?

- Are adequate financial resources available to support instruction? Are resources well and wisely used?

- How is the school budget developed, and are resources distributed in an equitable manner at the school?

- Are student and parent voices heard in matters related to the management of the school?

- Are the school's policies and procedures consistent with the districts?

- Are teachers clearly attuned to the underlying purposes of the school's policies and procedures, and are they supportive?

- Are behavior-related procedures designed to maintain a climate conducive to high student achievement?

(Illustrative issues: student attendance and course credit, academic credit and suspension, length of suspensions for various problems, etc.)

- Does classroom management support the school's mission, and is it consistent with a culture of success?

Stakeholder Involvement

KEY QUESTION: *Is the entire educational community aware of practices and procedures needed to support and sustain a systematic effort to assure that every student receives a superior middle school education which will lead to success in high school and beyond?*

- Is the school a welcoming place where parents and visitors feel valued and safe?

- Are parents and other visitors routinely seen at school?

- Is there a program of public information which informs all stakeholders of school issues-successes, needs, challenges, and opportunities for community involvement?

- Is there an active program of volunteerism beyond booster clubs for athletics and/or band or chorus?

- Is there an active and meaningful parent-teacher organization?

- Are provisions made for active involvement with the business community in manners beyond the perfunctory? Is there a school-business council?

- Are provisions to allow extra- or co-curricular opportunities for all students evident?

While this is not an all inclusive list of reflective questions, they do provide a beginning point for a valuable needs assessment and as a beginning point for a cultural analysis.

Takeaways

1. Leadership behaviors and expectations are the biggest contributors to learning culture development.
2. Reflection and self-assessment of one's behaviors lead to improved impact.
3. Monitoring cultural development is a process of dialogue, not one of direct instruction.
4. Developing leadership behaviors is a transformational process within itself.

Application

1. Develop, conduct and summarize a survey or focus group discussions dealing with leadership behaviors that lead to cultural development.

Chapter 11

Value-Added Theory

"If you give people tools, [and they use] their natural ability and their curiosity, they will develop things in ways that will surprise you very much beyond what you might have expected."

----*Bill Gates*

Direct value-added assessment. This method estimates institutional effect on student learning by measuring and comparing what students know and can do at two points in time—for example, at the beginning and end of a school term. The difference between the two measures represents the learning gain and serves as an estimate of the institutional contribution to student learning that can be compared across similar institutions. More complex models may be needed that take into account student academic abilities.

Indirect measures of value-added assessment. Rather than directly examining student learning, this approach measures the student behaviors and institutional actions that are known to correlate with student learning and success. These measures of "good practice" are treated as proxies for student learning—to the extent that they are in place, it is expected that greater student learning will occur. As demonstrated in the Gates study, student perception of the learning culture is a key piece of evaluating teacher performance. This supports the concept that effective teachers inspire a love of learning. It is indicated in the Gates[59] report that "students must experience the classroom environment as engaging, demanding and supportive of intellectual growth". The Gates group used student perceptions to provide teachers with data that would improve use of class time, the quality of comments on homework, their pedagogical skills, and their relationships with teachers.

Applied value-added models. Instead of examining what happens during the formal school years, this approach gauges the impact of the educational experience in an applied setting, after-the-fact. For example, alumni would be interviewed about the extent to which their education prepared them for jobs, and employers would be interviewed about the extent to which their employees have the necessary knowledge and skills for the job.

It is suggested in the model illustration early in this chapter that each of the above models be considered in the analysis. Determining the intent of the organization will determine the degree of model that may be necessary. Student gains cannot and should not be ignored while learning cultural indicators have more lasting sustainable impact on the organizational performance. Still relevant to the discussion and assessment is the question of responding to public accountability while focusing on organizational improvement. As mentioned previously, this model should not operate in isolation, meaning that elements of leadership will be a constant and consistent focus in the process of assessment.

Value-added experiences versus value-added outcomes. It is important to distinguish differences in value-added experiences and value-added outcomes as they are related to the models described above. Value-added experiences, as mentioned numerous times in this text, center on individualized and organizational plans based on measures of dispositions, professional experience, organizational structures, shared decision-making opportunities, and personal assessment. The suggested action research component implies a continuous inquiry into research based methods and continuous assessment of the impact of any implemented actions. The continuum is one of needs assessment, identified intervention and assessment of the impact of intervention. The process, even though termed action research, is not one of scientific endeavor. Rather, it is intended that the organization, as individuals or collective teams, collaborate on the process of continuous examination of proven strategies or programs. This is completed without losing the focus on organizational routines, learning language, and multiple relationships. Explanations of such theory would be part of the efficacy training targeted in the model. This would be an example of the applied value-added model. The "experiences" are intended to add value to the measures of individual and collective efficacy. Value-added outcomes would consist of the desired measures that the organization seeks for improved effectiveness, i.e., student growth indicators, teacher summative measures, organizational cultural measures, or other particular targeted goals. Student growth outcomes would be an example of direct value-added assessment. A measure of cultural conditions would be an example of indirect value-added assessment as it is well understood that the impact of cultural environments is significant to improved learning. The model is designed and intended to contribute to self-efficacy even in the planning of collaborative experiences. As benchmark self-efficacy assessments are gathered, the sharing of data and the planning for activities to address indicators in the data will enhance the professional experience, the organizational structures, and shared decision making components of the model.

Takeaways

1. *Value-added experiences are based on incremental changes in the key desired outcomes.*
2. *Multiple sources of data are needed for examining the connection between experiences and outcomes.*
3. *Value-added assessment is never ending and reflects the learning characteristic of the brain in that as learning occurs, the configuration and appearance of the organization changes.*

Application

1. Discuss differences in value-added experiences and value-added outcomes.

Chapter 12

Personal Assessment

"The most fruitful lesson is the conquest of one's own error. Whoever refuses to admit error may be a great scholar but he is not a great learner. Whoever is ashamed of error will struggle against recognizing and admitting it, which means that he struggles against his greatest inward gain."

----*Goethe*

In the five domains of a value added model, assessment skills are relevant to the learning culture of the teacher and leader. The fifth domain, personal assessment skills/ formative reflection, captures the essence of reflective practice in teachers and principals. Pedro[60] suggests that reflective practice in teacher education is one reform effort that has taken hold in the education community. Pedro[61] therefore, conducted a study of teacher reflective practice to better understand the significance in teacher preparation and to discover how pre-service teachers understand and interpret reflective practice.

Many teacher education programs have incorporated strategies to encourage pre-service teachers to think critically about their practice.[62] Pre-service teachers were used in the study in order to develop strategies to gain a strong start when they begin teaching. The study was guided by three main research questions, (a) how do the pre-service teachers perceive and understand the concept of reflection?, (b) how do the pre-service teachers describe how they learn to reflect on their practice?, and (c) in what context did the pre-service teachers engage in reflection?[63] There is relevance to this dialogue as these are excellent questions for the experienced teacher. Learning how to reflect on one's performance is key at all levels of experience. This model supported in this chapter proposes to implement a measure of the degree and ability to reflect based on judgments and the impact of any changes to instructional delivery. Even more important would be the process of sharing these reflections as part of the learning community development.

There are many links to other literature based on Pedro's research. Dewey[64] and others have researched reflective practice. Dewey believed that reflection precedes intelligence and is the act of careful and persistent consideration of any belief. Pedro[65] believes his views addressed practical problems allowing for doubt. This discussion leads a reflective practitioner to consider key constructs of such action. First of all, is the mere act of thinking about action and what has occurred. Secondly, the reflective practice must be considered and viewed as a problem-solving activity. Lastly, the reflective practice must consider more complex issues such as values and beliefs of the practice itself. The suggestion is that the reflective practices need to become a part of the culture.

Pedro details how viewing various authors' construction of meanings led to the theory of symbolic interaction. This theory/framework was used to develop a clearer understanding of how the pre-service teachers interpreted what they learned about reflective practice and how they used it.[66]

The participants in the study were from a graduate teacher education program and their ages ranged from 22 to 42 years. Data was collected qualitatively in a descriptive and interpretative design. The interpretation of the pre-service teachers' conceptions and understandings were captured through in-depth interviews and through examination of teachers' reflection journals.[67] Data was collected over three semesters allowing time for analysis and interpretation. The interviews were open-ended and lasted an hour. There were three interviews given throughout the study for each participant. Some sample interview questions include: What do you understand by the term reflection? When was the first time you heard the term reflection? And, give me an example of a time you engaged in reflection?

From the use of the interviews and journals, Pedro[68] was able to establish themes using words and phrases for the teachers' actions. Themes were used to identify similar responses given by the participants. Therefore, to interpret the results, the pre-service teachers acquired their perspectives on reflection by definitions, questioning, and using the opportunity to reflect, which answers the first research question. The second question dealt with how pre-service teachers described how they learned to reflect and it was discovered that pre-service teachers attributed their ability to reflect to their interaction with significant others in the program and they based their reflections on their personal beliefs as well as education theory.[69] The third question was answered by the pre-service teachers' involvement in many reflective activities in the university courses and the classrooms in which they practiced because they engaged in self, written, and verbal reflections.[70]

In conclusion, pre-service teachers had a general understanding of reflection. They used this conceptual device and study to build their teaching skills by using reflection. Pedro[71] believes that there are some implications in the study. Critical reflection and the development are areas that can be explored. Lastly, this study raised many questions: can reflective practice be taught in a more clearly articulated fashion? will the pre-service teachers continue to reflect on their practice as they begin teaching in the schools? and what other forms of writing reflections can teacher educators use to teach pre-service teachers to critically reflect on their practice?

Literature provides a multitude of teacher reflection; however, there are few studies that seek to understand the reflective practice in leaders/principals. Wright[72] conducted research in the area of principal reflection and provided conclusions in this area of study. Many principals are faced with various duties with the educational context which limits reflection. Wright[73] uses the swamp metaphor to suggest how some principals refuse to dive into the swamp, which is filled with dilemmas and conflicts, in order to be free of more problems that are brought to the table. Therefore, principals feel reflection is going into the swamp (in other words). These issues and dilemmas cause principals to shy away and avoid reflection. However, to calm fears, reflective practice is not something to do, rather it is a state of mind and a way of being a principal.[74]

Being reflective encourages principals to think critically about what is going on in their schools and effectively utilize teachers to develop strategies to improve their schools. Therefore, in order for teachers to take heed and be reflective, principals should strive for the same. Wright[75] states that she came to understand that if individual change is to be a precursor to collective change, reflection should involve the interruption of taken-for-granted behavioral patterns and unexamined assumptions that perpetuate the status quo. Further into her research, Wright discovered that reflexion is another term and a differentiated form of reflection. Reflexivity disrupts habituated patterns of thinking and interrogates beliefs and practices particularly around internalized structures and preoccupations based on one's position of power and privilege. It is assumed in this discussion that when principals practice reflexivity, they consciously take responsibility for their actions and the impact on others and school improvement efforts.

Although stated earlier, in the swamp lies issues and dilemmas; the swamp also produces possibilities, freedoms, and chances which are hidden without the use of reflection. Wright[76] also cites Dewey[77] and speaks of his views of open-mindedness and responsibility in a way to be reflective as a leader. Based on these views, an experimental cycle of reflective and reflexive practice is used to help principals develop this mindset. In the cycle, principals must identify a problem, observe, analyze and reflect, engage in reflexive observation and analysis, and re-conceptualize practice. Using this cycle will allow principals to see how assumptions and beliefs create contradictions in reflective practice. In the journal article, Wright[78] ends with explaining her research and giving some conclusions of leaders and reflective practice. Principals should regularly reflect on their decisions and moral purposes and space/time is necessary for reflection to support ongoing and complex change processes.

Ostermann et al.[79] provided a detailed explanation on the process of reflective practice for educators. The common misconception found was reflective practice was a meditative or relaxing process. On the contrary, reflecting in one's practice required a challenging, demanding process which produced the most effective results in a collaborative process. Even though reflective practice has been viewed in many different forms, Osterman suggests viewing reflective practice as a way to be enlightened on how one's self-awareness affects the nature and performance of creating opportunities for professional growth through the reflective process.[80]

Reflective practice was imperative for professional growth, according to Wagner.[81] Wagner collected data from three sources: a self-assessment instrument named the California Professional Standards for Educational Leaders, peers (other administrators), and teachers. The self-assessment tool was written by Orozco, a professor at California State University at Fullerton. The peer data was collected through interviews and teacher data collected through surveys and questionnaires. Through the data collection, it was found that successes needed to be celebrated and it allowed for a professional development plan. Often, successes are not celebrated due to the lack of reflection, while data collected allows for the creation of goals.[82]

Wagner[83] also stated the importance of being reflective with four key points. First, reflective practitioners made decisions that were data driven. Data pulled from multiple sources provided a true representation of reality which created a more valid process. Decisions were not made based on personal or collective whims or opinions. Second, reflective practices led to a well-defined professional development plan. Omitting reflective practice often resulted in skipping critical steps of the skill and knowledge building process. Third, reflective practices allowed for the identification of truly authentic strengths and weaknesses. Strengths were used most effectively and weaknesses were targeted for improvement. Finally, reflective practices led to innovative practices. It forced one not to stay in the same place because there was constant progress towards a goal.[84]

The comment from a former student of more teaching and less talking about reflective practice inspired Russell[85] to create an authentic approach to teaching the skill of being a reflective practitioner. Russell created an outline with five tables for the five points within the education program which aligned with each reflective assignment that was due. Each of the five tables had three columns to enhance students' thinking skills. The first column contained questions intended to foster the student's professional thinking skill. The second column contained responses and the third was Russell's response. Russell did not use the word reflection to describe the process until the end of the semester. Students were surprised to find out they were reflective practitioners. Russell's ratings were the highest of his career. Students enjoyed reflecting when taught to reflect and were not turned off by hearing the word reflection.[86]

Measuring or expressing reflective practice was a difficult task. Schon[87] explained that professional knowledge was based on experience in professional settings. Practitioners who were competent often knew more than they could put into words. They had the knowing-in-practice knowledge, most of which was implied or unspoken knowledge. Master teachers or administrators often were not able to express what made them successful. Reflective practitioners who struggled were often uncertain about their own behaviors and what was causing them to be unsuccessful[88] which reinforced Russell's conclusions of reflective practice needing to be taught.

McKnight[89] the teacher education placement coordinator at the University of Maryland, offered strategies or examples to use if one had to be a self-directed learner for the practice of reflection. Forms of self-guided reflections included thinking aloud, keeping a reflective journal, or the development of a professional portfolio. Competency continuum allowed for self-examination on the standards by which the teacher was held accountable. By using the prescribed teacher evaluation instrument to rate one's self, it allowed the teacher to reflect on limitations and what was holding the individual back from achieving a higher rating. The continuum or evaluation instrument could have been used as a discussion starter for the mentoring team or administrators. Another form that included data collection and action research provided a strategy to help produce a solution to a current problem. The individual teacher created an instrument to research and collect data on the problem and created a solution based on the data. Finally, the collaborative process was a crucial tool for reflection. In the natural flow of a conversation, one can use peers or others to talk about teaching and learning. This provided an opportunity to share ideas along with formally or informally sharing ideas.

Zeichner et al.[90] described five traditions of reflective practice. Generic tradition reflections involved an end means or summation of an observation. In education, a generic tradition example was reporting and reflecting on the events that occurred. Second, academic tradition stressed knowledge, content, and pedagogy within a discipline. Reflective practice in this domain involved examining strategies used and the effectiveness of those strategies. Reflection could have been based on alignment to national standards. Next, the social efficacy tradition relied upon research and the appropriate implementation of various pedagogical models. The individual's experience, values, and tradition played a role in the applications of the various teaching models. The most common form of this type of reflection was a portfolio (i.e., national board certification or graduate requirement). Fourth, the developmentalist tradition reflected upon the needs of the students and whether instruction was differentiated. The reflection examined how the students should be taught based upon their background, developmental level, interests, and understanding. Finally, the social reconstructionist tradition dealt with all the influences that were involved that affected what happened in the classroom. For example, the factors included the overall learning community, political reality, social reality, and ideological reality effective practices in the classroom.

The power of collaborative reflection and professional learning communities was displayed in Hipp's[91] description of the results in a case study that involved 10 urban high school principals. The 10 principals gathered periodically to discuss and reflect upon topics such as the values that had the greatest impact of their schools. The principals reflected upon the results of data collected at each of their respective schools. Data was collected to evaluate their level or skill at advocating for student learning, communicating, being a change agent, community building, and management of their organization. After reflecting upon and bringing their data to the group, the group created a shared vision for creating schools that reduced the achievement gap. Principals also shared their effective practices and experiences.[92] Unfortunately, the article was written immediately after the professional learning community was established and the results of where the school was, compared to where they grew to, were not available.

McAlpine et al.[93] collected data on six university professors two times. The second time they used three professors who were pre-tenure and three labeled as exemplary. They expanded the range of teachers for the second study to further validate it. In both studies, they videotaped the professors' undergraduate lessons, and then within a couple days of the videotaped lessons the professors were interviewed twice. The professors first described the class, and then watched the videotape to help stimulate memories from the lesson.

The analysis team created a three-tiered coding system. In the system, tier 1 was types of reflection, tier 2 was goals of reflection, and tier 3 was processes of reflection. Using the tiered system, McAlpine et al.[94] were able to establish three types of reflections and four types of goals. The first type of reflection was formative evaluation. This occurred when the professors were able to draw upon pre-existing knowledge about teaching after analysis of a specific aspect in their teaching. The second type of reflection was formative evaluation/advanced thinking. In this form of reflection, the subject still assessed him/herself related to a specific skill or course. But, it moved beyond the first type reflecting (formative evaluation) because the subject was able to form a hypothesis based on stated experiences. It was a type of reflecting-in-action that occurred during class. The third type of reflection was advanced thinking which involved purposeful questions, curiosity, and investigating beyond the class or course in general. This reflection was similar to formative evaluation because the subject drew upon existing knowledge and was similar to formative evaluation/advanced thinking due to a hypothesis being drawn. But, what separated advanced thinking from the previous two was that the subject drew a conclusion and built new knowledge based upon the experience. The four goals of reflection were assessing teaching effectiveness, improving teaching, assessing student learning, and fostering learning. Assessing students and fostering student learning fell into similar a category (learning) while the same was true for assessing teacher effectiveness and improving teaching (teaching). Decision making goals included fostering learning and improving teaching.[95]

Takeaways

1. *Being reflective encourages leaders to think critically about their organization, indicating a need to fully understand the alignment of standards and outcomes.*
2. *Personal assessment, as related to cultural transformation, requires a review of individual and collective contributions.*
3. *Personal assessment is challenging, demanding, and vitally important to a shared vision for the organization.*
4. *Personal assessment is a trainable skill, but requires support by effective habits.*

Applications

1. Find examples and list positive outcomes from personal formative assessment. Create a Spicy Node or other graphic to demonstrate your findings.
2. List and support theoretical underpinnings of reflective practice.
3. Examine and list barriers to reflective practice and include strategies to combat the barriers.

Chapter 13

Sustainability

"Concentration is inspiration. You must be completely overtaken by your work and your subject. Only then do all your influences and experience come up to the surface."
----Cesar Chavez

Modern organizations are sustained by belief systems that emphasize the importance of going beyond temporary gains in achievement to create lasting, meaningful improvements in learning found most prevalent in any learning culture. This implies that the effective leader will prepare the culture to survive in his or her absence by building skills in those in the organization. The absence can be temporary or permanent, but in either case, the culture continues to flourish due to the established norms and practices. Promoting learning with value-added experiences will more likely produce such cultures that will produce outcomes consistent with the vision of the organization. Consistent with the previous language of participative or distributive leadership through empowered practices, the organization will perpetually develop the ability to flourish. Such an environment not only responds to accountability, but it also creates a spirit of responsibility. A spirit of responsibility outlives any of the individuals in the organization. Examples of such spirit in the real world would be Duke University basketball, Notre Dame football, Harvard Law School, and other institutions built on a shared understanding of what is expected by all participants. Organizations are easier to establish and manage while institutions are built on the shared belief of what it takes to make the institution survive and in some cases dominate its peers. That is the type of attitude of responsibility that builds sustainability. Evident in the value-added model are the domains of what it would take to create such opportunities leading to a sustainable institution: dispositions, structures that support learning communities, shared decision making opportunities, relevant professional experience, and trained self-assessment skills. Key to the value-added model outcomes is the development of interactive systems that provide the necessary supports consistent with approaches to reform that in which all members of the organization do their work in the best interest of sustaining that ability to perform.

Sustaining cultures is far more than determining if particular actions can be replicated. Replication may be key to those activities that demonstrate success or effectiveness, but true sustainability is a management consideration with emphasis on succession driven by the principles, not the principals. Attaching desired success to an individual is a misguided understanding of sustainable action. Thus, the need for individual and collective efficacy deserves even more consideration for sustainability purposes. Even pre-service leadership programs contain a curriculum heavy in scripted behaviors. While important, the curriculum does not contain experiences in how to establish common social and environmental systems that perpetuate themselves. A value-added model allows for incremental assessment of the components and interactions of the components found in social and environmental systems. It is apparent that preparation for cultural transformation that will sustain in the future requires several key considerations.

1. A full understanding of global implications on current organizational need for transformation is imperative. Obviously, current social systems expand the bound-

aries of our individual environments. The world is continuously getting smaller. Creating and managing collective efficacy will depend on our understanding of the global skills needed for survival and its implications in preparing students for those skills.

2. Skills in assessing cultural characteristics are important especially related to metaphoric organizational patterns. Organizations have distinguishable patterns. Brains and organisms are examples of metaphoric labels. The value of considering this literature is that it provides us insight into the behaviors of individuals. Altering these behaviors through cultural transformation will be important to the ability to transform and the level the organization may reach in the transformation process.

3. In the complex organization life, leaders of cultural transformation must be skilled in promoting social and generational equity. Just as student bodies become more diverse, so do the faculties. Age variations bring about different needs in terms of personal and professional lives. What the leader may be faced with is the readiness level differences in generations and social groups for accepting the needed or identified transformational activities.

4. The ultimate driving force in cultural sustainability has to be the quality of life for the participants found and impacted by the culture. Quality of life is certainly a by-product of sustainability as the impact or outcome of transformation can perpetuate cumulative life experiences. Organizations with institutionalized environments flourish on the basics of human needs with high degrees of self-actualization.

5. Collaborative processes with full participation will enhance the passion needed for sustainable opportunities.

There certainly will be a balance of competitiveness and collaboration. The implications of such conditions are that if a balance between competition and collaboration can be created and can continue to exist, the passion will enhance the development of collective efficacy. What may occur is compensation tied to individual growth and unit growth that will naturally build on the passion to succeed, but succeed at a level that is comparable to others. This might appear to be a contradiction to full collaboration, but as new performance evaluation instruments are implemented, along with compensation models based on performance, the leader must deal with the competitive nature of such models.

6. At the root of sustainable education is quality teaching and quality learning. This is included so that leaders do not lose focus on the fundamental premise of transformation. Defining quality teaching and quality learning will be a challenge to some, but it is crucial to the discussion of collective efficacy.

7. Sustainability in education has to be a process of including the principles of sustainability in the thought and minds of members of the organization, not just inserted at a prescribed time. Sustainable language needs to be at the onset of the transformation process. The language of sustainability must be consistent, encouraged, and programmed throughout the organization. The language must be inspirational, but real to the members.

8. Within the model is the need for an attitude of taking risks that are best calculated to enhance the performance of the organization. This statement does not promote taking risks at the possible consequence of harming the organization. Rather, risks are based on

personal or group action research with control measures for damage.

9. Leadership for sustainability must be resourceful, especially during economic times that create burdens on society. Actually, resourcefulness validates the need for the value-added model and sustainable outcomes associated with the model.

10. A basic challenge of sustaining transformational excellence is highly systematic. It is important that systems support leaders that model sustainability. Systems support transformational leaders and leaders that can impact growth, but there is little language of promoting sustainability behaviors. Legacies need to focus on systematic change and sustainable change rather than standardized recognition for immediate change. A sustainable leader can inspire others, lead by a vision and are much less likely to "burn out".

This section of the text closes with sustainability for a purpose. The purpose is to avoid a temporary cultural change that does not have long-term impact. Thus, the idea of a value added model is to address the learning culture while focusing on the outcomes that politicians and society deem crucial to the indication of performance. The model is intended to create transformation that is not a "flash in the pan".

Takeaways

1. *Sustainability is contingent upon belief systems that are not only shared, but supported by skills that strongly encourage a language and commitment to responsibility.*
2. *Cultural transformation is impacted by the interaction of social and environmental systems.*
3. *Sustaining a viable culture is trainable with adequate curriculum and experiences.*
4. *Sustainability is more directly related to responsibility than accountability.*

Applications

1. Create a graphic that features strategies for sustainability. Provide specific examples.
2. Create a graphic that addresses interdependencies for social and environmental systems.

Section III: 21st Century Skills

Chapter 14

Who Are the Teachers in the 21ˢᵗ Century?

"We can whenever and wherever we choose, successfully teach all children... we already know more than we need to know in order to do that."
                              ----*Ron Edmonds, Educator*

Of a gifted teacher (she) "has an unfailing heart and eye for magical classrooms and who loses sleep over any sliver of work at less than the highest quality."
                              ----*Carol Ann Tomlinson*

Ron Edmonds and Carol Ann Tomlinson help us see the value in the disposition of "can" rather than "can't". Seeing the possibilities in the youngsters we serve is a critical ingredient to successful teaching and learning. Changing the culture of schools becomes a significant factor in the process of embracing Edmonds and Tomlinson's dispositions. Recruiting, selecting, and retaining teachers with the value-added components outlined in Chapter 11 becomes a necessary part of the selection process. Training prospective teachers and re-training present teachers allows teachers to become aware of skills and standards required of 21ˢᵗ century teachers. Aligning dispositions with current research-based practice becomes challenging.

Trying to answer the question posed in this chapter – Who are the teachers in the 21ˢᵗ century? - takes us back to the past and also brings us the present. Schools of yesterday were developed around the factory model in which students sat in rows and listened as the teacher taught lessons.

Testing was done at the end of a chapter or unit of study and grades were recorded in a grade book. A traditional high school encompassed four grades and taught basic and advanced subjects and vocational courses. Instruction involved teachers teaching and students listening. Tests were given at the end of chapters and units. Teachers were considered experts and valued as such. Through the years, schools were not faced with accountability issues. The "factory" continued to run with little or no change deemed necessary.

As the information age progressed in the 20th century, schools were expected to use current technology with little change to teaching and learning. As the end of the 20th century came into view, *A Nation at Risk (1983)*[1] was published (referenced again and elaborated upon in Chapter 20) and the findings were startling[1]. Contained in the report were the following facts:

- International comparisons of student achievement, completed a decade ago, revealed that on 19 academic tests American students were never first or second and, in comparison with other industrialized nations, were last seven times.
- Some 23 million American adults were functionally illiterate by the simplest tests of everyday reading, writing, and comprehension.
- About 13 percent of all 17-year-olds in the United States were considered functionally illiterate. Functional illiteracy among minority youth may run as high as 40 percent.
- Average achievement of high school students on most standardized tests was lower than when Sputnik was launched.

- Over half the population of gifted students did not match their tested ability with comparable achievement in school.
- The College Board's Scholastic Aptitude Tests (SAT) demonstrated a virtually unbroken decline from 1963 to 1980. Average verbal scores fell over 50 points and average mathematics scores dropped nearly 40 points.
- College Board achievement tests also revealed consistent declines in such subjects as physics and English.
- Both the number and proportion of students demonstrating superior achievement on the SATs (i.e., those with scores of 650 or higher) dramatically declined.
- Many 17-year-olds did not possess the "higher order" intellectual skills expected of them. Nearly 40 percent could not draw inferences from written material; only one-fifth could write a persuasive essay; and only one-third could solve a mathematics problem requiring several steps.
- There was a steady decline in science achievement scores of U.S. 17-year-olds as measured by national assessments of science in 1969, 1973, and 1977.
- Between 1975 and 1980, remedial mathematics courses in public 4-year colleges increased by 72 percent and constituted one-quarter of all mathematics courses taught in those institutions.
- Average tested achievement of students graduating from college was also lower.
- Business and military leaders complained that they spent millions of dollars on costly remedial education and training programs in such basic skills as reading, writing, spelling, and computation. The Department of the Navy, for example, reported to the Commission that one-quarter of its recruits could not read at the ninth grade level, the minimum needed simply to understand written safety instructions. Without remedial work they

could not even begin, much less complete, the sophisticated training essential in much of the modern military.

These deficiencies came at a time when the demand for highly skilled workers in new fields was accelerating rapidly. For example:

- Computers and computer-controlled equipment were penetrating every aspect of our lives--homes, factories, and offices.
- One estimate indicated that by the beginning of the 21st century millions of jobs involved laser technology and robotics.
- Technology radically transformed a host of other occupations. They included health care, medical science, energy production, food processing, construction, and the building, repair, and maintenance of sophisticated scientific, educational, military, and industrial equipment.

With this view from A Nation at Risk, a stronger prescription was placed in the lens of education. A myriad of programs began and teachers and schools were inundated with solutions. Within the field of education, new and exciting thoughts were beginning to emerge. Educators began to implement programs to try to solve the needs expressed in the report. Yet, all schools did not make needed change and students continued to fall behind. School leaders began to dialog among themselves to try to solve the problems. A myriad of thought began to take focus and thus began the discussion of 21st century teaching and learning. With an abundance of research-based information, we know enough today to begin to answer the following questions:

- Who do we hire to teach in the 21st century classroom?
- What does the 21st century curriculum look like?
- What are 21st century standards?
- How are 21st century skills integrated into the curricula?
- What instructional practices are necessary in a 21st century classroom?
- How has the learning environment changed in the 21st century classroom?
- In what ways do we conduct 21st century professsional development?

As educators review these questions and begin to discover answers, the framework of the 21st century school/classroom will be established. Within this model, notice the relationship of teacher qualities to actual work environments and the business world. By understanding new research and embracing updated strategies, teachers model qualities necessary for success in any work environment. The principal and administrative staff of the school and school system become accountable for empowering teachers to know and understand value-added practices in the classroom. By taking each question separately, we can provide a visual of required expectations of the 21st century classroom.

Let's begin by answering the overarching question: What are the characteristics we would expect to see in a 21st century Educator?

We know they are student-centric, holistic, and they are teaching about how to learn as much as teaching about the subject area. We know too, that they must be 21st century learners as well. But teachers are more than this. According to Andrew Churches, the vision of a 21st century educator looks like this graphic:

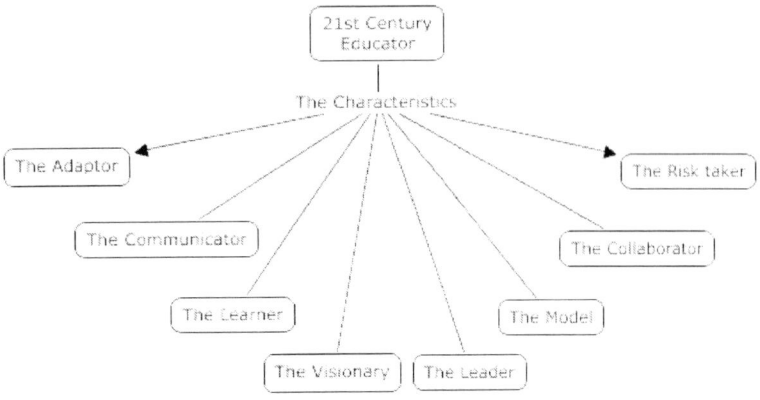

Characteristics of the 21st Century Teacher[2]

Let's take a closer look at each characteristic and its value in selecting great teachers to serve the youngsters in the schools.

The Adaptor

The 21st century teacher is an adaptor. Harnessed as we are to an assessment-focused education model the 21st century teacher must be able to adapt the curriculum and the requirements to teach to the curriculum in creative ways. They must also be able to adapt software and hardware designed for a business model into tools utilizable by a variety of age groups and abilities. As the lead actor in the "play of learning" the teacher must also be able to adapt to a dynamic teaching experience. When it all goes wrong in the middle of a class, when the technologies fail, the show must go on. Innovative, creative teachers adapt their teaching to meet this important disposition. As an educator, teachers must understand and apply different learning styles. Teachers must be able to adapt their teaching style to be inclusive of different modes of learning. Students must be taught to know and understand their own learning styles in order for them to work with new ideas in ways that assist them in learning. Teaching students how to learn is a critical strategy for the 21st century. In studying dispositions of today's educators, adaptability becomes a key ingredient in the teaching/learning process. Teaching students to learn how to learn is a value-added strategy.

Again, we look at a needed change in disposition for teachers and students. Knowing and understanding change models become clear to teacher trainers and university professors. The teacher today must embrace change on a regular basis and be prepared to embrace Eury's Value-Added model (as discussed in Section II of this text). The model creates a process in which educators can negotiate a new practice in schools and connect them to classroom learning.

A visionary educator provides the challenge to change and create new ideas about teaching and learning. This person presents challenges to teachers and requires others to think and create new models and strategies. As research about leadership styles informs us, educators must be equipped with or able to draw upon a variety of styles in order to get the work done. The visionary cannot work in a vacuum. At times, s/he must use participative leadership or change-oriented leadership. Leadership style practices assist in decision making and offer assistance to the visionary leader.

The Visionary

Imagination, a key component of adaptability, is a crucial component of the educator of today and tomorrow. Today's educator must use students to assist them in learning the potential in the emerging tools and web technologies, grasp these and manipulate them to serve their needs. Teachers are no longer masters of all they teach and every tool they use. Collaboration in classrooms creates opportunities for student leadership and creativity. If teachers look at the technologies currently emerging, how many are developed for education? The visionary teacher can look at others ideas and envisage how they would learn to use or actually use these in their class. At times, a short conversation with students helps the teacher understand the technology and can assist the teacher in conveying the process to the entire class. The visionary also looks across the disciplines and through the curricula. They collaborate and develop units that intersect with other disciplines. **They teach students the big ideas of the curriculum and utilize specific learning targets in their lesson planning.** They make links that reinforce and value learning in other areas, and leverage other fields to reinforce their own teaching and the learning of their students. To facilitate this process in a school, teachers and administrators must determine ways to provide interdisciplinary planning for teachers. Each school has teachers who know how to work with interdisciplinary teams or who want to learn to do this. Then teachers become collaborators.

The Collaborator

Teaching in most classrooms is a lonely profession. Teachers are often isolated and without planned collaboration. Expecting and planning for teams to work together is a critical piece of teaching and learning in the 21st century.

Students in the 21st century already understand Ning, Blogger, Wikispaces, Bebo, MySpace, and Second Life. As educators, teachers must be able to leverage these collaborative tools to enhance and captivate learners.

Teachers too, must be collaborators; sharing, contributing, adapting and inventing. Knowing what other teachers are using to teach and understanding how they utilize the successful strategies is one way to insure quality teaching in classrooms of the 21st century. Professional learning communities, better known as PLC's, serve as an excellent system to provide continuous collaboration and planning for teachers.

The Learner

Are you beginning to see that teachers must also be constantly learning? You ask - How can teachers know all these things? How can you teach teachers how to use them?

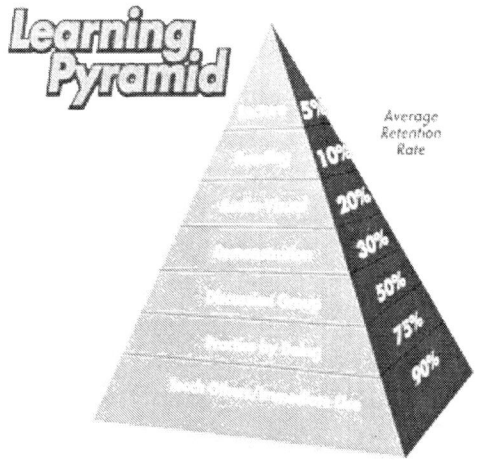

When teachers collaborate and begin to adapt to changes necessary, their ability to take risks can be enhanced. In 21st century teaching and learning there are so many innovative strategies and so much to learn. Teachers must take risks and sometimes surrender themselves to the students' knowledge. They must have a vision of what they want and what the technology can achieve, identify the goals and facilitate the learning. Teachers must use the strengths of the digital natives to understand and navigate new products, have the students teach each other. The learning pyramid[3] shows that the highest retention of knowledge comes from teaching others. Providing opportunities for students to teach the class can reap great rewards in learning. Trust your students. By reviewing the learning pyramid, we remind ourselves of how we retain our learning. Teachers want students to retain what is taught. The pyramid gives reminders of how that can be achieved.

The Communicator

"Anywhere, anytime" learning is a catchphrase used often today. Usually it's paired with "lifetime learner". To have anywhere, anytime learning, the teacher too must be anywhere and at anytime. It does not have to be the same teacher, but the 21st century teacher is a communicator. They are fluent in tools and technologies that enable communication and collaboration. They go beyond learning just how to do it, they also know how to facilitate it, stimulate and control it, moderate and manage it. Today's classroom is open to parents and the public. It is necessary and important that teachers, parents, and the community work together to prepare youngsters for life in the 21st century in a world environment. In this environment, teachers must be willing to facilitate opportunities for all parents to be involved in the classroom activities. This is an easily spoken assignment, but more difficult to implement.

The Model

Teachers must model the behaviors that are expected from students. Today and tomorrow more so, there is an expectation that teachers will teach values. We are often the most consistent part of a student's life. Teachers will see the students more often, for longer periods of time than their parents during the school year. This is not a criticism of the parents, rather a reflection. The 21st century educator also models reflective practice, whether it's the quiet, personal inspection of their teaching and learning, or through reflective practice via blogs, twitter and other medium, these educators look both inwards and outwards. Teachers also model a number of other disposition characteristics. Reflective practice is a part of the professional teaching standards. They model:

- tolerance
- acceptance
- a wider view than just their curricula areas
- global awareness
- reflection

The Leader

Teacher leadership is part of professional teaching standards. The 21st century teacher is a leader. Leadership, like clear goals and objectives, is crucial to the success or failure of any project. Vision, incentives, and action plans are all elements of leadership:

Churches continues with the following visual to capture the process of clear and lasting change in any organization.

vision + skills + incentives + resources + action plan = change
        skills + incentives + resources + action plan = confusion
vision +   incentives + resources + action plan = anxiety
vision + skills +   resources + action plan = resistance
vision + skills + incentives +   action plan = frustration
vision + skills + incentives + resources +   = treadmill

The 21st century teacher not only knows what to teach, but how to be certain students are learning. Using Churches' eight characteristics, the 21st century teacher must learn or re-tool skills and strategies that insure learning for the 21st

century student. Willingness to learn to use technology as a tool to effectively teach and to rely on students within the classroom for assistance, 21st century teachers must adopt a team approach to teaching and learning. Colleges and universities will also need to attend to training teachers for the 21st century. The "factory model" is no longer viable for today's teacher. We must know our subjects, be able to integrate subjects and teach students for mastery. Education is in the process of changing and 21st century educators will embrace the future with excitement and vigor.

To help each child prepare for successful employment and productive citizenship in the 21st century, all teachers must deeply know their subject areas, understand how children learn, use modern learning technologies effectively, and work closely with their colleagues to create rich learning environments that produce high-quality learning experiences for every child.

Decades of research confirm what we know from experience: At the heart of every high performing school, we find high quality teaching. Good teachers are the most important factor in the quality of a child's education. Investing in high quality teaching is the most important action America's schools can take to put our children's dreams within reach and prepare our nation for the future.

Schools in the 21st century will be laced with a project-based curriculum for life aimed at engaging students in addressing real-world problems, issues important to humanity, and questions that matter.

This is a dramatic departure from the factory model education of the past. It is abandonment, finally, of textbook-driven, teacher-centered, paper and pencil schooling. It means a new way of understanding the concept of "knowledge", a new definition of the "educated person". A new way of designing and delivering the curriculum is required.

The following new definitions for "School" and "Teacher" are appropriate for the 21st century:

- Schools will go from 'buildings' to 'nerve centers', with walls that are porous and transparent, connecting teachers, students and the community to the wealth of knowledge that exists in the world.
- Teacher - From primary role as a dispenser of information to orchestrator of learning and helping students turn information into knowledge, and knowledge into wisdom.

The 21st century will require knowledge generation, not just information delivery, and schools will need to create a culture of inquiry. Students will be at the center of the process. Teaching them to think and learn will be the highest priority.

Takeaways

1. Teachers in the 21st century will plan and teach differently from their predecessors in the 20th century. Their training and re-training will require innovative measures.
2. Teachers will be learners and students will be teachers. "Controlling" classrooms will be a lesser part of the teaching process. Keeping students involved in the learning process will be the main focus.
3. Classrooms will no longer be a place of four walls and a ceiling and floor. Classrooms will be international, online and organized in new ways of learning for students and teachers.
4. Teacher dispositions must match the needs of students and the educational environment.
5. Approaching teaching with willingness to adapt to the situation will be essential.
6. Displaying leadership and modeling sound affective dispositions will create more productive environments for students.
7. Training for new teachers will be a critical part of teacher training in the United States.

Application

You are asked to speak to a group of undergraduate students at a local college and are given the specific task:

Using a 21st century visual representation (not power point), design and describe in detail the critical qualities of a 21st century teacher.

Chapter 15

Who Are the 21st Century Learners and What is the Teaching-Learning Environment?

"You learn at your best when you have something you care about and can get pleasure in being engaged in."
----*Howard Gardner*

"The future is here. It's just not widely distributed yet."
----*William Gibson*

If we continue to look at teacher self-efficacy as it relates to learning, we begin to view the value of well-trained professional educators in each classroom. Teachers must be consistently involved in professional learning. Teachers must be willing to become part of the learning team that includes the students. At the present, educators often speak of how poorly high school graduates perform when entering college. Colleges and universities often complain of too many students having to take remedial courses before starting general requirements. Expressions of general concern about college freshmen readiness for college coursework can be heard on almost all campuses. Perhaps some of the perceptions may be accurate. However, one often wonders if the student's process of development on the maturity scale is a "work in progress." Often times, as college professors, we want students to learn and show mastery in the same ways the Baby Boomers experienced their learning. With the dawning of technology in the early 80's, student learning began to look different. Carie Windham describes the Net Generation in the words of students[4]:

- My computer is the nucleus of my workspace
- When I need information I go online
- Besides IM (i.e., instant messaging) or email my cell phone is my primary method of communication
- I'm usually juggling five things at once

As Diane Oblinger cites, "This is the Net Generation, students who were born after 1982 – students who have never known life without the internet. Although educators may see students every day, we don't necessarily understand their habits, expectations or learning preferences." She further asserts that these students use IM, text, and Google as verbs. The Net Generation involves technology in all phases of their lives. What does this knowledge do to inform the teacher?

The 21st century will require knowledge generation, not just information delivery, and schools will need to create a "culture of inquiry".[5]

In addition to the net generation description, students today are very different learners.

In the past a learner was a young person who went to school, spent a specified amount of time in certain courses, received passing grades and graduated. Today we must see learners in a new context as outlined by 21st century schools:

> First – we must maintain student interest by helping them see how what they are learning prepares them for life in the real world. This reflects the need for relevance and real world practice in the teaching/learning process.
>
> Second – we must instill curiosity, which is fundamental to lifelong learning.
>
> Third – we must be flexible in how we teach.

Fourth – we must excite learners to become even more resourceful so that they will continue to learn outside the formal school day. A quick view of Bloom's Revised Taxonomy will assist the 21st century teacher here. Use of appropriate questioning skills adds a multi-level dimension to the classroom.

So what will schools look like, exactly? What will the curriculum look like? How will this 21st century curriculum be organized, and how will it impact the way we design and build schools, how we assess students, how we purchase resources, how we acquire and utilize the new technologies. What does all this mean for us in an era of standardized testing and accountability?[6]

Twenty-first century curriculum has certain critical attributes for learners. It is interdisciplinary, project-based, and research-driven. It is connected to the community – local, state, national and global. Sometimes students are collaborating with people around the world in various projects. The curriculum incorporates higher order thinking skills, multiple intelligences, technology and multimedia, the multiple literacies of the 21st century, and authentic assessments. Service learning is an important component.

The classroom is expanded to include the greater community. Students are self-directed, and work both independently and interdependently. The curriculum and instruction are designed to challenge all students, and provides for differentiation.

The curriculum is not textbook-driven or fragmented, but is thematic, project-based and integrated. Skills and content are not taught as an end in themselves, but students learn them through their research and application in their projects. Textbooks, if they have them, are just one of many resources.

Knowledge is not memorization of facts and figures, but is constructed through research and application, and connected to previous knowledge, personal experience, interests, talents and passions. The skills and content become relevant and needed as students require this information to complete their projects. The content and basic skills are applied within the context of the curriculum, and are not ends in themselves.

Assessment moves from regurgitation of memorized facts and disconnected processes to demonstration of understanding through application in a variety of contexts. Real-world audiences are an important part of the assessment process, as is self-assessment.

According to Hal Portner,[7] Where does formal schooling take place? The response to this question is: *between the teacher and the student in the classroom.* Portner continues by saying the notion still holds true in general, but given the today's changing world and the definition of an educated student prepared to cope with these changes, this perception often falls short.

The classroom begins to display a different scenario. The teacher becomes the planner and the manager, and, at times, the facilitator of knowledge. However, we begin to see the sharing of teaching and learning begin to appear. Portner continues by asking us to drop preconceptions and let our imaginations expand the traditional concept of 'classroom' to include an additional range of virtual, as well as, actual options. An example he uses is - learning and teaching take place between and among students; the teacher assumes the roles of facilitator, resource, and coach; and students not only extend themselves technologically into cyberspace, but also physically in such real-world sites as the local community and beyond.

Wherever possible, activities and processes are carried out in an environment that develops and recognizes students' interests and abilities, and that relate them directly to real-world practices. When students are encouraged to dig for data on a topic they care about, the results can be enlightening and empowering. To paraphrase Harry S. Truman, *the best way to involve your students is to find out what they are good at and then allow them to do it.*

Portner's perceptions of the 21st century teaching and learning environment are on target. Treating teachers as professionals and allowing them sufficient time to plan and develop real-world practices is essential to the success of students. Deliberate planning at all levels becomes essential. Becoming a part of a planning group or PLC (i.e., Professional Learning Community) can be advantageous at this point. In lieu of longer planning time, teachers and students can enhance their learning if they are included in collaborative group work. Students, like teachers, can benefit from this timely collaboration.

Collaborative Group Work

Portner continues his description:

> "There are three basic ways people interact with each other as they work. They can compete to see who is "best," they can work individually toward a goal without paying attention to others, or they can work cooperatively with a vested interest in each other's contribution as well as their own. In most of today's public and private enterprises, especially the successful ones, collaboration is the most dominant of these three interaction patterns. Case in point: Google founders Larry Page and Sergey Brin see to it that most projects in the "Googleplex"

are implemented using development teams of 3-5 people.

It may appear that some successful individuals have been effective working alone – Einstein and Henry Ford, for example – however, even these innovative people often collaborated regularly. Thomas Edison, for instance, often worked together with Frank J. Sprague, a skilled mathematician, and Nikola Tesla, a talented mechanical and electrical engineer."

Students in the competitive world of today's schooling vie with other students within their own environment and beyond. They are faced with needing good grades, impressive course resumes, and high scores on college entrance examinations. Portner states that the Studies by the Center for Public Education and others show that students are "more satisfied, more academically productive, more likely to participate in school activities, better behaved, and less likely to drop out when they are organized into collaborative groups."

Portner summarizes with "many teachers avoid cooperative group work – perhaps because they worry about off-task behavior, aren't sure about how to grade individual students who work together, or are reluctant to change from their familiar methodologies."

From research we learn that student classroom time is spent listening to the teacher and often working alone. The latest research in successful teaching strategies tells us this is not the best way to teach. We know that the classroom strategy in which students work together in collaborative groups and tackle projects and problems can be highly successful.

Middle and High School Classes

The old model of pedagogy – teacher-focused, one-way, one-size-fits-all – makes no sense to young people who have grown up in a digital world. Today's middle and high school students expect a conversation rather than a lecture, and they're used to working in groups rather than toiling alone. Digital immersion has even affected the way they absorb information. They don't necessarily read a page from left to right and from top to bottom. They might instead skip around, scanning for pertinent information of interest.

Just because there is still a teacher and a classroom does not mean that the traditional model of teaching and learning needs to happen. The savvy 21st century middle and high school teacher functions as facilitator, coach and resource; the student functions as team member, researcher and creative problem solver; and the classroom may extend, virtually and actually, beyond its walls.

Getting students involved in their education is more than having them participate. The teacher's role is to connect students with their education by enabling them to influence and affect their own learning, and allowing them to become enwrapped and engrossed in their educational experiences.

Teachers have to learn and employ a new set of skills where the teacher is more of a questioner and a resource of knowledge than a giver of knowledge. There are, of course, occasions when lecturing or using other modes of giving information is appropriate. On the other hand, lectures can be listened to at home as a podcast. Students can listen to it as many times as needed and make notes of questions to ask in class.

The sort of teacher we are envisioning is a person on the move, checking over shoulders, asking questions and teaching mini-lessons for individuals and teams. Support is customized and individualized. S/he sets clear expectations, provides explicit directions, and keeps the process well structured and productive. S/he circulates, disciplines, questions, assesses, suggests, validates, facilitates, monitors, challenges, motivates, watches, moderates, diagnoses, trouble-shoots, observes, encourages, suggests, models, clarifies, directs, redirects, and knows when to get out of the way.

The teacher engages students by asking questions: How are you going to approach this problem? What are the resources that you're going to need? How would you know when you're successful? What are the steps in the process that you're going to take? The teacher helps students develop ways to monitor their own behavior, come up with criteria for governing themselves, and create internal strategies to monitor their progress. The teacher guides the students' reflections. 'What did you learn from this? What did you learn from this that you could apply to future activities? As you were engaged in this activity, what was going on inside your head? How did you know that you were being successful? What did you do when you met with frustration?'

To help the teacher carry out the role of facilitator/coach/resource, the classroom is set up so that the teacher is accessible to all groups and has room to walk easily from one group to another. When leaving one group to go on to another, the teacher leaves with a "challenge" aimed to raise the bar or to redirect their focus. Of course, the teacher must establish or negotiate "ground rules" around acceptable behavior and protocol.

Finally, as a teacher assumes the role of facilitator/coach/resource, s/he should expect to be kept on his/her toes and therefore open to fine tuning his/her own practice.

S/he will need to become a steward of his/her own professional development and his/her school district must provide appropriate professional development to support his/her needs.

Students are a few clicks away from being connected to a wealth of data. Google and Wikipedia, for example, have allowed us to find any piece of information or facts we would ever want to know. Why memorize what is right at your fingertips? The key is knowing what facts or information you need, where and how to find them, and whether or not they are accurate and complete.

Some educators decry the use of anything other than reference books and newspapers, and perhaps television news and documentaries as viable data sources. These media remain important sources of information. However, ignoring or demonizing technology that students willingly and actively use in every other aspect of their lives is not a winning educational strategy. Tapping into the capabilities of modern technology provides a powerful way to engage students and enhance learning both inside and outside of the classroom.

Teenagers tend to use social networks such as MySpace, FaceBook, Twitter, etc. to share and access information which may not be reliable. The teacher must insist upon and monitor the importance of original source and verification when accessing information. The teacher should also be aware that daily exposure to digital technologies such as the Internet and smart phones may lead to social awkwardness, an inability to interpret nonverbal messages, isolation and less interest in traditional classroom learning. Balance is critical in the daily practices in classrooms.

The Challenge

In his article "Preparing Creative and Critical Thinkers," appearing in the Summer 2008 edition of *Educational Leadership*, Donald J. Treffinger writes, "Once upon a time, educators might have said to their students, *If you'll pay close attention to what I'm going to teach you, you'll learn everything you need to know for a successful life.*"[8] It's doubtful that this message was ever entirely true, but it's certainly not true today. We don't know all the information that today's students will need or all the answers to the questions they will face. Indeed, increasingly, we don't even know the questions.

We have looked at the 21st century learner and the 21st century learning environment. As educators, we know the descriptions found in this chapter are not widely known in the public. Our responsibility becomes one of communicating the message and inspiring students to demonstrate their skills and abilities. Motivation on the part of educator to insure the public is knowledgeable and students are involved in teaching them lifts expectations to a higher standard. The students can be the exemplary teachers in the 21st century environment.

Takeaways

1. Students are multi-taskers and want to learn through multimedia. Teaching this student requires a vast array of knowledge and tools by the teacher.
2. Classrooms are without walls and reach around the world for the 21st century learner. Teachers need to know how this environment works.
3. Teachers assume different roles in the 21st century classroom – coach, communicator, resource guide, questioner, etc. Being prepared for the diversity in the classroom empowers teachers to be much more effective.
4. Teachers of 21st century learners must be prepared to use 21st century technology and know its benefit in the teaching /learning process.
5. School systems must equip schools/classrooms with technology for teachers and students to use to benefit the teaching/learning process.
6. Teacher training institutions need to focus on the needs of the 21st century learner and the environment necessary to teach and learn. Professors need to be up to date in the use of the vast array of technology and teaching strategies that are necessary in the 21st century classroom.

Application

You have been asked by the director of instruction in your school district to develop a 21st century lesson design to use in your school.

Using the information in this chapter, work with a partner to develop a lesson plan template to use in your school. In bold print in your template, designate 21st century approaches to learners.

Chapter 16

Critical Attributes of 21st Century Schools Curriculum and Instruction

"Yet we know from research that access to a challenging high school curriculum has a greater impact on whether a student will earn a four-year college degree than his or her high school test scores, class rank, or grades. And we know that low-income students are less likely to have access to these accelerated learning opportunities and college-level coursework than their peers."

----*Arne Duncan*

"A democratic education means that we educate people in a way that ensures they can think independently, that they can use information, knowledge, and technology, among other things, to draw their own conclusions."

----*Linda Darling-Hammond*

From the minds of Arne Duncan, Secretary of Education, and Linda Darling-Hammond, distinguished professor of education and published author, comes the importance of current teaching and learning and the effects on society. Duncan reminds us of what it takes to get students into college and higher education and Darling-Hammond reminds us of the importance of creating thinkers in the schools. The global classrooms of the 21st century create opportunities for students to interact and do project-based learning using targets of concern to the world. The following segment introduces current thought and practice to stimulate curriculum and instruction today.

Global Classrooms

Every day students from countries all over the world collaborate on important projects. The web site, ePals is a place where teachers and students can go to join or start a collaborative project with anyone in the world. According to ePals, Inc., "Our Global Community™ is the largest online community of K-12 learners, enabling more than 325,000 educators and 126,000 classrooms in over 200 countries and territories to safely connect, exchange ideas, and learn together. Award winning SchoolBlog™ and SchoolMail™ products are widely used and trusted by schools around the world."

As we have seen from our own experiences, from the media, from university research, and as it was demonstrated in the Did You Know? YouTube video, technologies, especially the Internet, have resulted in a globalized society. The world is now "flat". Our world has been transformed, and will continue to change at ever-increasing rates.

In order for our students to be prepared to navigate this 21st century world, they must become knowledgeable in 21st century literacies, including multicultural, media, information, emotional, ecological, financial and cyber literacies. Collaborating with students from around the world in meaningful, real-life projects is a necessary tool for developing these literacies. Students can learn that through collaboration, not competition, they can work together to make the world a better place. Students will use technologies, including the Internet, and global collaboration to solve critical issues[9].

21st Century Skills

As educators, we think of 21st century studies. In middle and high schools we attempt to provide students with a cross section of appropriate information to help them in the years to come. Mastery of core subjects and 21st century themes is essential for students of today (this topic will be discussed in more detail in chapter 26). Core subjects include:

- English, reading or language arts
- World languages
- Mathematics
- Science
- Economics
- Geography
- History
- Government and Civics
- Arts

In addition to these subjects, we believe schools must move beyond a focus on basic competency in core subjects to promoting understanding of academic content at much higher levels by weaving 21st century interdisciplinary themes into core subjects[10]:

- Global awareness
- Financial, economic, business and entrepreneurial literacy
- Civic literacy
- Health literacy
- Environmental literacy

Think tanks on peaceful co-existence come to the forefront. Students of the 21st century must be the guiding force in efforts to gain and sustain peace throughout the world.

Giving 21st century students knowledge and a desire to be involved becomes critical.

Relevant, Rigorous, Relationships and Real-world Learning

To bring all the skills necessary to the learning environment, teachers must embrace relevance, rigor, relationships, and real-world learning.

Defining Relevance

Relevance refers to learning in which students apply core knowledge, concepts, or skills, to solve real-world problems. Relevant learning is interdisciplinary and contextual. It is created, for example, through authentic problems or tasks, simulations, service learning, connecting concepts to current issues and teaching others.

Defining Rigor

Academic rigor refers to learning in which students demonstrate a thorough in-depth mastery of challenging tasks to develop cognitive skills through reflective thought, analysis, problem solving, evaluation or creativity. It's the quality of thinking, not the quantity, that defines academic rigor, and rigorous learning can occur at any school grade and in any subject.

Defining Relationships

An additional concept, relationships, dovetails with the two mentioned above. Relationships between students and teachers, students and students, and teachers and teachers add value to the learning. Special value comes from enhanced student – teacher relationships. Knowing the teacher cares often becomes a pivotal point for student learning and creates motivation for learning.

Most states have set curricula that lead public education in the United States. The process of developing a national curriculum and having it adopted by all states is a bureaucratic process that is in progress. In outlining standards for English (Language Arts) and Mathematics, or Common Core Courses as they are called, the new standards were prepared using 21st century qualities.

The Common Core State Standards define the rigorous skills and knowledge in English (Language Arts) and Mathematics that need to be effectively taught and learned for students to be ready to succeed academically in credit-bearing, college-entry courses and in workforce training programs. These standards have been developed to be:

Fewer, clearer, and higher, to best drive effective policy and practice; Aligned with college and work expectations, so that all students are prepared for success upon graduating from high school; Inclusive of rigorous content and applications of knowledge through higher-order skills, so that all students are prepared for the 21st century; Internationally benchmarked, so that all students are prepared for succeeding in our global economy and society; and research and evidence-based. The standards intend to set forward thinking goals for student performance based on evidence about what is required for success. The standards developed will set the stage for US education not just for next year, but for the next decade, and they must ensure *all* U.S. students are prepared for the global economic workplace. Furthermore, the standards created will not lower the bar but raise it for all students; as such, we cannot narrow the college-ready focus of the standards to just preparation of students for college algebra and English composition. Therefore we will seek to ensure all students are prepared for all entry-level, credit-bearing, academic college courses in English, mathematics, the sciences, the social sciences, and the humanities. The objective is for all students to enter these classes ready for success (defined for these purposes as a C or better). In order for teachers to begin to align themselves in subjects and grades, they must first find a common vocabulary.

Common Vocabulary:

Goal: The standards as a whole must be essential, rigorous, clear and specific, coherent, and internationally bench-marked.

Essential: The standards must be reasonable in scope in defining the knowledge and skills students should have to be ready to succeed in entry-level, credit-bearing, academic college courses and in workforce training programs.

Workforce training programs pertain to careers that:

1) Offer competitive, livable salaries above the poverty line
2) Offer opportunities for career advancement
3) Are in a growing or sustainable industry

College refers to two- and four-year postsecondary schools

Entry-level, credit-bearing, academic college courses (e.g. English, mathematics, sciences, social sciences, humanities)

Rigorous: The standards will include high-level cognitive demands by asking students to demonstrate deep conceptual understanding through the application of content knowledge and skills to new situations.

High-level cognitive demand includes reasoning, justification, synthesis, analysis, and problem-solving.

Clear and Specific: The standards should provide sufficient guidance and clarity so that they are teachable, learnable, and measurable. The standards will also be clear and understandable to the general public.

Quality standards are precise and provide sufficient detail to convey the level of performance expected without being overly prescriptive. (the "what" not the "how"). The standards should maintain a relatively consistent level of grain size.

Teachable and learnable: Provide sufficient guidance for the design of curricula and instructional materials. The standards must be reasonable in scope, instructionally manageable, and promote depth of understanding.

The standards will not prescribe *how* they are taught and learned but will allow teachers flexibility to teach and students to learn in various instructionally relevant contexts.

Measureable: Student attainment of the standards should be observable and verifiable and the standards can be used to develop broader assessment frameworks.

Coherent: The standards should convey a unified vision of the big ideas and supporting concepts within a discipline and reflect a progression of learning that is meaningful and appropriate.

Grade-by-grade standards: The standards will have limited repetition across the grades or grade spans to help educators align instruction to the standards.

Internationally benchmarked: The standards will be informed by the content, rigor, and organization of standards of high-performing countries so that all students are prepared for succeeding in our global economy and society[11].

Teachers, parents and community leaders have all weighed in to create the common core state standards. The K-12 Common Core State Standards are a breakthrough in focus and coherence. They allow students to understand what is expected of them and to become progressively more proficient in understanding and using English and Language Arts. At the same time, teachers will be better equipped to know exactly what they need to help students learn and establish individualized benchmarks for them. The common core standards focus on core conceptual understandings and procedures starting in the early grades, thus enabling teachers to take the time needed to teach core concepts and procedures well -- and to give students the opportunity to really master them.

With students, parents and teachers all on the same page and working together for shared goals, we can ensure that students make progress each year and graduate from school prepared to succeed and build a strong future for themselves and the country.

Writing:

The ability to write logical arguments based on substantive claims, sound reasoning, and relevant evidence is a cornerstone of the writing standards, with opinion writing—a basic form of argument—extending down into the earliest grades. Research—both short, focused projects (such as those commonly required in the workplace) and longer term in-depth research —is emphasized throughout the standards but most prominently in the writing strand since a written analysis and presentation of findings is so often critical.

Annotated samples of student writing accompany the standards and help establish adequate performance levels in writing arguments, informational/explanatory texts, and narratives in the various grades.

Speaking and Listening:

The standards require that students gain, evaluate, and present increasingly complex information, ideas, and evidence through listening and speaking as well as through media. An important focus of the speaking and listening standards is academic discussion in one-on-one, small group, and whole class settings. Formal presentations are one important way such talk occurs, but so is the more informal discussion that takes place as students collaborate to answer questions, build understanding, and solve problems.

Language:

The standards expect that students will grow their vocabularies through a mix of conversations, direct instruction, and reading. The standards will help students determine word meanings, appreciate the nuances of words, and steadily expand their repertoire of words and phrases. The standards help prepare students for real-life experiences in college and in 21st century careers. The standards recognize that students must be able to use formal English in their writing and speaking but that they must also be able to make informed, skillful choices among the many ways to express themselves through language. Vocabulary and conventions are treated in their own strand not because skills in these areas should be handled in isolation but because their use extends across reading, writing, speaking, and listening.

Media and Technology:

Just as media and technology are integrated in school and life in the 21st century, skills related to media use (both critical analysis and production of media) are integrated throughout the standards.[12]

In the 1950's President Kennedy led the United States in a resurgence of focus on mathematics and science in the curriculum. The Russians had launched Sputnik, the first un-manned space capsule and the United States found itself behind in the world space program. The latest study of academic proficiency of U.S. students in world competitions found U. S. students in the top 25 in most cases; however, countries such as China, Finland, and Singapore were at the top. At a time such as this, the United States needs to hasten a national curriculum and make additions for all subjects. The English/language arts outlined in the common core standards assists educators with a view of the changes. Although the standards are a good first effort, they do not assist teachers with differentiation in the classroom, especially for high achievers.

Also available are learning skills outlined by the Partnership for 21st Century Skills. Although the skills are not part of the common core standards, they are aligned with higher order thinking skills and practices and technology. With all of the resources available and new and innovative efforts in place to make a difference, the majority of schools are not preparing students for the 21st century. A glimmer of hope comes from such efforts as the North Carolina New Schools Project, funded in part by the Bill and Melinda Gates Foundation. The concept is to allow first time college students in families an opportunity to go to college and succeed. Students apply during 8th grade and, if accepted, begin school on the campus of the early college high school which is located within the local community college. In collaboration with the community college, students are registered for course work that will enable them to complete two years of college work by attending the early college for five years (this will be addressed in more detail in Section IV of this text).

What do we teach? becomes a state by state effort aligned to each state's standards. Although we have evidence of the need to require students to think and collaborate to solve problems, we know this is certainly an uphill movement which brings us back to the way we teach. How can educators improve instruction to insure student learning? What we teach and how we teach cannot be separated.

Takeaways

1. *Today's classroom should be a global world for students and should reflect that world in its planning and teaching.*
2. *The classroom teaching and learning should reflect relevance, rigor, and relationships to insure success for all students.*
3. *Core subjects will require custom textbooks and/or e-books that include the national curriculum standards and are easily accessed by teachers and students.*
4. *The common core standards establish a "staircase" of increasing complexity in what students must be able to read so that all students are ready for the demands of college- and career-level reading no later than the end of high school.*
5. *The standards also require the progressive development of reading comprehension and writing skills so that students advancing through the grades are able to gain more from whatever they read and write.*
6. *The standards mandate certain critical types of content for all students, including classic myths and stories from around the world, foundational U.S. documents, seminal works of American literature, and the writings of Shakespeare.*

Application

You are the lead adviser of an educational design team who has been assigned to develop the 21st century curriculum to use in a school. Because your research and advice to educators is so valued, the request also includes a need to develop teaching strategies that result in high levels of student learning.

Using the latest free online software, develop a movie that depicts the contents of the curriculum and also demonstrates teaching strategies that are effective in the 21st century school.

Chapter 17

How Do We Teach?

Mastery learning has long been in the vocabulary of most educators. We must continue to teach for learning with a different emphasis. Teaching students to think and develop solutions to problems and projects has been found much more effective than the "sit and get" method practiced in schools through the last century. Twenty-first century learners need and deserve a renewed paradigm. The first and most important ingredient in effective teaching is effective planning. Failing to plan is planning to fail. Using technology and dedicated time to work with other teachers in the planning process, teachers who work as effective teams find more success than some others. Having a plan for teaching and a way to evaluate is critical. Dr. Bob Kiznik gives some specific advice to teachers on developing effective plans:[13]

1. Preliminary Information

The development of a lesson plan begins somewhere, and a good place to start is with a list or description of general information about the plan. Although this may sound simple, this information sets the boundaries or limits of the plan. Here is a good list of these information items: (a) the grade level of the students for whom the plan is intended; (b) the specific subject matter (mathematics, reading, language arts, science, social studies, etc.); (c) if appropriate, the name of the unit of which the lesson is a part; and (d) the name of the teacher.

2. The Parts

Each part of a lesson plan should fulfill some purpose in communicating the specific content, the objective, the learning prerequisites, what will happen, the sequence of student and teacher activities, the materials required, and the actual assessment procedures. Taken together, these parts constitute an end (the objective), the means (what will happen and the student and teacher activities), and an input (information about students and necessary resources). At the conclusion of a lesson, the assessment tells the teacher how well students actually attained the objective.

In a diagram, the process looks something like this:

Input ======>Process=====>Output

Let's look at each part separately.

Input: This part refers to the physical materials, other resources, and information that will be required by the process. What are these inputs? First of all, if you have thought about what the lesson is supposed to accomplish, the inputs are much easier to describe. In general categories, inputs consist of:

1. Information about the students for whom the lesson is intended. This information includes, but is not limited to, the age and grade level of the students, and what they already know about and what you want them to learn.

2. Information about the amount of time you estimate it will take to implement the lesson.

3. Descriptions of the materials that will be required by the lesson, and at some point, the actual possession of the materials.

4. Information about how you will acquire the physical materials required.

5. Information about how to obtain any special permissions and schedules required. For example if your lesson plan will require a field trip, you must know how to organize it. If your lesson will require a guest speaker, you must know how to make arrangements for having that person be at the right place at the right time.

Process

This is the actual plan. If you have done the preliminary work (thinking, describing the inputs), creating the plan is relatively easy. There are a number of questions you must answer in creating the plan:

1. What are the inputs? This means you have the information (content description, student characteristics, list of materials, prerequisites, time estimates, etc.) necessary to begin the plan.

2. What is the output? This means a description of what the students are supposed to learn.

3. What do I do? This means a description of the <u>instructional activities</u> you will use.

4. What do the students do? This means a description of what the students will do during the lesson.

5. How will the learning be measured? This means a description of the assessment procedure during and at the end of the lesson.

As an example, below is a template that college and university teachers have used successfully to teach students to write lesson plans:

Lesson Plan Format:

Teacher_____ Subject_____
GradeLevel_____
Date_____

I. Content: This is a statement that relates to the subject-matter content. The content may be a concept or a skill. Phrase this as follows: I want my students to: (be able to [name the skill]) OR (I want my students to understand [a description of the <u>concept</u>]). Often times, this content is predetermined or strongly suggested by the specific <u>curriculum</u> you are implementing through your teaching.

II. Prerequisites: Indicate what the student must already know or be able to do in order to be successful with this lesson. (You would want to list one or two specific behaviors necessary to begin this lesson). *Some research indicates that up to 70% of what a student learns is dependent on his or her possessing the appropriate prerequisites.*

III. Instructional Objective: Indicate what is to be learned - this must be a <u>complete objective.</u> Write this objective in terms of what an individual student will do, not what a group will do. Limit your objecttive to one behavioral verb. Including information on what the student objective is critical. Make sure your objective relates to the content statement for the lesson. Be certain students know and understand their own learning targets.

IV. Instructional Procedures: Description of what you will do in teaching the lesson, and, as appropriate, includes a description of how you will introduce the lesson to the students, what actual instructional techniques you will use and roles for students, and how you will bring closure to the lesson. Include what specific things students will actually do during the lesson. In most cases, you will provide some sort of summary for the students.

V. Materials and Equipment: List all materials and equipment to be used by both the teacher and learner and how they will be used.

VI. Assessment/Evaluation: Describe <u>how</u> you will determine the extent to which students have attained the instructional objective. Be sure this part is directly connected to the behavior called for in the instructtional objective.

VII. Follow-up Activities: Indicate how other activities/ materials will be used to reinforce and extend this lesson. Include homework, assignments, and projects.

VIII. Self-Assessment (to be completed after the lesson is presented): Address the major components of the lesson plan, focusing on both the strengths, and areas of needed improvement. Determine here how you plan to collect information that will be useful for planning future lessons. A good idea is to analyze the differences between what you wanted (the objective) and what was attained (the results of the assessment).

Of course, there is an immense difference between being able to plan and actually being able to carry out the plan. However, if you have thought carefully about where you are going before you begin writing your plan, the chances of your success, as well as the success of your students, are much greater.

Dr. Sandra Kizlik's ideas for beginning teachers include the following:[14]

School curriculum (what is intended that students learn) is usually structured in units. The units can have themes or not, but they include many topics that are united by a common thread. These units, which may involve work for days or weeks, are subdivided into daily lesson plans.

Lesson plans are written by teachers to help them structure the learning for themselves and for the students. Unfortunately, more emphasis on lesson plans is found at the elementary level. All teachers need to understand the expectation that lesson plans are a standard part of teaching and learning at any school. Principals and school leaders must monitor and expect quality lesson plans.

Research indicates that all students benefit from and appreciate well-structured lessons.

All lessons are based on curriculum; that is, what is intended that students learn. Sometimes the curriculum reflects intended learning outcomes that are processes, like learning to research a topic, or learning long division. Sometimes the curriculum reflects learning outcomes relating to memorizing information, such as the multiplication tables, or the conditions that make a desert. Sometimes the curriculum outcomes are about creating a basis for judgments, like the qualities of being a good pet owner. Sometimes the curriculum outcomes relate to applying knowledge, like writing essays, or analyzing and solving problems, or analyzing economic relationships.

Daily Lesson Plans

Purpose

Lesson plans are not written for teachers to read to the class. They are used to structure the lesson and to help with the flow of the class, especially when something has occurred to distract everyone, including the teacher.

Thinking Parts

Lesson plans are first of all a thinking process. This thinking process basically is completed in four parts.

First, determine the curriculum; that is, what the students will learn, what they will be able to do upon completing the activities or work of the lesson.

Second, determine what the students already know, before beginning the lesson, that can lead into the new curriculum of the day.

Third, determine at least one way to assist the students in learning the new curriculum.

Fourth, determine at least one way to evaluate the learning outcomes of the students.

Written Format

There are many different formats that can be used to write daily lesson plans. Formats that are most useful are very simple to follow and are well structured. An outline format can be used very easily during class for quick references by the teacher. It can be followed and accessed very quickly by the teacher in case there is a distraction or in case the teacher loses his/her train of thought.

The following is one type of outline format for writing daily lesson plans.

First, write the student academic behavioral learning objective based on the thinking parts above (especially the first and fourth steps; that is, what the students will be able to *DO* upon completing the lesson, and what student academic knowledge will be evaluated as a result).

Second, follow steps A, B, and C as follows.

A: What the students enter the lesson already knowing (prerequisites)

Review any prerequisite knowledge that will lead easily into the new curriculum.

B: Core lesson (what the teacher and the students do)

Be sure to include the exact examples, problems, projects, or activities that will be used.

C: The NEW curriculum that the students exit the lesson knowing (objective of the lesson)

Review and stress again all of the most important points of the core lesson.

Note: The thinking parts involve thinking about A, B, and C above in this order. First determine C, then determine A (pretest if necessary), and finally determine and develop B.[14]

After effectively designing appropriate lesson plans, teachers must become aware of new tools for teaching. Strategies such as problem-based learning, inquiry based-learning, technology integration, interdisciplinary instruction, student projects, cooperative group work, and utilization of higher order thinking skills become essential tools for the 21st century teacher.

Problem–Based Learning: Motivation, relevance and context, higher-order thinking, learning how to learn, and authenticity describe problem-based learning. Essentially, students are faced with a problem that is ill-structured, can change with the addition of new information, is not solved easily, and doesn't have a "right" answer.

This student-centered, learning-centered strategy puts the challenge of discovering and learning on the student and puts the teacher in the role of a facilitator who asks questions and offers some guidance in order to minimize frustration.

Inquiry-Based Learning: An old adage states: "Tell me and I forget, show me and I remember, involve me and I understand." This is the essence of inquiry-based learning. Asking questions is natural for humans, especially children. Inquiry-based learning uses this curiosity to facilitate learning.

As our world becomes more fast paced, with information available in a key stroke, students need to learn how to discern information that is credible and serves their purpose, then use that information to satisfy their curiosity. Learning how to find and use information is becoming as important as learning to read and compute basic facts mentally.

Technology Integration: 21st century students spend much of their day on-line or texting. Utilizing technology as much as possible in the classroom lends itself to student interest. Teachers often struggle with the integration of technology into the classroom because of lack of availability. Federal and state governments that emphasize the need to utilize technology must provide appropriate infrastructure and hardware as well as software. Used as a tool for teaching, technology often provides the motivation for students to study.

Interdisciplinary Learning: Making learning more natural, meaningful, and less isolated by content lines, when appropriate, is the premise behind interdisciplinary instruction. Planning around a theme, piece of literature, or unit can lead students on a journey of discovery through the core subject areas and the arts. Educators know that the more times content is experienced the better students understand. And when the content is presented from different perspectives, the learning becomes deeper. When connecting topics across the disciplines, the focus is on making connections that are logical, natural, and appropriate.

Student Projects: Motivation, relevance and context, higher-order thinking, learning how to learn, and authenticity all describe problem-based learning. As students are faced with a problem to solve, they may also be faced with the challenge of how to communicate their answers in a coherent, effective presentation. Projects planned and worked on as a group with appropriate rubrics provided assist students in becoming leaders. Teaching other students about their project is also another way to insure learning of the presenter.

Cooperative Group Work: Cooperative Learning, sometimes called small-group learning, is an instructional strategy in which small groups of students work together on a common task. The task can be as simple as solving a multi-step math problem together, or as complex as developing a design for a new kind of school. In some cases, each group member is individually accountable for part of the task; in other cases, group members work together without formal role assignments.

According to David Johnson and Roger Johnson (1999), there are five basic elements that allow successful small-group learning:

- Positive interdependence: Students feel responsible for their own and the group's effort.
- Face-to-face interaction: Students encourage and support one another; the environment encourages discussion and eye contact.
- Individual and group accountability: Each student is responsible for doing their part; the group is accountable for meeting its goal.
- Group behaviors: Group members gain direct instructtion in the interpersonal, social, and collaborative skills needed to work with others occurs.
- Group processing: Group members analyze their own and the group's ability to work together.

Cooperative learning changes students' and teachers' roles in classrooms. The ownership of teaching and learning is shared by groups of students, and is no longer the sole responsibility of the teacher. The authority of setting goals, assessing learning, and facilitating learning is shared by all. Students have more opportunities to actively participate in their learning, question and challenge each other, share and discuss their ideas, and internalize their learning. Along with improving academic learning, cooperative learning helps students engage in thoughtful discourse and examine different perspectives, and it has been proven to increase students' self-esteem, motivation and empathy.

Takeaways

1. Mastery learning is a critical part of the teaching-learning process.
2. Failing to plan in the classroom is planning to fail. Students deserve better.
3. Utilizing a comprehensive lesson planning system is important.
4. Strategies such as problem-based learning, inquiry based-learning, technology integration, interdisciplinary instruction, student projects, cooperative group work, and utilization of higher order thinking skills become essential tools for the 21st century teacher.

Application

You are a teacher. In your teacher work room you have a plaque with the following words on it:
"Tell me and I forget, show me and I remember, involve me and I understand."

In your classroom, you strive for 100% mastery learning. Plan, individually or with a group of at least three, strategies that will insure understanding by your students. Report to the class the strategies you and/or your group selected. Demonstrate at least one strategy to your class.

Chapter 18

Are Students Learning?

"Assessment for learning can contribute to the development of effective schools. If assessments of learning provide evidence of achievement for public reporting, then assessments for learning serve to help students learn more. The crucial distinction is between assessment to determine the status of learning and assessment to promote greater learning."[14a]

----R. J. Stiggins

How do we know students are learning in the classroom? Assessing student knowledge and learning is a critical piece in the teaching and learning process in the 21st century. In their effort to "Race to the Top" (federal effort taking the place of No Child Left Behind), states and school districts are requiring teachers to utilize formative, benchmark, and summative assessment to assist students in learning. Formative assessment assists teachers in knowing what students already know or have currently learned about a topic. This type of assessment "forms" a basis for teaching and learning. Benchmark assessment is defined as a check at midpoint in a course or grade level to determine if students are on task for mastering the course/subject. Summative assessment is defined as the final test, product, presentation that summarizes the work of the course/subject. With an emphasis on all three areas, school districts, schools, and teachers are again asked to produce evidence of student learning. States are developing/adopting on-line programs for use with test data that gives projected gains for students. Test banks are available and ready for teachers to utilize in developing assessments. Teachers are being required to increase their knowledge of test and measurement, analysis of data, and planning related to the information they glean from the assessment. Professional development in school districts is being focused on assessment for learning. One of the outstanding researchers in this arena is Rick Stiggins.

Stiggins, founder and director of the ETS Assessment Training Institute (317 SW Alder St., Suite 1200, Portland, OR 97204), has completed extensive research on assessment for learning. Stiggins professes that instead of using assessment to clearly delineate winners and losers in the classrooms, teachers should use assessment to develop a winning scenario for all students. He developed a comparison of students who are involved in assessment on winning streaks and also on losing streaks. Refer to his outline below:[15]

The Assessment Experience For Students on Winning Streaks	For Students on Losing Streaks
Assessment results provide	
Continual evidence of success	Continual evidence of failure
The student feels	
Hopeful and optimistic	Hopeless

Empowered to take productive action	Initially panicked, giving way to resignation
The student thinks	
It's all good. I'm doing fine.	This hurts. I'm not safe here.
See the trend? I succeed as usual.	I just can't do this . . . again.
I want more success.	I'm confused. I don't like this - help!
School focuses on what I do well.	Why is it always about what I can't do?
I know what to do next.	Nothing I try seems to work.
Feedback helps me.	Feedback is criticism. It hurts.
Public success feels good.	Public failure is embarrassing.
The student becomes more likely to	

Seek challenges.	Seek what's easy.
Seek exciting new ideas.	Avoid new concepts and approaches.
Practice with gusto.	Become confused about what to practice.
Take initiative.	Avoid initiative.
Persist in the face of setbacks.	Give up when things become challenging.
Take risks and stretches - go for it!	Retreat and escapes - trying is too dangerous!
These actions lead to	
Self-enhancement	Self-defeat, self-destruction
Positive self-fulfilling prophecy	Negative self-fulfilling prophecy
Acceptance of responsibility	Denial of responsibility
Manageable stress	High stress

Feeling that success is its own reward	No feelings of success; no reward
Curiosity, enthusiasm	Boredom, frustration, fear
Continuous adaptation	Inability to adapt
Resilience	Yielding quickly to defeat
Strong foundations for future success	Failure to master prerequisites for future success

Stiggins also professes that assessment for learning turns every day assessment into a process that enhances student learning. He reminds us that we do not use assessment to merely monitor learning, but to encourage student growth and self-esteem. In one of the scenarios in this article, Stiggins likens classroom learning by students to outstanding athletes. He cites Duke coach Mike Krzyzewski and how he works with ball players to correct any mistakes they made in a previous game. Stiggins believes the immediate work by Coach K enables his players to go into the next game with self-assurance and knowledge of how to handle the situation. Classrooms are not unlike the sports arena and good teachers are certainly the best "coaches" for our students. Students need this stepped up motivation for success.

Teachers who work consistently to discern how to teach and re-teach students in need will create learning classrooms.

Learning is not a punitive process. It is our choice to decide if we will have winners or losers on our team.

Along with assessment comes grading. How do we grade students so parents and students know and understand how students are graded. Teachers in the 21st century are continuing to develop specific rubrics to use in the classroom in order for students and parents to know and understand the expectations of projects and activities. Teachers continue to work hard and to grade every homework assignment and assign several unit tests. Homework is a large part of the learning process. Educators are beginning to see new and revised thoughts on homework and grading. Several teachers in selected high schools in the United States are looking at a grading system that uses 1-4 and prorates it to the local grading system. Standards based grading is quickly becoming the norm.

Takeaways

1. Assessment abounds in the 21st century classroom.
2. Teachers know and understand how to use formative, benchmark, and summative assessment.
3. Determining rubric assessments creates a clearer understanding of assignments.
4. Re-evaluating your grading system is important. Do you need to make any changes?

Applications

Study Rick Stiggins' Assessment Experience and decide if your students are on a winning streak or a losing streak. List each student in your class and note if he/she is a **W** for winner or an **L** for loser.

Make a concrete plan to improve opportunities for students who are on a losing streak. Share your plan with a classmate and tell when and what you will be doing to enhance each student's experience.

Chapter 19

How Do We Improve?

"The illiterate of the 21st century will not be those who cannot read and write, but those who cannot learn, unlearn, and relearn."

----*Alvin Toffler*

"Nothing has promised so much and has been so frustrating wasteful for teachers and leaders as the thousands of workshops and conferences that led to no significant change in practice."

----*Michael Fullen*

Toffler and Fullen bring ideas to us about student and teacher learning. Learning, unlearning and relearning create opportunities for the student to bring creativity and new ideas into focus. As educators, we must also be willing to do the same thing. The issue in the newspaper this week was the possibility of new planets. This is a perfect example of one of the unlearning and relearning tasks for this week. As we grow and learn, we all are charged with the opportunity to change and learn new thoughts and ideas. The 21st century teacher will be on the cutting edge of technology tools and strategies to use in the classroom. Students will relate and find relevance in their instruction. We have opportunities through federal legislation to begin the process. The American Recovery and Reinvestment Act instituted by President Barack Obama cited specific changes to be made in public education. They are as follows:[16]

The Act provides $77 billion for reforms to strengthen elementary and secondary education, including $48.6 billion to stabilize state education budgets (of which $8.8 billion may be used for other government services) and to encourage states to:

- Make improvements in teacher effectiveness and ensure that all schools have highly-qualified teachers;
- Make progress toward college and career-ready standards and rigorous assessments that will improve both teaching and learning;
- Improve achievement in low-performing schools, through intensive support and effective interventions; and
- Gather information to improve student learning, teacher performance, and college and career readiness through enhanced data systems.

The Act provides $5 billion in competitive funds to spur innovation and chart ambitious reform to close the achievement gap.

The Act includes over $30 billion to address college affordability and improve access to higher education.

In other words, the federal government has money to spend on public schools. Why is the money not making a marked difference? How will classrooms change and improve?

This question brings us back to motivation to teach and learn. What are the habits of students and teachers who perform well in school? We know that time spent engaged in learning makes a significant impact on academic skills. Student and teacher collaboration as well as parent support and encouragement are all key factors. If we look at the Asian population in the U. S. public schools, we generally see higher student achievement. What is different about learning with Asian-American students? Again, quality time spent in study is significant. Time spent in entertainment is markedly different. In the on-line video "How to Improve Early Education?",[17] D. Quinn Mills, professor at Harvard Business School, uses this venue to describe his thoughts on the issue. He basically says that it is a decision of wills. What is each student willing to give to the effort to learn?

In Education Week, January, 2007, Lynn Olson in Gauging Student Learning reported several factors that directly affect student learning. Education Week publishes an annual report, Quality Counts, that outlines major issues that affect the quality of schools. The report in Olson's article monitors this information.[18]

School systems know and understand the need for preschool and early childhood programs for youngsters, particularly youngsters of poverty. Although initial levels of success are seen with these programs, it is not sustained throughout childhood and adolescence.

Through the years, *Quality Counts* has looked at the progress states have made in raising student achievement in elementary and secondary schools over more than a decade as measured by the National Assessment of Educational Progress, or NAEP, often known as "the nation's report card." When looked at over that longer time period, student achievement has gotten better, particularly in mathematics and for low-income and African-American and Hispanic students. But reading achievement has barely budged since 1992. High school achievement remains flat.

Achievement gaps by race and class remain a concern. Near the end of high school, African-American and Latino students have reading and math skills that are almost the same as those of white 8th graders. Poor and minority teenagers fail to graduate from high school within four years. And even those who do may not be ready for college. Despite calls for more young people who are trained in math and science, just over half of high school students took upper-level math courses in 2004, and just one in three took upper-level science courses.

What does this research tell us about the indicators for school success? The list is comprehensive and not unknown to educators. The Chance for Success Index developed by Education Week states that the following qualities directly affect graduation rates of students and their overall success in school.

- Parental education
- Parental employment
- Linguistic integration
- Preschool enrollment
- Kindergarten enrollment
- Elementary reading
- Middle school mathematics
- High school graduation
- Postsecondary participation
- Adult education attainment
- Annual income
- Steady employment

Although all of these issues directly affect student success in school, classrooms and schools across the United States continue to make a difference in the lives of students each day. As educators, we challenge you to find a successful school that is similar in demographics to your own school or school system and go to the school and determine why the school is successful. A practicing administrator was concerned about her students' ability to write well when they arrived at high school. After viewing many school districts across the state, she selected two or three districts with outstanding writing scores at high school. she contacted the school system and the particular school that was achieving and found an outstanding teacher who had developed a system to insure that all his students knew how to write well. He taught her school system how he had achieved the level of work at his school. His work involved teaching the students vocabulary, mechanics, and systematically working with the class to produce quality writing. His insight and determination were quickly understood by the teachers in her school district. We are not required to always be the best teacher, but to learn how to teach through collaboration and team work.

We already know how to accelerate student learning. The big question remains – are we willing to do the work that the challenge requires? Master teachers do just that. They are on a quest and will not take no for an answer. Their students are the biggest winners. Their own motivation is contagious.[19]

Professional Development for Educators

Describing the needs of today's learner, it is quite evident that the students of the 21st century will be accessing a variety of sources to find instant answers to their questions. A connected world makes their work somewhat easier. However, the amount of information and knowledge available to them is exponential and growing. With this environment for students, how do we begin to think about the professional development needs of teachers? Their needs are varied and have gained attention from educational researchers who are interested in what works for the future of professional development. With students learning through several venues, how will teachers cope? What does this mean for them?

It means that they should be constantly learning with and from accomplished colleagues and experts in the field, modeling for their students the collaborative learning and knowledge construction that is at the core of 21st century competencies.

Yet according to the most recent MetLife Survey of the American Teacher (2009), today's teachers work alone—they spend an average of 93 percent of their time in school working in isolation from their colleagues, and they continue to work alone during their out-of-school hours on preparation and grading. Their day-to-day work is disconnected from the efforts of their colleagues, and their pullout professional development is fragmented and poorly aligned with their students' learning needs.[20]

This fragmentation prevents any substantial education reform from gaining traction, because teachers are not given the support they need to collectively build a coherent body of knowledge and practice to improve student achievement. Today's new teachers are eager to work with their accomplished colleagues, but they find themselves working alone in self-contained classrooms where they are bound to the teaching practices of the past. Faced with a choice between working in the last century or the 21st century, they "vote with their feet". The young people we are counting on to teach for the future are leaving our obsolete schools at an alarming rate.

It is time to change this picture. Today's teachers want to team up to teach for the future. In survey after survey, teachers who are most satisfied with their careers and the contributions they are making to their students' lives are more likely to work in schools with higher levels of professional collaboration.

To expand on these survey findings, the National Commission on Teaching and America's Future (NCTAF), along with the support of the Pearson Foundation, has conducted an extensive review of research reports and practitioner case studies to document the specific learning-team principles and practices that improve teaching effectiveness and student achievement. Based on their findings, they have concluded that the nation has a pressing need, and an unprecedented opportunity to improve school performance by using learning teams to systematically induct new teachers into a collaborative learning culture—teams that embed continuous professional development into the day-to-day fabric of work in schools that are constantly evolving to meet the needs of the 21st century learners. This calls for a cultural shift in schools, a shift that is gaining momentum across the country.

NCTAF's review identified six learning-team principles and practices that are most effective in improving teaching and student achievement, described in the report "Team Up for 21st Century Teaching and Learning." While there is no magic formula, they found that highly effective learning teams have the following:

Shared Values and Goals: The team members have a common vision of student learning needs and a well-defined understanding of how their collective teaching capabilities can be orchestrated to meet those needs. They clearly identify a learning challenge around which the team can join forces to improve student achievement.

Collective Responsibility: Team members have appropriately differentiated responsibilities based on their experience and knowledge levels. They hold themselves mutually responsible for each other's success, and they are collectively accountable for improving the achievement of every student served by the team.

Authentic Assessment: Team members hold themselves personally and professionally accountable by using assessments that give them real-time feedback on student learning and teaching effectiveness. These assessments are valuable to them—not because they are linked to high-stakes consequences, but because they are essential tools to improve the team's teaching effectiveness, as measured by student learning gains.

Self-Directed Reflection : Highly effective learning teams establish a reflective feedback loop of goal-setting, planning, standards, and assessment that is driven by the learning needs of the students and the corresponding professional development needs of the teachers.

Stable Settings: Highly effective learning teams do not function within dysfunctional schools, but they can transform low-performing schools into successful learning organizations if they are given dedicated time, space, resources, and leadership for their collaborative work. Even the best teachers in the world can't turn around a low-performing school by working alone.

Strong Leadership Support: Highly effective learning teams are supported by school leaders who build a climate of openness and trust that empowers team members to make decisions on how to improve teaching effectiveness that are directly linked to student needs. This support must be balanced with appropriate, positive pressure to continuously increase school performance with improvements in teaching effectiveness that are explicitly linked to specific student learning needs.

Transforming American education is the rallying cry heard throughout the country today. The Obama administration has focused the nation's vision for education in 2020 on two basic goals: assuring that every student is college- and career-ready, and closing the achievement gaps for low-income students and children of color.

NCTAF is answering this call by creating "learning studios" for teaching the STEM subjects of science, technology, engineering, and mathematics that are based on the documented effectiveness of these six principles. Similar to architectural-design studios, these STEM Learning Studios enable learning teams composed of digital-age teachers, tech-savvy youths, veteran educators, and skill-based volunteers to develop innovative responses to complex learning challenges. Learning studios improve student achievement, increase teaching effectiveness, and amplify the impact of community resources.

Another shift in education is teaching students in same sex classrooms. Recent research by scholars in the United States and worldwide begin to display interesting findings.

As reported by the National Association for Single Sex Public Education (2009),[21] researchers at Stetson University in Florida have completed a three-year pilot project comparing single-sex classrooms with coed classrooms. All relevant parameters were matched: the class sizes were all the same, the demographics were the same, all teachers had the same training. On the FCAT (Florida Comprehensive Assessment Test), here were the results:

Percentage of students scoring proficient on the FCAT

boys in coed classes: 37% scored proficient

girls in coed classes: 59% scored proficient

girls in single-sex classes: 75% scored proficient

boys in single-sex classes: 86% scored proficient (2009).

These students were all learning the same curriculum in the same school. And, this school "mainstreams" students who are learning-disabled, or who have ADHD (2009).

In one study of 2,777 English high school students, girls at coed schools were found to lose ground to boys in science and vocabulary as they progressed through high school. Exactly the opposite occurred at single-sex schools: the girls at single-sex schools outperformed both the boys at single-sex schools and the boys at coed schools. Again, this study reported the familiar pattern: girls at single-sex schools on top, followed by boys at single-sex schools, then boys at coed schools, with girls at coed schools doing the worst. (Finn, 1980).[22]

Further research on single gender education needs attention and should add to the dialog of quality practices that insure student success in school.

This kind of teaching and learning represents ambitious goals. Making it happen will require changes that go beyond tinkering with today's schools. If all we do is to give today's students a better factory-era school, with stand-alone teachers who continue to deliver monolithic instruction in self-contained classrooms, the future is already over. It is time to team up to teach for the 21st century.[23]

Takeaways

1. *Seeking knowledge from exemplary students, teachers and schools should be part of every school's improvement plan.*
2. *Studying the Chance for Success Index and using the information to change schools and school systems should be on the agenda for all schools.*
3. *Using successful teachers to offer professional development and collaboration will provide schools with improved teacher learning.*
4. *Promoting teamwork in the school setting including students, teachers, parents and the community should bring better results in learning.*
5. *Teachers must collaborate and work in teams to focus on the teaching and learning of students.*
6. *A new look at single gender education needs attention and discussion.*
7. *We must teach all students well and have them college ready when they leave our schools.*

Application

In this chapter, when we look at the qualities that directly affect graduation rates of students and their overall success, schools usually have one or more areas of concern. When they review the list, school leaders can often be heard saying that they do not know what to do about low reading scores, the dropout rate, student absences and so on.

Larry Lezotte, quoting the late Ron Edmonds, an accomplished educator, states that we already know enough to do the job. What does he mean by this statement? How do we find answers to the questions that often come in the form of the above topics? Be prepared to discuss how you would attack each of the problem areas.

Section IV: Successful School Models

Chapter 20

The Challenges

"Our nation is at risk. Our once unchallenged preeminence in commerce, industry, science and technological innovation is being overtaken by competitors throughout the world. This report is concerned with only one of the many causes and dimensions of the problem, but it is the one that undergirds American prosperity, security and civility. We report to the American people that while we can take justifiable pride in what our schools and colleges have historically accomplished and contributed to the United States and the well-being of its people, the educational foundations of our society are presently being eroded by a rising tide of mediocrity that threatens our very future as a Nation and a people. What was unimaginable a generation ago has begun to occur—others are matching and surpassing our educational attainments."

----*A Nation At Risk: The Imperative for Educational Reform: Report by the National Commission on Excellence in Education. April, 1983.*

How prophetic!! Some 27 years later we are still struggling to bring relevance, rigor, ingenuity and a passion for curiosity to our educational institutions. While there has been much study and analysis which has led to many reform initiatives little has changed. In fact, one key measurement of academic success, high school graduation rates, have declined since the release of this April, 1983 report. This is not due to lack of extraordinary efforts by well meaning educators, politicians, business and community leaders. From changes in curriculum to types/means of assessment secondary education has experienced a plethora of changes. These changes have exacted a toll on administrators, teachers and students while resulting in no significant positive change in academic performance and career or post secondary readiness. Data from a recent report on college readiness of our high school graduates indicates that forty percent of all students who enter college must take remedial courses.[1] The high school graduation rate in the United States, which hovers around 70%, lags significantly behind many of the industrialized countries such as Japan (93%).[2] For those high school graduates who choose to enter the workforce nearly half are "deficient" in basic knowledge and applied skills according to a recent survey of some 400 employers.[3] The evidence continues to mount that the challenges are growing daily and the "product" of our secondary education is not meeting the needs of our society nor ready to tackle the global challenges of the 21st Century. Said another way, we collectively (educators, elected officials, business community and parents/guardians) are failing to produce a 21st century "educated" young citizen. It must be stated here that the student has a responsibility as well and later in the book that responsibility and accountability will be addressed.

Tony Wagner in his book, *The Global Achievement Gap: Why Even Our Best Schools Don't Teach The New Survival Skills Our Children Need- And What We Can Do About It*, offers up the notion that there are two achievement gaps in our educational system.[4] The first is the gap between the education our middle class children receive from the schools in more affluent neighborhoods and the education of the children that takes place in the economically disadvantaged neighborhoods. This has been well documented and widely discussed and debated for years. The gaps in student achievement between white students and students of color are real and significant. The second gap Wagner cites is the one between what our best schools teach and test on versus what they will need to know and execute on to succeed in this 21st Century global economy. In his book *The World is Flat*, Thomas Friedman asserts that the United States "made up for our deficiencies in K through twelve by being able to get all these good students from abroad".[5] This was an attempt to fill our top tier universities in critical fields such as engineering and computer science to meet the evolving needs of US businesses for example, Intel. This sad indictment is only more evidence that the achievement gap is affecting our global competitiveness as a country.

Educators understand the importance of foundational skills such as writing, reading and math. Much emphasis has been placed on improving the performance of high school students and for that matter elementary school students as well. A myriad of programs/initiatives have found their way into the classroom over the years addressing these fundamental skill needs. For a variety of reasons which will be discussed later in the book these efforts have not met the intended objectives/expectations. Our students struggle in these very basic skills. Additionally, our students are lacking in the "soft" skills such as leadership, teamwork, and initiative. These skills facilitate the learning and application of the "hard" skills referred to as foundational skills above. In a forum on education a CEO of a Fortune 500 company lamented the fact that so many of the company's new hires had difficulty expressing themselves and struggled in communicating succinctly when asked to report on project status. He cited an example which he stated is all too common in industry today where one of his employees, a recent college graduate, wrote him a lengthy memo to request funding for a particular project. After reading the seven page memo (replete with grammatical and syntax errors) he could not ascertain what the employee was asking for. How often have we experienced a similar situation? Being able to formula a question to elicit a response to what we want/need to know is at the heart of effective communications skills as well as a key ingredient in fostering/promoting curiosity. In the classroom, educators talk about the essential question(s) associated with each lesson. The essential question(s) frames the learning process for students with respect to that lesson and student responses provide a quick assessment of understanding.

There is an expression and at one time it was a national educational campaign that "reading is fundamental". Perhaps the most serious challenge we face in educating our youth as it relates to skill development is the lack of effective reading skills. The evidence is in State test scores not only in language arts but in science, social studies and even math as there are word problems which require reading and understanding so one can set up the math problem to solve. As with any skill one develops it through practice. There is a strong correlation between reading and effective writing and for that matter curiosity. Little if any progress has been made in improving literacy since the publication of Rudolf Flesch's book, *Why Johnny Can't Read* some 50 years ago. Mastering the 3 Rs has dominated education at the elementary and secondary levels for years. The troubling news is that even with that attention our students are still struggling to meet basic standards and we know that even meeting those standards is necessary but not sufficient given the needs (perhaps better stated, the demands) on the 21st century employee.

Where is student assessment and how is it serving our needs in understanding how effective our instruction is and how prepared our students are for postsecondary education or career readiness? The most common form of student assessment at the State level to determine mastery of the subject matter is standardized testing using multiple choice and true-false questions. Some States have instituted writing tests such as North Carolina which examine students' writing and critical thinking skills. Often times, students can master these objective-based tests through memorization/recall of key names, dates, events, etc. According to Wagner, "the majority of college professors surveyed report that what is taught in high school does not prepare students for college. One major reason is that the tests students must take in high school for State-accountability purposes usually measure 9th or 10th grade-level knowledge and skills. Primarily multiple-choice assessments, they rarely ask students to explain their reasoning or to apply knowledge to new situations, so neither teachers nor students receive useful feedback about college-readiness".[6] These types of assessments allow students to operate in the lower levels of Bloom's taxonomy (for example, remembering and understanding) and achieve a false sense of mastery of the content. To get to the higher order learning modes/skills of analyzing, evaluating and creating instruction must focus on developing and fostering critical thinking skills. Assessments must be designed to determine whether the student truly has mastered the content. Unfortunately assessments can drive counter-productive behavior such as teaching to the test. This is not intended to demean those who prepare these assessments or the teachers who administer these tests. The vast majority of teachers and administrators want to do what is in the best interest of the students!!

Suffering from a multitude of "reform" initiatives it is no wonder that many teachers are cynical and doubt the efficacy of the next initiative. It becomes the proverbial "program de jour". Inherently, the risk grows when that happens as the stakes increase for producing positive results. Additionally, even if the initiative has merit, grounded in substantial research and successfully implemented in pilot programs, the will to see it through to successful completion has been lacking. We too often are victims of our own high level of impatience to "get results". This leads to the discussion on accountability and expectation setting. In Brian D. Biro's book, *Beyond Success*, he speaks of the power of setting expectations.[7] He relates expectation setting to the essence of empowerment. "The term Pygmalion effect describes the transformative power of expectation. As we communicate the vision we have for others and the expectations we hold for them, we create an almost magnetic pull that draws them in the direction of those expectations."[8] There is a process for expectation setting. It begins with setting clear, concise and realistic expectations. Ones that are based on sound judgment. The expectations must be communicated in a timely manner to all that are affected. Next is to ensure that the expectations are aligned with ones (an organization) vision, goals and objectives. The alignment also applies to ensuring that everyone on the team both "up and down the organization" understand the expectations and the reasons for them. There needs to be consequences, positive and negative, associated with executing on these expectations and finally there needs to be follow-up. This brings to mind the adage, you get what you *inspect* not what you *expect*. When expectations are not met as we have seen too often in secondary education reform initiatives, the failure can be attributed to breakdown in the process noted above. Expectations and accountability go hand in hand. Wagner addresses the breakdown over the years in accountability in the broadest sense as well a more focused discussion on accountability systems.[9] As he states, "most teacher evaluation systems are checklists of teachers' techniques, which must be filled out periodically by school administrators. Is the purpose of the lesson and the homework assignment on the board? Are the content standards to be covered in the lesson made clear to students? And so on. Rather than look only at what teachers are doing, I try to assess what students are being asked to do: the specific skills and knowledge that students are expected to master and the level of intellectual challenge in the lesson. What the teacher does is the means by which the students learn— not the end."[10] Wagner has it right on several counts. We, as a society, too often measure "motion" and not "momentum". We focus on the means and lose sight of the end goal. That has been the nemesis of many of the educational reform initiatives over the years. Couple that with the breakdown in the expectation process and overlay a high level of need for instant success (lacking in a warranted amount of patience) and the ever-changing environment, it is no wonder that educators (teachers, administrators, and yes, parents/guardians) and elected officials are frustrated with the lack of real progress.

With the societal changes over the past 50 years schools are assuming more and more of the role of the parent in providing support in the form of encouragement, advice, mentoring and monitoring to the students they serve. This increase in "responsibility" has added challenges to the educational process and some would say has significantly contributed to the stagnation in student achievement and the persistently high drop-out rates and the corresponding low graduation rates in the United States.

That said, let there be no mistake, there are many parents, guardians, grandparents and relatives who have essentially dedicated their lives to supporting in every possible way their children in school. From volunteering at school to sitting at home with their children at night (after many long hours at work) assisting them with homework assignments and/or helping them through the latest spat with a friend these parents/guardians are role models in supporting the development of their children.

With the many and varied challenges noted above facing our teachers, professional development, for those already in our classrooms, and education programs offered by Colleges and Universities, for those prospective teachers, are critical components for success. With respect to on-going professional development there is a strong sense supported by both empirical and anecdotal evidence that too often it is not focused on proven tactics to effect positive change in the classroom. As teachers have expressed, it comes at you at 10,000 feet and we're operating at ground level. Too much theory and not enough applied practice is the common lament. With constant budget constraints and the need to do more with less, training (professional development) finds its way to the top of the list for reduction. In a later chapter we will discuss different approaches to more effective professional development and one which is more cost effective as well. Lack of adequate teacher preparation and the needed support once in the classroom has been identified as one of the leading causes for an inordinately high teacher turnover rate in the United States. Wagner cites studies that show that approximately 50 % of the teachers who start out in the classroom quit after five years. He goes on to say that according to the National Commission on Teaching and American's Future "estimates that the cost of this teacher dropout problem is over $ 7 billion dollars a year".[11] Furthermore, he quotes from recent research by Arthur Levine in his 2006 report, Educating School Teachers, which is based on surveys of education school graduates, principals, and faculty in addition to Levine's many visits to College and University programs around the country. One such quote is "many students seem to be graduating from teacher education programs without the skills and knowledge they need to be effective teachers. More than three out of five (62 percent) report that schools of education do not prepare their graduates to cope with the realities of today's classrooms".[12] Levine concludes that one of the major reasons for this is that education school faculty lack an updated understanding of the current challenges in school classrooms. Additionally, it has been stated that education school faculty are too far removed from what is needed in preparing teachers to prepare our students for 21st Century problem solving. Equipping the United States citizens of tomorrow for this daunting set of challenges should be job one for these schools of education. Administrators and experienced teachers, especially those who serve as mentors, have their own experiences from working with new teachers and it corroborates findings of Dr. Levine. Again, there are exceptions and you don't need to look very far to name names and cite examples of outstanding new teachers. However these are in the minority of all teachers entering the profession. As stated earlier there is no doubt that the vast majority of these new teachers want to do an excellent job in educating their students. They mean well and their intentions are honorable. This is also the case with the faculty members in these schools of education. They too want to do their best in preparing these prospective teachers. With willing parties, change can occur that will produce more effective teachers and better prepared students. First though, we collectively must recognize and acknowledge that the process needs fixing and that all involved parties (colleges, universities, school systems, and students in these programs) are ready and willing to make the necessary changes to effect positive results. We will delve into this more in a later chapter. The intent here was to identify the challenge and the need to change for the betterment of the students we serve.

Priorities and the setting of priorities have contributed to the challenges of secondary education reform. Whether it is in our personal lives or in our jobs, establishing and executing on a set of priorities (that is, first things first) is essential to orderly, systematic approach to meeting challenges. In his book, *The 7 Habits of Highly Effective People*, Stephen Covey discusses the importance of setting priorities and sticking to those priorities.[13] He emphasizes the need to be clear and concise about your priorities and to ensure that the important (ones that make the most difference...greatest impact) are at the top.

Reflecting on secondary educational reform over the years it has been unclear what those priorities were let alone what was first, second, etc. The mission to improve education rides on a set of priorities which must be clear, concise, measurable and communicated. They must be communicated in concert with the expectations referenced earlier in the chapter. With a finite set of resources and an infinite number of "opportunities" to positively impact student achievement the need to zero in on the levers that will produce the greatest effect is essential. That is best accomplished by implementing and conducting a rigorous priority setting process. This is not a static event but an on-going exercise that is reviewed and updated as conditions change. All too often we fixate on a list of "to do" projects only to discover later that things changed and the expected results will not be achieved.

Perhaps one of the greatest challenges educators face is student apathy or the perceived lack of passion for learning by the students. It has been widely documented that students feel detached from the instruction that is taking place in the classroom. Failing to tap into that innate inquisitiveness that we all possess has led to tuning out or worst yet dropping out. Wagner lists curiosity as one of his seven survival skills.[14] He also believes that students drop out of school because they are bored. The challenge is to uncover the students' passion while relating it to the learning in the classroom. A few years ago at the invitation of a friend a school administrator visited a kindergarten class. She wanted him to see the work her students were doing on a science project she had assigned. He arrived at the school a little early that morning and sat in the back of the classroom waiting for his friend and the students to walk through the door. What happened next was an eye opener for him and an experience he shares with others in seminars and other education forums. From the time Anne, the teacher, entered her classroom to the time she placed her tote bag on her desk (all of 15 feet in distance) she was besieged by 18 excited youngsters who were peppering her with question after question. Some related to the project at hand but most were random, general interest type questions. The fascinating aspect was the high level of curiosity exhibited by essentially every one of those students. That inquisitiveness seemed to be contagious and it lasted the entire class time. The friend commented to Anne after the class how impressed he was with the quality of the projects and shared with her his observation of her students' level of curiosity. She remarked that this is an everyday phenomenon. How refreshing to experience this wonderment by our youngest students. Somewhere along the education continuum this high level of curiosity dissipates and in some cases rather rapidly. In many high school classrooms, the teacher has to drag the questions out of the students. This is at the heart of improving education today. That is, finding ways to motivate students through tapping in to their passions and leveraging that across the content areas. As mentioned earlier, this can be done by making those "levers" relevant.

Takeaways

1. Despite many well meaning initiatives over the years academic achievement at the secondary level has stagnated or declined.
2. Students are struggling to master basic skills, such as reading, writing and math.
3. 21st Century skills are placing greater emphasis on the "soft" skills e.g., collaboration, leadership, creativity.
4. Many high school graduates who enter college are not ready academically to meet the rigors of post secondary education and must take remedial courses.
5. The need to establish a clear set of expectations and hold educators accountable for student academic growth and achievement is essential to any reform initiative but often is lacking.
6. Effective training of our educators along with a support system, especially for new teachers has been problematic and resulting in low retention rates.
7. The myriad of priorities often times conflicting provides for a de-focused effort resulting in failed attempts to gain momentum in reforming secondary education.
8. The need to tap into students' passion(s) and to ignite or reignite their inquisitiveness is at the core of student engagement and effective teaching and learning.

Application

In your school (or school you are familiar with) what are the top 5 challenges to improving student achievement?

Chapter 21

Responses/Actions Taken

"Action is eloquence."
----*William Shakespeare*

There has been a plethora of reform initiatives focused on secondary education at the federal, state & local levels over the years. Reform initiatives have focused on five major areas; curriculum, instructional delivery, resourcing/personnel, organizational structure and assessments. Some were targeted approaches and others were broadly implemented. These initiatives have had varying levels of success. We'll look briefly at these efforts with the intent of understanding the whys and wherefores.

In the area of curriculum, over the past 30 years the course offerings at the secondary level has expanded. With the Carl D. Perkins Vocational and Technical Education Act, authorized by the federal government in 1984, a robust set of vocational and technical courses were added to the high school course offerings. This provided some diversity to the core academic course offerings and a step toward preparing those students who intended to enter the workforce immediately after graduating from high school. This early attempt to address career readiness provided a foundation to build on in later years. Students have increasingly sought out these courses (currently referred to as Career and Technical Education or CTE). These course offerings include courses such as computer applications, principles of business, drafting, consumer science, auto mechanics, masonry, marketing and electronics to name a few. In North Carolina, during the past five years more than 70 percent of its high school students have taken at least one CTE course each year.[15] Administrators and CTE teachers often comment that the vast majority of the students who take a CTE course will take additional CTE courses. This became a very popular expansion of the secondary curriculum and as noted in a later chapter a contributor to higher high school graduation rates in at least one State.

In the area of core academic courses the high school curriculum over the past 30 years has added more advanced subjects as well as more remedial courses most notably in language arts and math. Also, many high schools offer multiple "tracks" for students. Typically, there is the college/university preparation pathway, the technical/ vocational/general education pathway and the occupational/ remedial pathway. Students select or in some cases are "placed" in the respective pathway. The level of rigor in both the course offerings and the instructional delivery is substantially different. This becomes problematic as the rigor associated with learning, embracing and using these 21st Century skills as outlined previously are mission critical for students no matter what they intend to do after high school. A program designed to provide a boost to those students who were in the academic middle ("C" average students) was developed in 1980. Advancement Via Individual Determination (AVID) is intended "to close the achievement gap by preparing all students for college readiness and success in a global society".[16] AVID programs are in more than 3,386 schools in 48 states and 15 countries.

Some of the courses that were considered "high school" courses were included in middle school course offerings such as algebra I. This provides the student the opportunity to take higher level math courses during their high school years. Adding more advanced and remedial courses to the high school curriculum was and is an attempt to meet the varied needs of the students it serves. This is certainly an admirable objective. However, evidence is mounting and becoming overwhelming that our schools are not adequately preparing our students for a career or post secondary education. The curriculum appears fragmented and disjointed. Often times not aligned with the stated objective of preparing students for college or the workforce. As noted in previous chapters it is a multi-dimensional challenge and curriculum is only one element but an important one in the equation for success. We'll explore how curriculum can be used as a lever for success in student achievement in a later chapter.

Much has been written about class size and how it impacts student achievement. According to the Center for Public Education, the national average number of students per teacher was 15.5 in 2007.[17] The trend for many years was steady to declining as secondary education funding increased from federal, state and local governmental units. Generally speaking, class sizes for the advanced level courses and the lower level/remedial courses have enjoyed the smaller class sizes at the secondary level. The standard level courses usually have the largest class sizes. With recent budget constraints the class size has begun to increase across the board. This has ignited the debate on the correlation between class size and student achievement.

With increases in education spending over the past 20 plus years it has afforded the school systems the opportunity to hire academic coaches, curriculum specialists, special populations coordinators, career development counselors/coordinators, school based psychologists, social workers. These support positions were created to support the academic needs of the students and to assist in leveling the "playing field" for all students. The belief was by providing specialists the classroom teacher could focus on the course content areas and have at their disposal "experts" to assist in addressing the barriers that are holding back a student academically or proactively assisting the student in planning for their future (that is, post secondary education or the workforce).

Reform initiatives have also involved changing/modifying the design and structure of the entire high school program. One notable example is the introduction of 9th grade (freshmen) academies. Often times, this involves separating these students physically from the rest of the high school population and focusing the curriculum on core subjects only such as language arts, math and science. Some of the high schools who have adopted 9th grade academies have rigid standards for "graduating" from the academy and moving into 10th grade. A certain level of subject matter mastery has to be achieved by the student to demonstrate proficiency and the "right" to enter the 10th grade. A more perhaps radical approach to redesign of high schools with respect to reform initiatives is the small within large comprehensive schools, the thematic schools (for example, Science, Technology, Engineering and Math [STEM]) and the early college and middle college programs. All of these design initiatives are intended to 1) increase student achievement, 2) prepare students for college or the workforce and to 3) increase high school graduation rates. Many of these schools have been in operation for 10 years or less. While the jury is still out on their ultimate success the results look promising.

Some schools as part of their reform efforts have adopted a 12 month or year round school calendar. This is in response to strengthening the continuity of learning by reducing the "down" time of the summer months. The current calendar that provides for a 2 or more month hiatus from school is based on yesterday's needs. The families needed their children to help with the harvest on the farms during the summer months. Today our needs are much different as a society which provides educators an opportunity to revisit the calendar. This will be explored in more detail in a later chapter.

In the past 25 years much work has been done in the area of student assessments in an attempt to measure academic growth and mastery in the higher order thinking skills. Still most state proficiency tests such as end of course exams are multiple choice exams and rely on student recall/memorization. Some states have instituted a senior project where students have to prepare a research paper, a project based on the paper, present and defend the project and document in a portfolio the experience. While this provides educators an opportunity to assess a student's higher order thinking skills it is not universally implemented and where it exists it sometimes falls short of the necessary rigor to make it meaningful. Much more needs to be done in the area of student assessments. The adage that you get what you measure is so true here. We need to teach and assess our students' mastery of 21st Century skills. That said, Dr. Richard Hersh, an influential pioneer in testing, says "life is not a multiple –choice test". With support from many foundations, he worked with the Rand Corporation in developing a tool to measure the "value-added" of a college education by trying to determine how much students learned from their freshman year to their senior year. The tool is known as the Collegiate Learning Assessment (CLA).[18] The CLA measures a student's reasoning, problem-solving, analytical and writing skills. It has been well received at the collegiate level. Based on that reception and the burning need to assess high school students' readiness for post secondary education, Dr. Hersh and his colleagues have developed a high school version called College and Work Readiness Assessment (CWRA).[19] The feedback from those schools that are using it is extremely favorable. Much needs to be done in truly assessing students' readiness. The good news is that there are promising efforts underway such as CWRA to get us to where we need to be.

Takeaways

1. Reform initiatives have focused on five major areas; curriculum, instructional delivery, resourcing/personnel, organizational structure and assessments.
2. Secondary education curriculum has expanded over the past 30 years with significant additions in the area of vocational education to assist with career readiness. However, too often it is fragmented.
3. Targeted programs such as AVID have been designed and implemented to address the college readiness challenges.
4. With increased spending on education over the past 30 years, class sizes in general have declined but in recent years that trend has reversed.
5. Additional specialized resources have been added to assist the classroom teachers in preparing students for success.
6. Major structural changes to secondary education have been instituted such as 9th grade academies, year round schools, STEM schools and early colleges.
7. Student assessment methods/techniques have changed over the years in an attempt to measure student achievement. More emphasis has been added in recent years to zero in on measuring students' higher order thinking skills.

Application

1) Reflecting on school reform initiatives you have been involved with which ones, in your opinion, were successful and why?
2) Which ones were not successful and why?

Chapter 22

Results/Impact of Initiatives

"People love chopping wood. In this activity one immediately sees results."
----Albert Einstein

"However beautiful the strategy, you should occasionally look at the results."
----Winston Churchill

When speaking or thinking about results one is reminded of these two salient quotes above that capture, in simple thought, the challenges presented by measuring effectiveness of our best efforts (and intentions) with respect to initiatives we have planned and implemented. Often times, our biases interfere with an objective assessment of "how is it working". Vested interests in making sure our programs are "successful" undermine what is really important and that is, is the initiative making a positive difference and is it meeting/exceeding our stretch, noble objectives? As we have often heard and perhaps expressed ourselves, you can make the numbers say whatever you want them to say/prove. Keeping our eye on the primary goal and that goal being preparing every high school student to be ready for college, a career(s) and a productive life in society and the 21st century economy. In this chapter, we'll look at results in four key areas; student achievement, college and/or career readiness of students, quality of work life for school personnel and velocity of change.

As noted previously, high school graduation rates in the United States hover around 70%. That has not appreciably changed in the last 10 years. As a country we are well behind other industrialized countries such as Denmark (at 96 %) and Japan (at 93 %).[20] Many of our college students must take remedial courses their first year in college. It has been cited that as high as 50% of all students who begin college never complete any kind of postsecondary degree program.[21] According to a 2009 U.S. Department of Education report, U.S. 9th grade students' scores in math now lag behind those of 31 countries.[22] Additionally, there are current studies that document student achievement gaps across demographic groups. These gaps are most evident in math and reading.[23]

According to the National Assessment of Educational Progress' 2008 Long-Term Trend report, reading performance levels for 17-year-olds has steady declined over the past 20 years and the math performance levels for 17-year-olds has been relatively flat over the past 12 years.[24] In reading, less than 10% of the students scored at the highest level (<u>Learn from Specialized Reading Materials</u>). Students reading at this level can extend and restructure the ideas presented in specialized and complex texts. Examples include scientific materials, literary essays, and historical documents. Perhaps more troubling is that less than half of the students were proficient in understanding complicated information. Some 20% of the students were not able to synthesize ideas and make generalizations. This is serious cause for concern as it impacts student learning in all subjects, not just language arts courses. With respect to math, less than 60% of 17 year-old students can solve moderately complex procedures and reasoning and only 6 % can apply a range of reasoning skills to solve multistep problems.[25] The driving concern is that with a global economy/society the United States needs to be producing students prepared to compete for the 21st Century jobs. In a recent Programme for International Student Assessment (PISA) tests of scientific and mathematical literacy developed by the Organization for Economic Co-operation and Development pointed out how severely unprepared our students are in these vital subjects when compared with the youth of fifty-five other countries.[26] In the area of math, PISA has adopted the definition of mathematical literacy as "an individual's capacity to identify and understand the role that mathematics plays in the world, to make well-founded judgments and to use and engage with mathematics in ways that meet the needs of that individual's life as a constructive, concerned and reflective citizen".[27] The U.S. students performed poorly on this test. They placed 35th out of the fifty-five countries that participated.[28]

Often expressed (and the most visible) as the greatest skill deficiency for high school students is in the area of communication skills. This includes students' ability to clearly and concisely express a thought verbally and/or in writing not to mention the need for passion and energy in the delivery. This too has been cited by employers as a major hindrance in employee performance. The lack of adequate, if not strong, communication skills hampers the performance of high school students in all their courses, and continues through their college years and into their careers. In industry, all too often it has been observed that very competent subject matter experts coming out of some of the best graduate schools in the country are not able to convey their thoughts, opinions, positions in an organized, focus and succinct manner. Clarity of thought is an essential prerequisite to effective communications. It is so apparent when that is lacking. For that reason at least one Fortune 100 company instituted a program (Power in Communication) which was essentially a remedial course on communication skills specifically oral presentation and written communication skills. This 4 day intense session equipped these new hires with the skills to not only survive but to thrive in the corporate environment. One of the major tenets of the program was to make sure your audience (recipient of a letter, memo or listener) in a matter of 2 or 3 sentences and 1 or 2 minutes into a presentation knew the purpose of your communication....why am I writing to you or speaking to you today and what do I need from you. Certainly this was targeted to the needs/demands of that company but it has value in everyday life for the individual as a productive citizen. Tony Wagner in his book The Global Achievement Gap cites a study by the Partnership for 21st Century Skills which states that "80.9 percent of employer respondents report high school graduate entrants as 'deficient'".[29]

In a report entitled The Condition of College Readiness 2009 prepared and issued by ACT, an independent, not-for-profit organization that provides a broad array of assessment, research, information and program management in the areas of education and workforce development, about 67% of all ACT-tested high school graduates met the English College Readiness Benchmark in 2009.[30] Furthermore, only 23% met all four College Readiness Benchmarks in English. Just slightly over half (53%) of the graduates met the Reading Benchmark, while 42% met the Mathematics Benchmark. In science, 28% met the College Readiness Benchmark.[31]

In a recent article in the Charlotte Observer newspaper (which was based on an article in the New York Times) it cited a warning from the College Board that Americans lag in attaining college degrees and the gap between the U.S. and other countries "threatens to undermine U.S. economic competitiveness".[32] The article states that now the U.S. ranks 12th among 36 developed nations. The U.S. in the past has led the world for many years in the number of 25- to 34-year-olds with college degrees. Approximately 70% of all high school graduates in the United States enroll in college within two years but only 57% of the students who enroll in a 4 year degree program graduate within six years. It further states that less than 25% of students who begin at a community college graduate with an associate's degree within three years.[33]

Teacher satisfaction surveys indicate a growing discontent with the quality of work life. Teacher turnover has continued to be high and costly despite many initiatives including increase pay, bonuses and expanded professional development opportunities. The Alliance for Excellent Education research indicates that for every school day across the country nearly a thousand teachers leave the field of teaching and another thousand teachers change schools, "many in pursuit of better working conditions".[34] The article cites the main reasons for the high attrition rates which are lack of or insufficient planning time, problematic student behavior not dealt with adequately and lack of influence over school policy. It states that nearly 50% of all teachers who enter the profession leave it within five years. In the exit interviews the departing teachers consistently cite lack of support from the administration and poor working conditions as the primary factors for their resignation.[35] In any other profession this rate of attrition for an extended period of time would be considered an epidemic and an untenable condition that must be addressed promptly and in a comprehensive manner. In a later chapter we'll explore initiatives to address this daunting challenge that is at the core of improving student achievement.

Takeaways

1. U.S. high school graduation rates hover around the 70% level despite a concerted effort to change that dynamic. Many initiatives have been launched to address this crisis over the past several years.
2. Many high school graduates entering college must take remedial courses to build the necessary mastery to be successful at the collegiate level.
3. Major student academic deficiencies still exist in reading, writing, math and science despite the increased emphasis placed on improving these shortcomings over the past 10 years.
4. Communication skills of our high school and college students are lacking. This challenge not only undermines ones pursuit of career readiness but also producing productive, effective citizens of our society.
5. Teacher turnover due to job dissatisfaction is inordinately high and even though there have been a number of initiatives to counter this growing crisis it still plagues us to this day.

Chapter 23

Common Denominators among Successful Schools

"Smarts and action are on the same side of the equation where the sum is success."
----*Garrett Hazel*

"Success is like a beautiful flower; first you must cultivate the soil and then plant the seed and water it frequently with encouragement, support and a heavy dose of persistence."
----*Author Unknown*

In searching for those common threads that make high schools successful an awarding winning school principal when asked what made you and your school so successful stated, without hesitation, "there are no silver bullets, only heavy lifting day in and day out". That is so true in education and life in general. Often times, we seek to find that one answer/solution that will fix the situation. Experience tells us that it is elusive because it frequently does not exist. However, there are many building blocks when put together form a successful school. These building blocks are strategies/initiatives which are strongly supported by all constituents and aligned with the overarching goal of improving student achievement for all students. From school calendar and school day to professional development and school leadership the successful schools have much in common. It all begins with creating a culture of excellence grounded in trust and mutual respect.

Phillip Schlechty in his book, *Working on the Work*, lists twelve standards that define a successful school where students are highly engaged in learning.[36] The standards are 1) patterns of engagement, 2) student achievement, 3) content and substance, 4) organization of knowledge, 5) product focus, 6) clear and compelling product, 7) safe environment, 8) affirmation of performances, 9) affiliation, 10) novelty and variety, 11) choice, and 12) authenticity. He frames the discussion of these standards in terms of the overall school culture. Establishing and communicating expectations of teachers, principals, superintendents, school boards, parents and students is fundamental to creating and sustaining a culture of excellence.

Schlechty speaks of "beliefs shape visions, and visions drive missions".[37] From missions come strategic goals which are associated with specific actions/tasks to meet those goals. While it sounds so basic it frequently is not practiced. That is not the case for those schools experiencing success across the board from student achievement and academic growth to teacher satisfaction/delight and staff retention. The successful schools build on that culture of excellence in everything they do. They are true to their mission and obsessed with seeking perfection but not letting it be the enemy of the good. School culture is the underpinning of all the programs, initiatives, interactions that comprise the institution. Ken Robinson describes culture as "a system of permissions. It's about the attitudes and behaviors that are acceptable and unacceptable in different communities, those that are approved of and those that are not."[38] This gets at the heart of expectation setting and another common denominator of successful schools and that is reflection and reaction. Professionals committed to life-long learning constantly reflect on their performance and react (adjust) accordingly. For successful educators it is part of their DNA. In a post observation session with a teacher she shared with the principal a copy of her marked-up lesson plan from the class he observed. She had written comments in the margin on what she will do differently next time based on her reflection of what might work better in terms of student learning. She had incorporated feedback from the students based on "exit tickets" she collected as the students left class that day. This commitment to continuous learning and improvement is essential in creating and sustaining a culture of excellence. It also is contagious. Both her colleagues and her students have embraced this practice of self reflection.

Another common denominator of successful high schools is a rigorous curriculum (Honors level and Advanced Placement courses in each subject area) that also provides the flexibility for students to place out of courses and to accelerate through a course if capable. These schools offer comprehensive support programs such as daily tutoring and student mentoring. Using the curriculum as a tool not as a constraint is the key here. There are schools that offer "progressive" courses where students start out at basic levels and move as quickly as they can through higher levels of complexity. Math, science and language arts courses lend themselves to this approach. In math, for example, creating a course that allows students to move from Fundamentals of Math to Algebra I and onto Algebra II all in one semester provides students an opportunity to move through the content area as quickly as they can master the material. Challenging students along the way is an essential tenet of the progressive courses.

Professional development and collaboration is front and center at successful schools. It is part of the culture mentioned above. The driving need for continuous improvement coupled with constant self reflection serves as the catalyst for the teachers, counselors and administrators to seek out opportunities to "sharpen the saw".

Administrators provide for these opportunities and teacher and administrator include these development opportunities in their respective personal development plans. This then becomes an integral part of the individual's evaluation. Collaboration is the life-blood of a successful professional development model. Tony Wagner identifies collaboration as one of his seven survival skills.[39] Daily interaction between and among teachers on student achievement is a strong indication of a high performance team. Collaboration is a powerful force that differentiates the ordinary faculty from the extraordinary. Collaboration must be all inclusive. That is, it must involve the entire team. All faculty members must be sharing their experiences. It can be one on one, one to many or many to many.

In terms of the classroom, the successful schools have instituted an "open door" policy. They are committed to making classroom instruction/learning a public domain. Teachers freely move in and out of colleagues' classrooms for the purpose of gaining insight into what they can do and to offer suggestions to their colleagues. This is part of their culture which as stated earlier is based on trust and mutual respect. This takes collaboration to the next level in these schools. In a later chapter we'll explore best practices in this area.

The final two common denominators among successful high schools are effective, proactive leadership and community alliances (for example, outreach programs). As in any organization, leadership is a major differentiator in whether the organization will be successful in meeting its objectives or not. Some would argue that it is the dominant factor determining success. Leadership is more art than science. There have been many books written on leadership and the qualities of leadership. The one that comes to mind is Stephen Covey's book entitled *Principle-Centered*

Leadership. In it he speaks of his "true north" principles and the characteristics of principle-centered leaders.[40] Embedded in that discussion are the five leadership qualities that are essential as it relates to leading high school reform initiatives. They are 1) it starts with a vision of what you want the organization to accomplish/achieve, 2) communicating that vision & associated expectations and ensuring alignment up & down the organization (superintendent to faculty, staff, students/parents and community), 3) empowering the organization, 4) measuring (and communicating) how well you are doing against those expectations and adjusting accordingly and finally being willing to take calculated risks. It is the calculated risk element that is too often missing when it comes to school reform. Change engenders fear. That is, fear of the unknown and fear of failure create emotional paralyses. Leaders weigh the risk with the potential reward always mindful of the impact on the organization, both positive and negative. Transformation sometimes requires bold action at times that is unsettling but necessary to reach higher levels of performance. In a later chapter we'll explore specific transformative initiatives that will require such actions.

Engaging the community in actively supporting the school's vision, goals and objectives is a commitment successful schools have embraced. This is a long term initiative but progress can and needs to be made in the short term. From involving community members in the school's leadership teams to proactively communicating with the community through newsletters, speaking engagements and newspaper articles successful schools have found this constituency as a powerful force in supporting school reform and ultimately higher student achievement.

Takeaways

1. There are no silver bullets in transforming high schools into a paragon of excellence.
2. Creating a culture of excellence is job # 1. That is established by laying "one brick at a time" to build that foundation.
3. Successful high schools have implemented a rigorous curriculum for **all** students and supported that through effective and timely professional development.
4. Faculty and staff collaborate frequently (daily) focused on improving student achievement for **all** students.
5. Classroom instruction is "public". That is, there is an open door policy for any faculty member to drop in on another class to observe. This is not only supported by all faculty members in successful schools but encouraged by the faculty.
6. Leadership connotes many qualities essential to the success of the school including calculated risk-taking.
7. Successful schools have reached out to the community for support. This has been a powerful force for supporting school initiatives.

Application

Reflecting on your school and Phillip Schlechty's 12 standards that define a successful school, identify specific evidence(s) of excellence with respect to each standard. How does your school rate?

Chapter 24

Keys to Success

"Don't be discouraged. It's often the last key in the bunch that opens the lock."

----*Author Unknown*

In the research for this book it was quite clear that schools that experienced sustained success over several years were ones that had an intense focus on improving student achievement and annual academic growth for every student. These schools set high expectations for administration, faculty and students and measured their performance against those expectations. From the superintendent to the office assistant in the respective schools the conversations centered on "what are we doing to improve student achievement". Every ounce of energy was expended on making that happen. In a conversation with a principal of a very successful high school she mentioned that the district's monthly meeting always began with a conversation about student performance. She went on to say that a considerable portion of the meeting was dedicated to discussing ways to increase student achievement including citing success stories in their schools. At the school level, all actions taken were viewed through the prism of what was in the best interest of the students and their academic growth. From curriculum design to bulletin board displays the message was unambiguous.....we (administration, faculty, staff and students) are here to increase student achievement. She stated that in every meeting with parents the focus was on how their son or daughter was doing academically and what specific actions needed to be taken to improve their performance. This discussion took place even if it was a meeting on a disciplinary infraction. This unwavering and laser-like focus on academic excellence establishes the foundation for high performing schools. Everything, that is, all actions, emanates from this student achievement core. According to the Department of Defense (DOD) Education Activity, organization charged with educating the children of military and civilian personnel working for DOD throughout the world, the #1 goal in their Community Strategic Plan is "highest student achievement".[41] All other goals are subservient to this goal.

Student achievement and student academic growth are "companion" goals. Focusing on increasing student academic growth by content area will result in increasing student achievement. Regardless of where the student resides on the proficiency continuum measuring that student's growth is the great equalizer. The US Department of Education (No Child Left Behind legislation) places significant emphasis on academic growth through the measurement of adequate yearly progress (AYP) at the school level.

Much research has been done on the correlation between student academic growth and dropout rates/graduation rates. Keeping the attention on "moving the achievement needle" upward for each student is a major lever in achieving success at the school level.

The North Carolina New Schools Project (NCNSP), a public-private catalyst for education innovation, has identified *personalization* as one of its five design principles for innovative high schools in North Carolina.[42] Personalization, as defined by NCNSP, is the "affective and academic support each student receives during the school day and that every student is known well by the adults in the school".[43]

Developing those relationships with each and every student is the linchpin in creating a high expectations, caring environment. As mentioned earlier in the text students don't care what you know until they know you care. How true that is!! There are so many inspiring stories of teachers and administrators who went the "extra mile" in addressing the emotional and financial needs of their students. This caring attitude is also evident between teachers, staff and administrators. A culture of caring is a hallmark of successful schools.

Collaboration is another quality of successful schools. That is, teachers working together with the support of the administration in pursuit of continuous improvement in student achievement. Re-enforcing skills from another class, aligning lesson plans (across disciplines) wherever possible and coordinating project-based learning opportunities are a few examples of teacher collaboration that foster increased student performance. It also has the potential to make the learning more relevant for the students. In large, comprehensive high schools it becomes a challenge to coordinate planning periods within departments such as math, language arts, etc. However, teachers can seek out those within their department with the same planning period as well as engage faculty members who teach grade-specific courses that their students are currently taking(for example, English II and a social studies class) for purposes of collaboration. In the schools who have made collaboration a priority many have also "adopted" the notion of making teaching/learning "public". Teachers regularly enter each other's classrooms to observe and provide feedback again focusing on continuous improvement in student achievement. This serves as a learning experience for the "drop-in" teachers as well. If there is a teaching technique that another teacher has mastered than this can be a learning laboratory for those teachers seeking to improve pedagogy in that specific area. Making teaching/learning public is a powerful force and one that is embraced by successful schools.

There are five additional keys that contribute in a major way to successful high schools starting with aligning on the vision and mission of the school by all stakeholders. This sounds Pollyanna and/or too cosmic but is essential in attaining long term, sustainable success. Successful schools not only seek and ensure alignment on the vision and mission but proactively promote (and yes, defend where necessary), educate and hold each one accountable for their actions consistent with their schools' vision and mission. This is not an easy task. It takes time and a commitment to a "greater good" for the betterment of the institution. This vision and mission needs to drive the strategies (curriculum design, instructional, outreach initiatives, etc) and the tactics (budgets, lesson plans, etc). In a conversation with a high school principal he mentioned that before every significant purchase the school makes he along with his leadership team first evaluates it with respect to their mission and strategies. That is, does it support what they are all about and will it contribute to their attaining their overall goals. He stated that it was more than a mental exercise but a dialogue amongst the team members culminating in "boxes to be checked off" on a budget form.

Much has been written about creativity and the need for innovation in education today. This need is not unique to education. Listening to noted economist, business and political leaders the evidence is there that the United States is falling behind in the "world of innovation". From the number of patents to the number of inventions we are losing our world leadership in this critical area. In education, one doesn't need to look too hard at our schools in general from curriculum to school calendars and everything in between to recognize not a lot has changed in the past 100 years or more. It deserves mentioning here that there are several examples of successful innovative approaches to education which are resulting in unparallel gains in student achievement and growth. These schools are fighting the odds and winning!!! Unfortunately these approaches have not been leveraged across the wider spectrum. It is viewed erroneously as a "one off" situation that "can't work on a larger scale". It is that attitude that must be addressed and refuted. Wagner speaks of creating a culture of innovation.[44]

It is a mindset. It starts with being inquisitive. We want our students to be inquisitive for good reason and we must model that behavior in executing our roles as educators. The Bill and Melinda Gates Foundation has been and continues to be in the forefront of secondary school reform. The Gates Foundation promotes innovation and risk taking (which is an inseparable companion to innovation) which we'll discuss a little later in this chapter. As with any significant change (and secondary education reform will require significant change) there needs to be a process and models (exemplars if you will) for change along with "change agents". Again, we'll discuss this in more detail in a later chapter. The role of innovation and the need for it in high school reform cannot be overstated or underestimated. It is a key lever for success.

The next key to success in high school reform is one of emotion. It is the passion to make a difference and the will power to persevere. In Dr. Ken Robinson's book, The Element, he speaks of passion as "I love it" phenomenon.[45] Refusing to be denied of what you are pursuing (that is, the vision and mission) is the essence of passion. We all have seen or experience passion in action. It is a sight to behold. How many times have we heard, "gee that person is really passionate about that subject, hobby, (you name it). Passion is contagious and that "infection" is one we want to spread to our students and colleagues.

As referenced earlier, the need for risk-taking is paramount to any successful initiative worth pursuing. There is an expression many of us are familiar with and perhaps experienced and that is "there is no gain without pain". Risk-taking is a staple for successful schools. It is inherent in every decision they make and every initiative they pursue. We know with risk there is a chance for reward or a possibility of failure. It is too often the latter that motivates us to seek the path that minimizes or eliminates the prospect of failure and thus limits our potential to be all we can be as a person and as a school. Risk aversion is the enemy of school reform. Risk can be mitigated substantially if pursued in a methodical manner. It is a **calculated** risk we should be willing to take for the prospect of substantial "returns". Keeping the (Calculated) Risk–Reward equation in balance is the key to success here.

As we develop our next steps in a later chapter we will identify specific actions that will require calculated risk-taking in pursuit of successful and sustained high school reform.

The last key to success is leadership. Having strong leadership at all levels from school board members and superintendent to local school administration is the catalyst in instituting education reform.

The number of books on leadership could fill a school gymnasium. You could distill each of them into 4 or 5 principles that constitute effective leadership. According to Donald Thomas and William Bainbridge in their treatise entitled *School Leadership 101*, educational leaders need the following leadership qualities/competencies: 1) listen effectively, understanding both content and feeling, 2) validate the accuracy of information received, 3) speak frankly and clearly and speak directly to the issue, 4) be positive about life, about self, and about one's work, 5) keep current, to synthesis knowledge and to utilize research, 6) self-motivate and to inspire colleagues, 7) try new ideas, take risks and encourage others to do so, 8) articulate purpose, to establish a vision and to inspire confidence in schools.[46] Thomas and Bainbridge go on to state in this article that educational leaders need to express idealism and practicality.[47] Leaders need to empower others and that is so essential in leading any initiative especially one that involves reform. A decentralized decision-making model predicated on a strong alignment on vision, mission and goals with an accountability element is what successful schools have adopted. Turning loose the creative energy of the faculty and staff and driving decision-making closer to the students is a model for success.

Takeaways

1. There are a handful of common factors, call them keys to success, which are resident in schools that have significantly increased student performance to levels of mastery over a sustained period of time.
2. The major factors contributing to schools that have excelled in student achievement and academic growth over a sustained period of time are:
   - Intense focus on student achievement/academic growth that permeates throughout the school community,
   - A culture of relationship building, caring for one another, student to student, teacher to teacher, administration to teacher, teacher to student, etc.,
   - Promoting and supporting collaboration and making instruction "public",
   - Aligning on vision, mission and goals of school and staying true to that alignment,
   - Encouraging creativity/innovation in addressing challenges and rewarding behavior that fosters inquisitiveness,
   - Burning passion to make a difference... administration, faculty, staff, students, parents alike,
   - Being calculated risk takers and to celebrate/reward such actions,
   - Strong leadership with decentralized decision-making.
3. The highest priority is student achievement and academic growth by all students. Setting high expectations for administration, staff, faculty and students and measuring performance against those

expectations underpins the culture of excellence in those successful schools.
4. *Change agents and models (exemplars) for the "new environment" are integral to successfully implementing reform.*

Application

You have recently been assigned to a new school in your district as its 1st principal. At the 1st faculty meeting you intend to stress the need to build a culture of excellence from day one. What are the keys to success in creating that culture that you will emphasize in your presentation.

Chapter 25

Next Steps/Recommendations (Short Term)

"The pessimist sees difficulty in every opportunity. The optimist sees the opportunity in every difficulty."
---- *Winston Churchill*

"They always say time changes things, but you actually have to change them yourself."
---- *Andy Warhol*

The need for change is indisputable. The evidence is overwhelming and growing that our high schools are not meeting the evolving needs of the students they serve. In an article in the September, 2010 issue of U.S. News & World Report magazine, entitled <u>Getting Kids Set for College</u>, it re-enforces the "troubling and dismal trends" a decade after the Federal No Child Left Behind legislation was enacted.[48] The article cites the continuing inordinately high dropout rates and states that graduation rates have remained the same since the early 1960s. Furthermore, "only 40 % of students in the United States who do manage to graduate from high school go on to earn a two-or four –year college degree, meaning that many more are unable to finish the work once they get to the university gates."[49] This has been chronicled in an earlier chapter but bears repeating here.

That said, we must not lose sight of the fact that there are high schools that are shining examples of success which are truly paragons of excellence. These schools are our exemplars. They have much to offer those schools that are struggling with low student achievement, high dropout rates and staff dissatisfaction. In this chapter we'll explore specific measures these challenged schools can embrace and implement immediately (within 1 year) and in the next chapter discuss longer term initiatives they can undertake positioning them for success. The ultimate goal is to create a high performance team of administrators, faculty, staff and students culminating in high student achievement, 100 % graduation rates, high morale.... a place where excellence is the norm.

There are 6 key actions that will lay the foundation for success which can be implemented in 12 months or less. These coupled with the 7 longer-term initiatives outlined in the next chapter can serve as the blueprint for transformation.

Aligning on a concise and easy to understand vision and mission for your school by all constituents is a prerequisite for what is to follow. Clarity around what your priorities are and where you intend to expend resources is a product of your vision and mission. Too often we compose and embrace eloquently expressed mission statements and then give lip service to how we will operationalize it.

Peter Senge in his book Fifth Discipline states that "the practice of shared vision involves the skills of unearthing shared pictures of the future that fosters genuine commitment and enrollment rather than compliance. In mastering this discipline, leaders learn the counter productiveness of trying to dictate a vision, no matter how heartfelt".[50] By clearly stating as a team what your vision is for the school and why you exist (mission) you have set the foundation for the strategies and tactics you will implement. There are two key points here. The first is to develop concise vision and mission statements. Ones that are challenging and will meet the needs of those you are serving (that is, students, parents, community, etc.). The second is to gain alignment among all the constituents. This can be done through school leadership teams, Outreach programs or any forum where school administration, faculty, parents, students and community members come together periodically. As stated above, this will be the basis for developing strategies, tactics and the corresponding budget(s). This will require setting aside an ample amount of "quality time" for discussion and a commitment to actively engage all parties culminating in an alignment on the school's vision and mission.

As with perfecting any process whether that be industrial (making computer chips), athletic (mastering the tennis serve) or educational (student learning) you start with understanding the basics. In education, the four fundamentals arguably are reading, writing, math and inquisitiveness. A laser-like focus on teaching (re-teaching) and re-enforcing the fundamentals of reading, writing, math and science in the 9th grade is essential in laying the foundation for what is to follow. There are several programs in existence that have produced very positive results for school districts across the country in meeting head on this critical need. One of those programs is the Advancement Via Individual Determination (referred to as AVID). With a concentration on reading, writing, math and organization skills the goal is to prepare students to be college ready. Some school districts have implemented "freshmen academies" where the focus is on mastering these fundamental skills before the students can move on to the next grade level. Some districts have designed "progressive" courses where students must master specific skills before they progress to the next (read higher) level of under-standing. Others have included a "GOALS" class in their curriculum where the emphasis is on grammar, organization and leadership skills. Students must attain mastery before advancing into English I. So there are a number of approaches to meeting the challenge of ensuring high school students early on have mastered the basic skills necessary for them to succeed in higher level courses and truly be college ready. As mentioned in an earlier chapter because of deficiencies in these basic skills 40% of all students who enter college must take remedial courses (principally in the area of math and language arts).[51]

Faculty collaboration and relevant professional development are essential ingredients in achieving and sustaining academic excellence. Schools that have arranged time for faculty members during the instructional day to collaborate have benefitted greatly in enhancing teacher effectiveness and morale. This can be accomplished in part by coordinating where possible "planning periods". In larger schools a few teachers from one department (for example, math) can meet with a few teachers from one or more other departments. If it can be done on a grade level basis (say 9th grade teachers) that would be even more effective. This is not intended to supplant the monthly department meetings where all the subject-specific teachers meet. These meetings also play a vital role and should be focused not on administrative detail but on how to increase student performance. During these collaboration sessions teachers exchange on a real time basis what is working for them in their classrooms and what is not and where they can use assistance/support in being more effective. An extension of these collaboration sessions is the peer observation. This should be an informal drop-in or a request to drop-in visit and can be most effective in "evaluating" an instructional activity. An administrator overheard a teacher in a collaboration session say to one of her peers who was struggling with organizing a project-based activity that she was starting one in her class tomorrow and for her to drop in on her class. In the subsequent collaboration session they were able to analyze and dissect what had transpired in the observed teacher's class for the benefit of the observing teacher. In this case, the session served as an exemplar for the observing teacher. Seeing it in action is a powerful learning experience. Making teaching and learning "public" is both a necessary and vital step in improving education. It needs to be non-threatening, caring and constructive. Creating a culture where faculty members reach out even beyond their school to collaborate with teachers who have demonstrated instructional excellence is another sign of a high performance team. This action is contagious. Success breeds success.

Relevant professional development (PD) on an on-going basis positions the faculty for success. Professional development and collaboration are synergistic. Providing contemporary and timely training on instructional strategies and tactics enables the faculty to sharpen their execution of instructional preparation and delivery. All too often professional development has been infrequent, irrelevant and/or non specific. Frequently the best professional development is teacher-led. Professional development that is focused on best practices and steps to get you from where you are to the best practices operating level is the definition of relevant professional development. Successful school districts identify teachers that have demonstrated instructional excellence and work with them to develop and deliver professional development sessions. These sessions need to be followed up with a support structure for those attending as they return to their classrooms to implement the newly acquired learning. The purpose of the support structure is to assist the PD recipient in implementing the strategies learned and to assess the effectiveness of the implementation. The support structure could be a teacher mentor.

Empowerment of faculty and staff is central to operating as a high performance team. Providing the requisite professional development and ensuring a vibrant communications process will establish an environment conducive to empowerment. Faculty need to participate in and make decisions that impact them. Decisions on curriculum design, instructional strategies, non-instructional school related activities, are areas ripe for faculty input and determination. The teacher is the instructional leader in their classroom and a co-leader at the school level. Empowerment breeds creativity and innovation which is contagious.

Embracing the belief that data is our friend, successful schools operate from a data driven discussion perspective. Using student performance data to target areas of deficiencies and areas of mastery is fundamental to creating new or adjusting existing instructional strategies/tactics. Identifying the data that is the most relevant and that is determinate is the key here. Also, there often is a fine line between getting the data you need to make an informed decision and letting the data paralyze the decision-making process. There are several tools and databases to utilize in the data gathering process. The significant effort required is turning this data into "knowledge" to make the informed decision.

An integral part of this key measure (once data/intelligence is at hand) is to focus on student academic growth. That is, how much growth does a student achieve from one year to the next in major content areas (for example, language arts, math, etc)? While composite scores such as % of students on grade level, above grade level, below grade level are important indicators more critical is the student growth data. This data will indicate whether the student made the academic progress consistent with one year's growth. No matter where the student started (below grade level for example) the growth factor will indicate whether s/he made adequate (1 year) progress in that class. Isn't this what we are about as educators? Often, too much attention is focused on the composite scores at the expense of student growth. That is short sighted.

After setting into motion the 1) development and alignment on the school's vision/mission, 2) focusing on the academic basics, 3) creating and implementing an environment of collaboration supported by relevant professional development, 4) empowering the faculty/staff and 5) instilling a passion for data and data analysis the final short term initiative involves establishing student mentors. Successful schools have detailed student education plans (Personal Education Plans or PEPs) for every student. These plans include an annual needs analysis, student grades, academic growth metrics, national test scores (for example, Scholastic Aptitude Test), academic accommodations (if needed), student interests, extracurricular activities, letters of commendation/awards. Additionally, students are afforded tutoring opportunities either during the school day or before or after school. Students also have access to guidance counselors. Generally the sessions with the counselor are focused on courses they need to graduate, college selection and any required testing for college entrance. The PEP, the tutoring opportunities and the access to guidance counselors are necessary but not sufficient. Students need academic mentors. These mentors can be the linchpin for student success. Working with the student to ensure they are receiving the support they need, providing the support where possible, serving as a voice of encouragement and as a sounding board for challenges they are comforting. These mentors are faculty members, community/church representatives, and local business representatives.

Takeaways

1. There is scrutable and compelling evidence that schools are not meeting the academic needs of our children and thus our society and the rate of decline is alarming.
2. There are many high schools that are centers of excellence and there are common denominators that contribute to their successes.
3. The six key actions that will provide the foundation for success are:

   - Developing, communicating, aligning on and implementing a clear and concise vision and mission from school board to faculty, students, parents and community.
   - Intense focus on the fundamentals (language arts, math and science), most critically in that first year of high school.
   - Institute a culture of collaboration between and among school administrators, faculty, students, parents and the community. Couple the collaboration with a heavy dosage of relevant and timely professional development.
   - Empowerment is the energizer in all successful transformation initiatives.
   - Data driven decision-making needs to be a routine exercise not an afterthought. "Data is our friend" mentality must exist.
   - Establishing a student mentoring program which supports, encourages and serves as a lifeline for all students.

Application

Your school board has asked you to provide a recommendation on how to improve teacher efficacy as well as student achievement in your school. What specific recommendations would you communicate to the board?

Chapter 26

Next Steps/Recommendations (Longer Term)

"We lose almost a million students from our high schools each year to the streets."
---- Arne Duncan, US Secretary of Education

"No problem can be solved by the same consciousness that created it. We need to see the world anew."
---- Albert Einstein

"We need a metamorphosis of education-from the cocoon a butterfly should emerge. Improvement does not give us a butterfly only a faster caterpillar."
---- Author Unknown

In a recent Wall Street Journal and NBC poll 58% of the respondents indicated that a major overhaul of schools is needed and gave schools an overall D+ grade.[52] In that same article which included the poll results, US Secretary of Education Arne Duncan stated that the US has fallen to 20th in the world in math and science and has dropped to 9th in the world in college graduates from 1st in just one generation.[53]

The need for a major overhaul has been characterized by many as a crisis of monumental proportions. As the quote above implies continuing to reform around the edges will not produce the desired and essential results that are needed to right the ship of education. It will take dramatic changes. These changes need to be phased in over a 3 to 5 year period of time with check-points established throughout the timeline. Borrowing from industry quality assurance initiatives the operative cycle for program implementation is Plan-Do-Check-Act.

This will require a full court press by all the constituents to make these changes in a timely manner and to be prepared for "bumps in the road". There are no silver bullets, only a lot of heavy lifting by all parties. The mantra is the three Rs. This translates into 3 phases as well. We need to <u>rethink</u> what we are doing and what we need to do to lead the world in educational excellence. We need to <u>rebuild</u> the educational construct and we need to prepare for the <u>rebound</u>. Let's explore the rethink and rebuild phases and later in this chapter we'll explore in more detail the rebound phase.

We'll tackle these two phases through the lenses of structural changes, curriculum modifications, accountability, professional development, community involvement, learning laboratories, and linkage to and role of post secondary institutions.

Much has been written about the length of the school calendar over the years. For a number of reasons there has been a great reluctance to embrace a longer school year and in many cases a longer school day. In the US our school year (for primary and secondary education) is approximately one month shorter than the countries who lead the world in producing students highly proficient in math and science. The school year has not changed appreciably over the past 75 plus years. Based on an agrarian economy the school year provided for school age kids to assist with farm duties during the summer months when crops were ready for harvest. With a global and technology based economy the need for "summers off" has vanished. Time magazine ran a cover article in its August 2, 2010 edition on the case for a year round school year.[54] The article focused on the need to keep kids/students engaged in the learning process during the summer months to avoid what it refers to as the "summer learning loss". This has a deleterious effect on students' academic progress from year to year. One program it references is the Summer Advantage program in Indiana where students are actively engaged in a variety of learning experiences and not tied to a classroom setting.[55] Another such program is the Fifth Quarter in a Cincinnati, Ohio school system.[56] Again, students learn about life experiences and are able to cultivate those life success skills such as adaptability, communications, inquisitiveness, critical thinking and entrepreneurship. While immensely important in the education process, the development of these skills is often neglected due to "time constraints" during the school year. These summer programs noted above are often funded by foundations and corporations with little or no financial support required from the respective school system. There are school systems that have implemented summer "boost" programs where low performing students are immersed in series of skill development sessions focused on "catching the students up" prior to entering the next grade level. These types of programs are admirable and can be expanded to include all students. There are examples of schools that have created a summer curriculum for all students and part of the instructional day for the accelerated students is to tutor the lower performing students in key subject areas with teacher oversight. These summer programs can include internships, field trips to educational sites, art/drama programs, recreational activities (beyond the 9th grade Physical Education class there is very little in the way of physical activity for all high school students). Those school systems who have implemented year round school calendars have had very positive experiences. The continuity of learning is so vital to the educational process. The summer hiatus sometimes referred to as the "summer slide" or "summer learning loss" is a significant contributor to the achievement gap. According to the Time magazine article the summer slide affects millions of low income students negatively as often the higher income students have access to mind stimulating experiences during the summer months that are not available to the lower income students. From a cost and expense perspective, a year round school calendar has the potential to save on facility costs (better utilization) and personnel if properly planned over the long term. This leads to the discussion of "seat time" that is the amount of time students need to spend in school each year. Most jurisdictions require 180 school days a year for students. This perhaps made sense for many years but today needs to be revisited. Much research has been done on student learning along with instructional best practices on differentiated instruction based on how students learn (for example, visual, auditory, kinesthetic). The pace of learning differs from student to student. Today those students who are "accelerated learners" are often slowed down by the pace of instruction and become bored in the process. Likewise those students who struggle with the pace, which is generally geared toward the average learner in the class, fall behind. Quite often these students are less apt to ask clarifying questions or acknowledge that the pace is too fast for them. That said, offering courses that are progressive in nature will serve **all** students better. With the support of technology (computers) and associated applications that provide teachers an opportunity to put their lessons and instruction on-line students can progress at their own level. If the student can demonstrate mastery of a lesson or series of lessons they can move on to the next one. If they can complete the course in 6,8,or 10 weeks rather than the "hardwired" 18 weeks (typical semester course) than they move to their next course. This also works well for the learner who struggles. If it takes 20 weeks to master the course than 20 weeks is allocated. The pace in which one learns needs to be factored in to the course length. The objective is to let mastery drive the length of the course and to use technology as the equalizer for scheduling purposes.

As referenced in a previous chapter, our high school students need more exposure to math (at least 5 courses including higher levels such as quantitative analysis) and science (at least 5 courses). Getting back to basics is essential in any high school reform initiative. For illustrative purposes, below is a program of study of suggested required courses that would (and in many cases today is) meet the academic needs of our high school students (that is, preparing them to be college or career ready).

Language Arts: 6 courses (English I thru IV plus journalism/creative writing and communications)

Math: 6 courses (Algebra I & II, Geometry, Calculus, Quantitative Analysis & Statistics)

Science: 6 courses (Earth and Environmental, Biology, Physical Science, Chemistry, Physics & Astronomy)

Arts: 2 courses (select from Theater, Art History, Music Appreciation, Design, etc)

Second (Foreign) Language: 2 courses

Social Studies: 4 courses (Civics & Economics, World History, US History, Contemporary Events/Topics*)

*Debate skills/techniques/practice would be incorporated into the course syllabus

Physical Education: 2 courses (one would be Health)

Electives: 2 courses (e.g., additional foreign language, arts or Career and Technical Education / vocational courses).

At first glance, one might think this curriculum is a "bridge too far" for our high school students. There would be concerns that the rigor of the course material would be too much for all of our students to master. Some might say that this would be appropriate for our "gifted" students but not the "average" student. This is where the commitment to establishing high expectations and leaving no students behind is really tested. It is a universal truth that we need to and want to hold our students to high expectations. By adopting a rigorous curriculum one that positions them for a successful experience in a post secondary educational environment or in a career we are "walking the talk".

Perhaps the one area that has drawn much attention in recent times as being ripe for reform is accountability. These discussions take the shape of pay for performance (AKA, merit pay) evaluation/appraisal systems or objective setting sessions (Management By Objectives). In a Time magazine poll (August 17-19, 2010) 71 % of the respondents support merit pay that is paying teachers on the basis of their effectiveness and 64 % believe student standardized-test scores should play a role in teacher-performance evaluations.[57]

The magazine article mentions that there are seven states that have enacted laws to "remove firewalls between student achievement and teacher evaluations" and that there are 12 states that have passed laws requiring student progress data to be used in preparing teacher evaluations or tenure decisions.[58] The US Department of Education is weighing in on this drive toward greater accountability through its Race to the Top initiative. This competition is pressing school districts throughout the country to raise academic standards and to, in part, evaluate teachers based on how much their students have learned. The momentum is building here and rightly so. While care must be taken on how the teacher evaluation instrument is constructed it is an imperative in instituting school reform. That said, there also needs to be a linkage in objectives, corresponding results and performance pay from the classroom teacher to the principal ending with the school superintendent. That "golden thread" is essential. The accountability model, referred to as the value-added model in a previous section of the book, must 1) be appropriately balanced between risk and reward, 2) include linkage, 3) contain an evaluation instrument that weighs appropriately four components (student academic growth [50 %], student achievement as measured by standardize tests [30 %] and teacher development [20 %]). In that same Time magazine poll 80 % of the respondents indicated that merit pay, better teacher training and mentoring by more experienced teachers would improve teacher effectiveness the most.[59] Before addressing the last two findings, which deserve more discussion as too often it has been given lip service or just ignored, the survey results regarding merit pay warrant further discussion. This text will begin to frame the topic as well as set up a more comprehensive dialogue for a future treatise on this burning issue. Let's begin by briefly defining what merit pay, again also referred to as pay for performance (PFP), is and why it is front and center in the discussion and debate on school reform. Merit pay is compensating the employee (in this case, the teacher and school administrators) for meeting and exceeding their objectives. These objectives are specific, measurable, achievable, realistic and timely. They should be resident in the employee's annual performance plan (MBOs as noted earlier) and tied to the school's improvement plan. That is the golden thread cited above. This also pertains to school administrators. At the heart of the teacher objectives should be student achievement and academic growth. This is not to imply that other factors/objectives are not important such as professional development, community involvement, etc. They too should be part of the employee's plan in the form of objectives. Pay scales are pegged to the performance of the individual versus their stated objectives. Quite simply, if the employee meets his/her objectives they receive one level of compensation and if they exceed their objectives they receive a higher level. On the contrary if they fall short of their objectives they receive a lower level of compensation. Compensation here is defined as salary and bonuses. There are a plethora of nuances here such as how much one exceeds (or misses) their objectives and its impact on pay levels (the element of progressivity), the weightings of each of the objectives, etc. These all need to be well defined upfront and the process needs to be very transparent.

For purposes of outlining the topic let's look at a few of the often mentioned pros and cons of merit pay. Starting with the positive reasons, below are a few frequently cited;

- It will assist in the recruitment and the retention of the best teachers and administrators. These individuals have other opportunities outside of public education that are competing for their talent.
- It will serve as an incentive for teachers (administrators) to work harder to produce better results.
- It will position the teaching profession to be more competitive (and consistent) with other professions. Most professions recognize outstanding performance through their pay structure.
- It will address the grossly underpaid condition that exists in the teaching profession. Many teachers would

- qualify for increased levels of compensation in a merit based pay structure.
- It will confront the growing belief that education promotes mediocrity by not rewarding those who "perform" and not penalizing those who don't. This also plays into the need to change the paradigm. Doing what we are doing today over and over again has not worked for our students and our schools and, thus, calls for a different approach.

That said, this is only one of several initiatives outlined in this book that need thoughtful consideration for implementation.

For the negatives, listed below are a few of them most often cited;

- It will dampen cooperation and collaboration among teachers.
- It will lead to cheating and dishonesty in order to "get the results". We have heard about a few examples of this happening.
- It will result in creating a larger bureaucratic structure to implement and maintain costing classroom teacher positions.
- It will be arbitrary and capricious as setting objectives for different circumstances such as special education students, exceptional students, ESL (English as a Second Language) students, "slow learners," etc is a very difficult process.
- It will deflect attention from what is really needed and that is just pay teachers more as they are underpaid by most standards today.

The pros and cons need to be examined closely and evaluated on the merits of their arguments.

Unfortunately, merit pay/PFP has been politicized and ideology has taken hold. Special interests groups on both sides have "dug in their heels" each losing sight of the bigger picture and that is, how we increase student achievement and academic growth. This proposition deserves a full and honest "hearing"/assessment. That includes discussion and debate on the advantages and disadvantages as well as experimenting with it. Establishing a prototype and trialing it in a controlled environment should be an integral part of the assessment process. This has been and continues to be done by a number of school systems across the country. The assessment should address the following dimensions/criteria;

- Fairness. Is it tied to individual performance plans? Are objectives specific, measurable, achievable, realistic (& relevant) and are they timely? What is the formula/algorithm for capturing the overall results/performance of each teacher/administrator? Is there consistency across the entire faculty with respect to difficulty of objectives and has leveling of the playing field been taken into consideration?
- Inclusion. Have teachers and administrators been actively engaged in the development and implementation of the plan?
- Linkage. Is the model linked to the school's improvement plan/objectives? Is it linked to the school administrator's merit plan? This is the "golden thread" concept.
- Logistics/mechanics. Is the process (systems) in place to objectively measure results and compute compensation in a timely manner? Are the budgets aligned with the merit pay plan?
- Communication. Has the plan be communicated to all the school's constituencies?
- Quality Control (QC)/feedback. This is the **Plan**, **Do**, **Check**, **Act** QC process. Has the plan worked according

to its objectives? What needs to be changed and how will it be changed?

This represents only a high level outline of what needs to be the basis for an assessment of a merit pay plan. The discussion needs to focus exclusively on the facts while attempting to suppress the emotions and biases (for and against).

Let's return to the Time magazine findings with respect to better teacher training and teacher mentoring. Teacher preparedness is really on two levels. The first level is official training that takes place in colleges and universities leading up to teacher certification (for both standard and lateral/alternative entry teachers). More and more education departments in our colleges and universities are revisiting the effectiveness of their programs. Too many of our teachers are not prepared for the challenges that lie ahead. The consequences are devastating for our students and our new teachers. Studies show that 50 % of our new teachers leave after just 5 years. The National Commission on Teaching and America's Future (NCTAF) estimate the national cost of this teacher dropout problem is over 7 billion dollars a year.[60] Three key elements of this challenge of not being adequately prepared are teacher expectations, classroom management and differentiated instruction. Teachers want to make a difference and they want their students to excel. It is a great feeling as a principal to see these newly hired, first time teachers meet their students at the door on that first day of school. They are a little nervous but full of enthusiasm and that "can do" spirit which is infectious.

The second level is training (professional development) received during their teaching career.

A recent McKinsey & Company, a consulting firm, study of the twenty-five highest performing school systems in the world concluded that "the experiences of these top school systems suggests that three things matter: 1) getting the right people to become teachers, 2) developing them into effective instructors, and 3) ensuring that the system is able to deliver the best possible instruction for every child".[61] Professional development has too often been viewed as a nice to do activity and not a must do requirement to retain ones position. Quality initiatives in industry and in education such as the Baldrige National Quality Program, Six Sigma all contain the tenet that training is the life blood of continuous improvement with perfection the goal. Every teacher (and administrator as well) should have as an integral part of their Personal Development Plan (PDP) a detailed description of what actions they will take in the form of courses, seminars, etc over a period of time. Administrators, once agreed upon with the individual teacher, should include the costs in the budget. Even in these very difficult budgetary times there are economical ways to provide access to professional development for the faculty. This needs to be a priority for the administration. Furthermore, this also should be part of the teacher's evaluation process. High performing schools tap into the learning that takes place in these professional development sessions by arranging for the teachers upon return to share with their colleagues what they have learned and how it will benefit them in becoming a better teacher. Also, high performance schools set aside time each month for faculty sessions dedicated to an aspect of instructional excellence. Instructional excellence is a moving target. To consistently hit that target it requires a commitment to continuous improvement and professional development is at its core.

Community involvement in schools has made a positive difference especially in improving the performance of those schools that are struggling academically. From parents to concerned citizens and the business community at large, schools have experienced an outpouring of support in the form of volunteering to perform administrative tasks, serve as chaperones for extracurricular school activities, mentor students, serve on school leadership teams, attend PTA meetings, organize fund raisers and a plethora of other roles. The willingness to help is there. High performing schools seek out and encourage community involvement. Taking this to the next level by establishing professional learning communities (PLC) whereby the classroom practice is extended into the community, bringing community personnel into the school to enhance the curriculum and learning tasks for students as well as engaging students, teachers and administrators simultaneously in learning. According to Richard Dufour, a recognized expert in Professional Learning Communities, the essence of PLCs is to focus on learning rather than teaching, work collaboratively, and hold yourself accountable for results".[62] The power of collaboration in support of a common mission is a game changer. Teachers, counselors and staff working together focused on student achievement coupled with support from administrators is the mark of a high performance school. As noted in the previous chapter school administration needs to provide the environment conducive for collaboration to take place. This includes engineering schedules to provide time for teachers to meet on a regular basis. This can be accomplished through common planning periods, teacher work days, "working lunch", etc. The tie-in to professional development and the benefit derived by the participants in collaboration sessions is especially noteworthy. Strengthening camaraderie among the faculty and staff while sharpening the skills/understanding of the individual participants in support of student achievement are two likely outcomes.

It has been said that the true method of knowledge is experiment. Industry relies on experimentation for perfecting products, processes, strategies to increase the odds of success. It is an invaluable exercise which protects the company from catastrophic failure. As we ponder major reform initiatives some of which are radical departures from what we have been doing over the past 50 plus years in education we need to first embrace the "do no harm" oath as it relates to student achievement. To mitigate downside risk on any major reform initiative it will be prudent to establish learning laboratories or incubators for perfecting them before general implementation. Depending on the size, scope, difficulty of the reform measure the incubator could be a classroom lesson(s) or an entire school. Some States have adopted the Early College model where high school students matriculate on a college campus (oftentimes it is a community college), take college courses and graduate in either 4 or 5 years with a high school diploma and an associate's degree. In North Carolina the Early Colleges have become learning laboratories where experimentation is a common occurrence. Partially funded and supported by the Bill and Melinda Gates Foundation and in North Carolina under the superb direction of the New Schools Project, a statewide private-public partnership, the Early Colleges have flourished. From dropout rates to graduation rates and overall student achievement and growth measures the results are outstanding. The Early Colleges are truly centers of excellence where best practices are on display. They provide opportunities for traditional high schools in North Carolina to learn from them and for school districts to use them as incubators for reform initiatives prior to wholesale implementation. Many school districts in the State have taken full advantage of this golden opportunity.

Another area which holds great promise for substantially increasing student achievement for all students involves community colleges and 4 year colleges and universities. Today many community colleges and 4 year colleges and universities are actively partnering with school systems across the country. One example of those very successful partnerships is the Early College model where, as stated above, the high school students matriculate on the community college or college/university campus and take college courses. With budget constraints at all levels (local, State and Federal) funding is and will continue to be a serious challenge. School systems across the US are consolidating schools and reducing teacher (& staff) positions while enrollment in many cases is increasing. This too is true for colleges. States and local jurisdictions are funding the predominant share of the secondary and post secondary schools' budgets. The opportunity to share space and administrative functions, at a minimum, deserves our full consideration. From strictly a funding perspective it has real merit. That said, perhaps the most compelling reason to pursue this model are the benefits the Early Colleges are enjoying as a result of this arrangement. These benefits, beyond the cost savings due to synergies, are direct access to college faculty for collaboration between high school teachers and college instructors on a frequent basis to ensure "college readiness" for the high school students, easier access to college courses (seated), an environment that promotes the acceleration of the maturity process and contributes to a aura of high expectations. This is not to imply that high schools do not promote high expectations or can't accelerate the student's maturity process only that sitting in class as a high school student with a bunch of college age students creates a greater likelihood that it will happen and sooner. The power of the college campus and its impact intellectually, socially and psychologically on high school students cannot be overstated. The Early College experience is a testament to this phenomenon. Furthermore, there is significant evidence to support the claim that Early Colleges have made the transition to college seamless and therefore has increased the probability of success. States should commission a blue ribbon panel of educators (Superintendents, College Presidents, etc), business community representatives, parents and public officials (Department of Education/Public Instruction, State legislators, county commissioners, School Board members) to study the feasibility of implementing such a model. The Early Colleges have served as a learning laboratory for this model as well as an "incubator" for newly created processes and can be a case study for this task force.

The final long term recommendation for transforming education involves teacher compensation. It is a major component in elevating in our society the teaching profession. There is a strong correlation between teacher compensation and the quality of those attracted to the profession. According to a September, 2010 study by McKinsey & Company entitled **Closing the Talent Gap**, top performing nations recruit 100 % of their new teachers from the top third of the class.[63] In the U.S., it's 23 % and 14 % in high poverty schools. Three of the countries highlighted in the study for their educational excellence were Singapore, South Korea and Finland. In each of these countries teachers are drawn from the top third of their cohort, are hugely respected and are well paid. In South Korea and Singapore, teachers on average earn more than lawyers and engineers. In the U.S. starting teachers earn on average approximately $39,000. The McKinsey study estimates that to fill most new teaching positions in high needs schools with graduates from the top third of their classes it would take $65,000. Through more efficient utilization of existing funds as well as placing a higher priority on teacher pay at the State and local levels along with a modest increase of funding this can be accomplished. As mentioned in earlier chapters many school districts across the country are exploring a pay for performance model to compensate teachers for their performance based on a number of factors centered around student achievement. As noted in a previous chapter this deserves further study prior to full implementation as it has the potential to improve teacher performance and ultimately student achievement. Raising the stature of the teaching profession in the United States is an imperative and increasing teacher pay is a major step in that direction. The U.S. needs the best and brightest professionals teaching our children.

The rebound involves the compilation of initiatives some of which are noted in this chapter. There must be an alignment of all constituents as States and school districts move forward. It will take a heavy dosage of leadership, perseverance, critical thinking, communication, risk-taking and most of all courage of one's convictions.

There is little room for being dogmatic and much room for pragmatism. Bold and audacious goals are in order. Keeping alignment through active communication channels and measuring progress are key tactics to the overall success. Constantly asking what is in the best interest of the students and "why can't we" constitute the clarion call for meeting the goals of transforming education as we know it today. The rebound may be "uneven" at first. That provides an opportunity to leverage the successful elements and rework those that are less successful. It is the quality mantra of "plan, do, check/modify, act" repeated over and over again. Celebrate successes!!!

Takeaways

1. *The need for a major overhaul in the high school educational experience is well documented.*
2. *It is time to rethink, rebuild and rebound with respect to the current secondary educational construct.*
3. *The school year needs to be lengthened to mitigate "learning loss" and to increase focus on "success skills."*
4. *Concentrate curriculum on the fundamentals of math, science and language arts.*
5. *Strengthen accountability through pay for performance merit pay/value-added plans based on an evaluation that includes student academic growth, student achievement and teacher development. Develop a framework that is based on fairness, inclusivity, practicality, and a commitment to revisit/adjust.*
6. *Re-dedicate efforts to improve teacher preparedness for prospective teachers in colleges/universities and for current teachers through a robust professional development program.*
7. *Institute professional Learning Communities (PLC) to foster collaborative learning among colleagues focused on increasing student achievement.*
8. *Establish learning laboratories or incubators for accessing the efficacy of reform initiatives prior to general implementation.*
9. *Recruitment of top tier college students to the teaching profession is an imperative. A major component in making this a reality is increasing teacher pay.*
10. *Leverage to the fullest the relationship between school districts and the local community colleges and 4 year colleges/universities.*

11. *The rebound will come. It will require tweaking some of the initiatives. We can't let perfection be the enemy of the good.*
12. *Celebrate successes!!*

Epilogue

It cannot be overstated the criticality of the crisis we face in education today in the United States. It seems like every day we are reminded how far we have fallen behind other countries in educating our youth. From declining student achievement (compared to other industrialized countries) to high dropout rates there is significant evidence that our schools are failing to prepare our students for the 21st Century careers. With a global economy our students are competing for jobs with students from China, India, Japan, South Korea, France, and so forth. The Broad Foundation cites that "American students rank 25th in math and 21st in science compared to students in 30 industrialized countries."[1] It further cites that 68 % of 8th graders cannot read at their grade level and very likely will never recover.[2] Norman R. Augustine, the retired CEO of Lockheed Martin, has been quoted to say, "since 1995 the average mathematics score for fourth-graders jumped 11 points. At this rate we catch up with Singapore in a little over 80 years…assuming they don't improve". While chronicled in previous chapters it deserves repeating that the time to act is now and boldly. It will require strong and passionate leadership from all the constituents from elected officials to parents and the business community. There will need to be tough decisions made and it will not come without confrontation and vigorous debate but it must happen. The movie *Waiting for Superman* was a poignant reminder of the "victims" those who need to be saved by a superman which are our kids. This heart wrenching documentary points out the travesty we have tolerated and perpetuated year after year. Yes, we all hope it will get better but hope is not a strategy!! We must develop plans that will truly re-invent our schools (rethink, rebuild, rebound) and have the courage to make them happen. A few months ago, Michelle Rhee, former embattled chancellor of the District of Columbia schools, formed StudentsFirst, a national movement to transform public education in the United States. StudentsFirst mission is to defend and promote the interests of children so that America has the best education system in the world. It has the potential to be a powerful voice, a catalyst and a strong advocate for our children. It has been said that public education reform is the civil rights issue of our time. We must engage our communities and our constituents in a dialogue leading to a call to action by all. Aligned in purpose and energized to fight for what is right. We cannot shy away from conflict. It is inevitable. Debate is healthy but it must be constructive that is, moving the ball forward. That said, there is a time for debate and there is a time to act. Let us not confuse motion with momentum. We must not let debate and lingering conflict paralyze us or we will lose that needed momentum. With **rethinking** what we are doing in education and preparing a plan to **rebuild** the educational construct based on the needs of the 21st Century economy/society there will be no doubt we will **rebound** to the level of preeminence in the world we all seek. That is the legacy we will leave to the generations that follow.

Endnotes

Endnotes for Section I

[1] Robinson, Ken. *The Element*: How Finding Your Passion Changes Everything. NY: Penguin Group, 2009.

[2] Quoted from an article entitled "Student Motivation and Attitudes: The Role of the Affective Domain in Geoscience Learning" appearing in a publication from the Science Education Resource Center at Carleton College. It can be accessed along with the complete article at http://serc.carleton.edu/NAGTWorkshops/affective/motivation.html

[3] Heider, Fritz. The Psychology of Interpersonal Relations. NY: John Wiley & Sons, 1958.

[4] Quoted from http://psychology.about.com/od/theoriesof personality/a/self_efficacy.htm

[5] Ibid.

[6] Quote from http://www.absoluteastronomy.com/topics/Self-Determination_Theory

[7] Readers can learn more about the New Empowerment Theory by Soren Lauritzen online at http://www.selfgrowth.com/articles/the- new -empowerment-theory-and-how-it-will-help-you-experience-your-best-life-ever

[8] Quoted from an article by Ibtesam Halawah entitled "The Effect of Motivation, Family Environment, and Student" available online at http://findarticles.com/p/articles/mi_m0FCG/is_2_33/ai_n16608929

[9] Quoted from an article entitled "Student Motivation and Attitudes: The Role of the Affective Domain in Geoscience Learning" appearing in a publication from the Science Education Resource Center at Carleton

College. It can be accessed along with the complete article at http://serc.carleton.edu/NAGTWorkshops/affective/motivation.html

[10] Davis, Barbara Gross. Tools for Teaching. San Francisco, CA: Jossey-Bass, 1993.

[11] Covey, Stephen R. The Seven Habits of Highly Effective People. NY: Free Press, 1989.

[12] This material came from Mansfield University and can be accessed in full on the website: see Mansfield.edu/.../TeacherEducationDispositionfinal208.pdf

[13] Ibid.

[14] Ibid.

[15] This material came from the website: www.NCATE.org/Public?Newsroom/NCATENewsPressReleases/Tabid/669/EntryId/55/NCATE-Defines-Disposition-As-Used-in-Teacher-Education-Issues-Call-to-Action.aspx

[16] Quote came from an article in The Language Educator publication entitled Why Teacher Dispositions are Crucial Aspect of Student Success by Maura Kate Hallam in January 2009 edition. This material along with more information on this topic can be accessed via the website: http://www.actfl.org/files/TLE_Jan09_Article.pdf

[17] Ibid.

[18] Ibid.

Endnotes for Section II

[1] Hunzicker, J. (2010). Characteristics of effective professional development: a checklist. Retrieved from ERIC database on January 29, 2011.

[2] Hargreaves, A., & Fink, D. (2006). The ripple effect. Educational Leadership, 63, 16-20.

3. Race to the Top initiative.
4. Information found at http://www.schoolstowatch.org
5. Fives, H. (2003, April). *What is teacher efficacy and how does it relate to teachers' knowledge?* Paper presented at the American Educational Research Association annual conference, Chicago, IL.
6. Tschannen-Moran, M. & Woolfolk-Hoy, A. (2001). Teacher efficacy: Capturing an elusive construct. *Teaching and Teacher Education, 17*, 783-805.
7. Hattie, J. (2003). Teachers make a difference: What is the research evidence? *Australian Council for Educational Research*, Auckland, Australia. Retrieved March 25, 2008, from http://acer.edu
8. Ibid.
9. Darling-Hammond, L. (2000). Teacher quality and student achievement. *Educational Policy Analysis Archives, 8*, 1.
10. Lightfoot, S. L. (1986). On goodness of schools: Themes of empowerment. *Peabody Journal of Education, 63*(3), 9-28.
11. Schmoker, M. (2006). *Results Now: How we can achieve unprecedented improvements in teaching and learning*. Alexandria, VA: Association for Supervision and Curriculum Development.
12. Bandura, A. (1997). *Self-Efficacy: The exercise of control*. New York, NY: W.H. Freeman & Company.
13. Ibid.
14. Bandura, A. (1994). Self-Efficacy. *Encyclopedia of Human Behavior, 4*, 71-81.
15. Bandura, A. (1997). *Self-Efficacy: The exercise of control*. New York, NY: W.H. Freeman & Company.

[16] Lawler, E., III. (1986). *High-involvement management*. San Francisco: Josey-Bass.

[17] Bandura, A. (1997). *Self-Efficacy: The exercise of control*. New York, NY: W.H. Freeman & Company.

[18] Ibid.

[19] Bandura, A. (1994). Self-Efficacy. *Encyclopedia of Human Behavior, 4*, 71-81.

[20] Bandura, A. (1997). *Self-Efficacy: The exercise of control*. New York, NY: W.H. Freeman & Company.

[21] Ibid.

[22] Ibid.

[23] Ibid.

[24] Bandura, A. (1994). Self-Efficacy. *Encyclopedia of Human Behavior, 4*, 71-81.

[25] Collins, J. C. (2001). *Good to great*. New York: Harper Collins Publishers, Inc.

[26] Bandura, A. (1994). Self-Efficacy. *Encyclopedia of Human Behavior, 4*, 71-81.

[26a] Eury, A. D., Shellman, D. & Hemric, M. (2009). Correlations Between Perceived Teacher Empowerment and Perceived Sense of Teacher Efficacy. *AASA Journal of Scholarship and Practice*, Spring, 2020.

[27] Ansalone, George (2001). Schooling, tracking, and inequality. *Journal of Children & Poverty, 7(1)*, 33-47. doi: 10.1080/10796120120038028

[28] Scribner, J., Truell, A., Hager, D., & Srichai, S. (2001). An exploratory study of career and technical education teacher empowerment: Implications for school leaders. *Journal of Career and Technical Education 18*, 1.

[29] Glickman, C.D. (1999, August). *School based authority and responsibility*. Issue paper presented to the Governor's

commission on Education: Committee on Accountability, Athens, GA.

30 Lightfoot, S. L. (1986). On goodness of schools: Themes of empowerment. *Peabody Journal of Education, 63*(3), 9-28.

31 McGraw, J. (1992). The road to empowerment. *Nursing Administration Quarterly, 16*(3), 16-19.

32 Kanter, R. (1993). *Men and women of corporation (2nd ed.)*. New York, NY: Basic Books.

33 Short, P., & Johnson, P. (1994). Exploring the links among teacher empowerment, leader power, and conflict. *Education, 114*(4), 581-593.

34 Bandura, A. (1977). Self-efficacy: Toward a unifying theory of behavioral change. *Psychological Review, 84*, 191-215.

35 DuFour, R., & Eaker, R. (1998). *Professional learning communities at work: Best practices forenhancing student achievement*. Alexandria, VA: Association for Supervision and Curriculum Development.

36 Lawler, E., III. (1986). <u>High-involvement management</u>. San Francisco: Josey-Bass.

37 Ibid.

38 Sowell, T. (1980). Knowledge and decisions. New York: Basic Books, Inc.

39 Ibid.

40 Gaines, G. F., & Cornett, L. M. (1992). School accountability reports: Lessons learning in SREB states. Atlanta, Ga. Southern Regional Education Board. (ERIC Document Reproduction Service No. ED 357 471

40a Learning Communities: Creating Connections Among Students, Faculty, and Disciplines; Gabelnick, et al., 1990 p. 92.

[41] DuFour, R., & Eaker, R. (1998). *Professional learning communities at work: Best practices forenhancing student achievement.* Alexandria, VA: Association for Supervision and Curriculum Development.

[42] Bandura, A. (1997). *Self-Efficacy: The exercise of control.* New York, NY: W.H. Freeman & Company.

[43] National Center for the Study of Adult Learning and Literacy. (2003). How Teacher Change: A Study of Professional Development in Adult Education. http://ncsall.gse.harvard.edu

[44] Helm, C. (2007). Teacher Dispositions Affecting Self-Esteem and Student Performance. *Clearing House*, 80(3), 109-110. Retrieved from EBSCO*host*.

[45] Good, T. L. & Brophy, J. E. (1971). The Self-Fulfilling Prophecy. *Today's Education.* April, 1971. Pp 52-53.

[46] Cole, R. 1990. Teachers who make a difference. *Instructor 110:58-59.*

[47] Harme, B. K., and R. C. Pianta. 2001. Early teacher-child relationships and the trajectory of children's school outcomes through eighth grade. *Child Development 72:625-38*

[48] Woolfolf, A. 2004. *Educational Psychology.* 9th ed. Boston: Pearson Education.

[49] Davies, J. and I. Brember. 1999. Self-esteem and national test in two years and six. *Educational Psychology* 19 (3): 337-45.

[50] Wayda, V., and J. Lund. 2005. Assessing dispositions: An unresolved challenged in teacher education. *Journal of Physical Education, Recreaction and Dance* 76 (1):34-41.

[51] Wakefield, A. 1993. Learning styles and learning dispositions in public schools- some implications of preference. *Education* 133 (3):402.

[52] Jung, E., & Rhodes, D.M. (2008). Revisiting disposition assessment in teacher education: Broadening the focus. Assessment & Evaluation in Higher Education, 33(6), 647-660.

[53] Ibid.

[54] Ibid.

[55] North Carolina Turnaround Project: Instituted by North Carolina Department of Public Instruction to address low-performing high schools and middle schools.

[56] Ibid.

[57] Bandura, A. (1997). *Self-Efficacy: The exercise of control.* New York, NY: W.H. Freeman & Company.

[58] Leadership Group of the Carolinas. Permission granted by co-owners of this organization to use the template of categorical prompts for cultural assessment. Any additional use by permission only.

[59] MET project. A research paper presented by Gates Foundation. (2011). Learning about teaching. Bill and Melinda Gates Foundation. http://www.metproject.org

[60] Pedro, J.Y. (2005). Reflection in teacher education: exploring pre-service teachers' meanings of reflective practice. *Reflective Practice*, 6(1), 49-66.

[61] Ibid.

[62] Ibid.

[63] Ibid.

[64] Dewey, J. (1933). *How we think: a restatement of the relation of reflective thinking to the educational process.* Boston: D.C. Health.

[65] Pedro, J.Y. (2005). Reflection in teacher education: exploring pre-service teachers' meanings of reflective practice. *Reflective Practice*, 6(1), 49-66.

[66] Ibid.

[67] Ibid.

[68] Ibid.

[69] Ibid.

[70] Ibid.

[71] Ibid.

[72] Wright, L.L. (2009). Leadership in the swamp: Seeking the potential of school improvement through principal reflection. *Reflective Practice*, 10(2), 259-272.

[73] Ibid.

[74] Ibid.

[75] Ibid.

[76] Ibid.

[77] Dewey, J. (1933). *How we think: a restatement of the relation of reflective thinking to the educational process.* Boston: D.C. Health.

[78] Wright, L.L. (2009). Leadership in the swamp: Seeking the potential of school improvement through principal reflection. *Reflective Practice*, 10(2), 259-272.

[79] Osterman, K., & Kottkamp, R. (1993). *Reflective practice for educators.* Newberry Park, CA: Corwin Press, Inc.

[80] Ibid.

[81] Wagner, K. (2006). Benefits of reflective practice. *Leadership*, November/December. Retrieved from http://ehis.ebscohost.com.

[82] Ibid.

[83] Ibid.

[84] Ibid.

[85] Russell, T. (2005). Can reflective practice be taught? *Reflective practice*, 6(2), Retrieved from http://ehis.ebscohost.com.

[86] Ibid.

[87] Schon, D.A. (1983). *The reflective practitioner: how professionals think in action*. London: Temple Smith

[88] Ibid.

[89] McKnight, D. (2002, November 20). *Reflective practitioner*. Retrieved from http://www.education.umd.edu/teacher_education/sthandbook/reflection.html

[90] Zeichner, K. & Liston D. (1996). *Reflective teaching: an introduction*. Mahwah, NJ: Lawrence Erlbaum.

[91] Hipp, K.H., & Webber, P. (2009). Developing a professsional learning community amoung urban high school principals. Journal of Urban Learning, Teaching, and Research, 4. Retrieved from http://www.eric.ed.gov/PDFS/EJ837804.pdf

[92] Ibid.

[93] McAlpine, L., Weston, C., Berthiaume, D., Fairbank-Roch, G., & Owen, M. (2004) Reflection on teaching: types and goals of reflection. *Educational Research and Evaluation 10(4-6)*.

[94] Ibid.

[95] Ibid.

Portions of Chapter 7 attributed to the dissertation work of Doug Eury.

Eury, A. D. Assessing the effects of data on the shared decision making processes in three high schools. (1996).

Portions of Chapter 7 are also attributed to:

Eury, A. D & Ratchford, V. F. (2006). Empowering Teams for Decision-Making. *AASA Journal of Scholarship and Practice*, 2 (4), 45-49.

Endnotes for Section III

[1] National Council for Excellence In Education. 1983. *A Nation at Risk*. Washington, DC: U.S. Department of Education.

[2] Eight Habits of Highly Effective 21st Century Teachers http://www.masternewmedia.org/teaching-skills-what-21st-century-educators-need-to-learn-to-survive/#ixzz0wbk8BtRW

[3] Learning Pyramid http://xnet.rrc.mb.ca/glenh/new_page_37.htm

[4] Carie Windham. Educating the Net Generation. NC State University Graduate School Colloquiun, September 14, 2007.

[5] http://partners.becta.org.uk/upload-dir/downloads/page_documents/research/emerging_technologies08_chapter1.pdf.

[6] www.21stcenturyschools.com/What_is_21st_Century_Education.htm

[7] Portner, Hal, Teachers Net Gazette, March, 2009, *The 21st Century Teaching-Learning Environment (Think Outside the Classroom Box)*.

[8] Treffinger, Donald. *Preparing Creative and Critical Thinkers*, Educational Leadership, summer 2008 edition.

[9] *Introduction – Education in the 21st Century*, 21st Century Schools, August, 2008.

[10] http://www.p21.org/index.php?option=com_content&task=view&id=57&Itemid=120, Partnership for 21st Century Skills, 2004.

[11] http://www.corestandards.org/assets/Criteria.pdf

[12] http://www.corestandards.org/assets/KeyPointsELA.pdf

[13] Kiznik, Dr. Bob, Six Common Mistakes in Writing Lesson Plans, http://www.adprima.com/mistakes2.htm

[14] Kizlik, Dr. Sandra, Lesson Plans the Easy Way, http://www.adprima.com/easyless.htm

[14a] Stiggins, R. J. 2002. Assessment Crisis: The Absence of Assessment FOR Learning, in *Phi Delta Kappan* Vol.83, No.10 pp758-765.

[15] Stiggins, Rick, Best of Educational Leadership 2006-2007, Volume 64, Assessment Through the Student's Eyes, pp. 22-26.

[16] American Recovery and Reinvestment Act, 2009, http://www.recovery.gov/About/Pages/The_Act.aspx

[17] Video http://video.answers.com/how-to-improve-early-education-291038344

[18] Olson, Lynn, Gauging Student Learning, Education Week, January 4, 2007.

[19] Education Week, Chance for Success 2007.

[20] http://www.metlife.com/about/corporate-profile/citizenship/metlife-foundation/metlife-survey-of-the-american-teacher.html?WT.mc_id=vu1101

[21] National Association for Single Sex Public Education (2009). www.singlesexschools.org.

[22] Finn, J. (1980). Sex differences in educational outcomes: a cross-national study. *Sex Roles*, 6(9), 25.

[23] Carroll, Thomas G., Fulton, Kathleen, and Doerr, Hanna, Team Up for the 21st Century Teaching and Learning What Research and Practice Reveal about Professional Learning, National Commission on Teaching and America's Future, June 2010.

Endnotes for Section IV

1. Report prepared by David Conley for the Bill & Melinda Gates Foundation, "Toward a More Comprehensive Conception of College readiness", available online at http://www.gatesfoundation.org/UnitedStates/Education/ResearchAndEvaluati/Research/HSImprovement.htm, (accessed June 1, 2010).

2. Report entitled "Education at a Glance 2003" prepared by Organisation for Economic Co-operation and Development (OECD), available online at http://www.oecd.org/document/52/0,2340,en_2649_33723_13634484_1_1_1_1,00.html (accessed June 1, 2010).

3. Report entitled "Are They Really Ready to Work?"commissioned by The Conference Board, Corporate Voices for Working Families, the Partnership for 21st Century Skills and the Society for Human Resource Management; available online at http://21stcenturyskills.org/documents/key_findings_joint.pdf (accessed June 1, 2010).

4. Wagner, Tony. The Global Achievement Gap: Why Even Our Best Schools Don't Teach the New Survival Skills Our Children Need-And what We Can Do About it. NY: Basic Books, 2008.

5. Friedman, Thomas L. The World Is Flat: A Brief History of the Twenty-first Century. NY. Farrar, Straus and Giroux, 2005.

6. Wagner, Tony. The Global Achievement Gap: Why Even Our Best Schools Don't Teach the New Survival Skills Our Children Need-And What We Can Do About it. NY: Basic Books, 2008.

7. Biro, Brian D. Beyond Success: The 15 Secrets to Effective Leadership and Life. NY: Perigee Book, Published by The Berkley Publishing Group, 1997.

[8] Ibid.

[9] Wagner, Tony. The Global Achievement Gap: Why Even Our Best Schools Don't Teach the New Survival Skills Our Children Need-And What We Can Do About it. NY: Basic Books, 2008.

[10] Ibid.

[11] Wagner, Tony. The Global Achievement Gap: Why Even Our Best Schools Don't Teach the New Survival Skills Our Children Need-And What We Can Do About it. NY: Basic Books, 2008.

[12] Ibid.

[13] Covey, Stephen R. The 7 Habits of Highly Effective People: Powerful Lessons in Personal Change. NY: Free Press, 1989.

[14] Wagner, Tony. The Global Achievement Gap: Why Even Our Best Schools Don't Teach the New Survival Skills Our Children Need-And What We Can Do About it. NY: Basic Books, 2008.

[15] North Carolina New Schools Project in Collaboration with State Superintendent June Atkinson. The Third Way: Education Innovation in North Carolina and Bridging the Divide between Preparation for College and Career. May, 2010.

[16] This information was obtained from the California Department of Education website: see http://www.cde.ca.gov/ci/gs/ps/avidgen.asp (accessed June 5, 2010).

[17] From the report "What is our average class size?" The center for Public Education, available online at http:/www.centerforpubliceducation.org/site/apps/nlnet/content3

[18] Wagner, Tony. The Global Achievement Gap: Why Even Our Best Schools Don't Teach the New Survival Skills Our Children Need-And What We Can Do About it. NY: Basic Books, 2008.

[19] Ibid.

[20] Wagner, Tony. The Global Achievement Gap: Why Even Our Best Schools Don't Teach the New Survival Skills Our Children Need-And What We Can Do About it. NY: Basic Books, 2008.

[21] Ibid.

[22] U.S. Department of Education: U.S. Performance Across International Assessments of Student Achievement: Special Supplement to 'The Condition of Education 2009'.

[23] Wagner, Tony. The Global Achievement Gap: Why Even Our Best Schools Don't Teach the New Survival Skills Our Children Need-And What We Can Do About it. NY: Basic Books, 2008.

[24] For more information about the National Assessment of Educational Progress, please consult their website: http://nationsreportcard.gov/ (accessed July 22, 2010).

[25] Ibid.

[26] Wagner, Tony. The Global Achievement Gap: Why Even Our Best Schools Don't Teach the New Survival Skills Our Children Need-And What We Can Do About it. NY: Basic Books, 2008.

[27] PISA 2006 Results, Executive Summary, available online at http://www.oecd.org/dataoecd/pdf (accessed July 23, 2010).

[28] Ibid.

[29] Wagner, Tony. The Global Achievement Gap: Why Even Our Best Schools Don't Teach the New Survival

Skills Our Children Need-And What We Can Do About it. NY: Basic Books, 2008.

[30] For information on the report The Condition of College Readiness 2009 please consult their website: http://act.org/research/.../pdf/TheConditionofCollegeReadiness.pdf (accessed July 22, 2010).

[31] Ibid.

[32] "Americans Now Lag in Attaining College Degrees", Charlotte Observer, July 23, 2010, available online at http://www.charlotteobserver.com/2010/07/23/1578309/nation-world.html (accessed July 23, 2010).

[33] Ibid.

[34] From the report "Teacher Attrition: A Costly Loss to the Nation and to the States", Alliance for Excellent Education, available online at http://www.all4ed.org/files/archive/publications/teacherattrition.pdf (accessed July 23, 2010).

[35] Ibid.

[36] Schlechty, Phillip. Working on the Work: An Action Plan for Teachers, Principals, and Superintendents. CA: Jossey-Bass, 2002.

[37] Ibid.

[38] Robinson, Ken. *The Element*: How Finding Your Passion Changes Everything. NY: Penguin Group, 2009.

[39] Wagner, Tony. The Global Achievement Gap: Why Even Our Best Schools Don't Teach the New Survival Skills Our Children Need-And What We Can Do About it. NY: Basic Books, 2008.

[40] Covey, Stephen R. Principle- Centered Leadership. NY: Simon & Schuster, 1990.

⁴¹ This information came from the Department of Defense Education Activity website: http://www.dodea.edu/pubs/csp2006.

⁴² The reader can learn more about the North Carolina New Schools Project online at http://www.newschoolsproject.org.

⁴³ Ibid.

⁴⁴ Wagner, Tony. The Global Achievement Gap: Why Even Our Best Schools Don't Teach the New Survival Skills Our Children Need-And What We Can Do About it. NY: Basic Books, 2008.

⁴⁵ Robinson, Ken. *The Element*: How Finding Your Passion Changes Everything. NY: Penguin Group, 2009.

⁴⁶ From the report "School Leadership 101" authored by M. Donald Thomas and William Bainbridge, available online at http://www.schoolmatch.com/articles/SMESPRO1.htm.

⁴⁷ Ibid.

⁴⁸ Anna Mulrine, "Getting Kids Set for College", U.S. News & World Report magazine, September, 2010.

⁴⁹ Ibid.

⁵⁰ Senge, Peter. The Fifth Discipline: The Art and Practice of the Learning Organization. NY: Doubleday, 1990.

⁵¹ Wagner, Tony. The Global Achievement Gap: Why Even Our Best Schools Don't Teach the New Survival Skills Our Children Need-And What We Can Do About it. NY: Basic Books, 2008.

⁵² Readers can learn more about this poll online at http://blogs.wsj.com/washwire/2010/09/26/wsjnbc-survey-a-c-grade-for-schools/ (accessed October 22, 2010).

⁵³ Ibid.

54 See "Case Against Summer Vacation", Time magazine, August 2, 2010, available online at http://www.time.com/time/nation/article/0,8599,2005654,00.html (accessed October 22, 2010).

55 Ibid.

56 Ibid.

57 Amanda Ripley, "A Call to Action for Public Schools", Time magazine, September 20, 2010.

58 Ibid.

59 Ibid.

60 See "The High Cost of Teacher Turnover" (Washington, DC: NCTAF, 2007), available online at http://nctaf.org.zeus.silvertech.net/resources/research_and_reports/nctaf_research_reports/documents/CTTPolicyBrief-FINAL_000.pdf (accessed June 11, 2010).

61 See the Executive Summary of "How the World's Best Performing School Systems Come Out on Top", McKinsey & Company, September 2007, available online at http://www.mckinsey.com/clientservice/social_sector/our_practices/Education/Knowledge_Highlights/Best_Performing_School.aspx (accessed June 11, 2010).

62 Richard Dufour, "Schools as Learning Communities", Educational Leadership, Volume 61 (May, 2004).

63 From the study "Closing the Talent Gap", McKinsey & Company, available online at http://www.mckinsey.com/clientservice?Social_Sector/our_practices/Education/Knowledge_Highlights/Closing_the_talent_gap.aspx.

Endnotes for Epilogue

[1] From the Broad Foundation website: http://broadeducation.org/about/crisis_stats.html (accessed December 10, 2010).

[2] Ibid.

Index

Academic college courses, 152
Academic Excellence in high-performing schools, 28–30
Academic mentors, 245
Academic rigor, 150
Academic tradition reflection, 108
Accountability model, 255
Achievement gaps in educational system, 196–197
Action research, 99
Adequate yearly progress (AYP), 230
Advanced thinking, 110
Advancement Via Individual Determination (AVID), 210, 241
Advocacy, 15
Affective contributions, 49–50
American Recovery and Reinvestment Act, 181–182
Applied value-added models, 98
Assessment, 138
Assumed similarity, 47
Attributions, 5
Attribution theory, 5
AVID. *See* Advancement Via Individual Determination (AVID)
AYP. *See* Adequate yearly progress (AYP)

Bandura, Albert, 6
Basic skills, 207
Benchmark assessment, 173
Bidirectional quality, 73
Bloom's taxonomy, 137, 199
Blue ribbon panel of educators, 264

Career and Technical Education (CTE), 209–210
Caring, culture of, 231

Change theory, 38
Churches' eight characteristics, 131
CLA. *See* Collegiate Learning Assessment (CLA)
Classroom, 137, 138
Class sizes, 211
COE. *See* Colleges/schools of education (COE)
Coed classrooms, 189, 190
Collaboration, 38–39, 128, 226, 231–232, 261
Collaborative group work, 139–140
Collaborative reflection, 109
Collaborative tools, 128
Collective professional experiences, 73, 75
Collective self-efficacy, 51
College, 152
College and Work Readiness Assessment (CWRA), 214
Colleges/schools of education (COE), 16
Collegiate Learning Assessment (CLA), 213
Common Core State Standards, 151–157
Communication skills, 219, 222
Community involvement, 260–261
Compassion, 15
Conduct, professional, 14
Continuous improvement, 39
Controlling boards, 40
Cooperative group work, 170–171
Cooperative learning. *See* Cooperative group work
Covey, Stephen, 10
Creativity, 38
CTE. *See* Career and Technical Education (CTE)
Cultural shift, 187
Cultural transformation sustenance, 114–117
Curiosity, 15
Curriculum, 137
CWRA. *See* College and Work Readiness Assessment (CWRA)

Darling-Hammond, Linda, 44, 147
Data-driven decision making, 67–68
Davis, Barbara Gross, 9
Decision implementation action plan, 69–70
Decision makers' accountability, 70
Decision making, effective, 63
Decision making goals, 110
Dedication, 16, 81, 84
Department of Defense (DOD), 230
Developmental responsiveness in schools, 30–31
Digital technologies, 143
Direct value-added assessment, 97
Discussion for decision making, 68–69
Disposition assessment, 82
Dispositions, 13–16, 17–18, 19, 79, 80
DOD. *See* Department of Defense (DOD)

Early College model, 262–264
Educating School Teachers, 202–203
Educational evaluation, 67–68
Education fundamentals, 241
Education, innovation in, 232–233
Education level at 20th century, 122–124
Educator, challenges for, 144
Efficacy development, 79
Employee compensation, 256
Employee's plan, 255–256
Empowering school participants, 60–61
Empowerment, 6–7, 11, 53, 54, 60, 83
Empowerment structures, 55
Empowerment without information, 65–66
ePals, 148
Essential question(s), 198
Expectation setting process, 200
Extrinsic motivation, 4, 11

Faculty collaboration, 242–243
Faculty empowerment, 244
Fairness, 16
FCAT. *See* Florida Comprehensive Assessment Test (FCAT)
Florida Comprehensive Assessment Test (FCAT), 189
Formal schooling, 138
Formative assessment, 173
Formative evaluation, 110
Formative evaluation/advanced thinking, 110
Foundational skills, 197
"Freshmen academies", 241

Gates Foundation, 233
Generic tradition reflections, 108
Global classrooms, 148
"GOALS" class, 241
Goals of reflection, 110
Grade-by-grade standards, 153
Grading, 178
Grouping for learning, 53

"Hard" skills. *See* Foundational skills
Heider, Fritz, 5
Hersh, Dr. Richard, 213
High expectations, 15
High-level cognitive demand, 153
High quality teachers, 44, 51
High school classes, 140–14
High school curriculum, 210
High school graduation rate, 196, 217, 222
High school study program, 253–254
Homework, 178
Honesty, 16

Ideals, 67
IM. *See* Instant messaging (IM)
Imagination, 127
Indirect value-added assessment, 97–98
"Individuals influenced by decisions make decisions", 64–65
Industrialized countries, 218
Information availability for decision making, 65–67
Information sources, 143
Inquiry-based learning, 169
Instant messaging (IM), 136
Instructional excellence, 260
Instructional strategies, 9–10
Interdisciplinary learning, 170
Interpersonal relationships psychology, 5
Intrinsic motivation, 4, 5, 11
Isolation, 59

Kanter's theory of structural power, 61
Knowledge, 138
Knowledge-based decision making, 67
knowledge transmitting capacity, 68

Leadership, 85
Leadership development, 39–40
Leadership effectiveness assessment, 87–94
Leadership self-efficacy, 86
Leader's role, 86
Learner, 136–167
Learning, 37
Learning-centered strategy, 169
Learning community, professional, 73
Learning, degree of, 37
Learning pace, 252
Learning pyramid, 129, 130
Learning-team principles and practices, 187–188
Lesson plan, 162–164, 166–168

Lesson plan development, 161
Lesson plan format, 164–165

Mandated policy system, 64
Mastery, 44–46
Mastery learning, 161
Mathematical literacy, 219
Merit pay, 254, 255, 256–257, 258
Middle school classes, 140–14
Mission statements, 39
Motivation, 4, 11

NAEP. *See* National Assessment of Educational Progress (NAEP)
National Assessment of Educational Progress (NAEP), 183
National Commission on Teaching and America's Future (NCTAF), 186–187, 259
National Council for Accreditation of Teacher Education (NCATE), 16
National Network for the Study of Educator Dispositions (NNSED), 17
"Nation's report card, the". *See* National Assessment of Educational Progress (NAEP)
Nation's vision for education in 2020, 188
NCATE. *See* National Council for Accreditation of Teacher Education (NCATE)
NCNSP. *See* North Carolina New Schools Project (NCNSP)
NCTAF. *See* National Commission on Teaching and America's Future (NCTAF)
Negative attitude, 83
Negative social persuasion, 48
Net Generation, 135–136
NNSED. *See* National Network for the Study of Educator Dispositions (NNSED)
Nonverbal persuasions, 48

North Carolina New Schools Project (NCNSP), 230

Organizational empowerment, 61, 71
Organizational knowledge development, 74
Organizational learning, 42
Organizational learning indicators, 39–41
Organizational planning, 41
Organizational structures and processes in schools, 32–34
Organizations *vs.* institutions, 113–114

Parent's responsibility, 201–202
Participative decision making, effective, 65
Passion, 3, 79, 233–234. *See also* Empowerment
Pay for performance (PFP), 255. *See* Merit pay
PDP. *See* Personal Development Plan (PDP)
PD support structure, 243
PEPs. *See* Personal Education Plans (PEPs)
Performance recognition, 37
Personal assessment skill, 101
Personal Development Plan (PDP), 260
Personal Education Plans (PEPs), 245
Personalization, 230
Personal mastery, 44
PFP. *See* Pay for performance (PFP)
Physiological and affective contributors, 49
PISA. *See* Programme for International Student Assessment (PISA)
Plan-Do-Check-Act, 250
Positive attitude, 83
Positive attributes, 54–55
Power sharing, 64
Pre-service teachers, 101–102
Proactive, 10
Problem–Based Learning, 169
Professional development (PD), 59, 76, 243, 260

Professional development and staff utilization assessment, 90–91
Professional development for educators, 185
Professional development in adult education, 74–75
Professional experience, 73
Professional learning, 59
Professional learning communities (PLC), 55, 77, 109, 129, 139, 261, 266
Programme for International Student Assessment (PISA), 218
"Progressive" courses, 241
Pygmalion effect, 200

QC. *See* Quality Control (QC)
Quality Control (QC), 258

Reading performance levels, 218
Reculturing schools, 85
Reflection, 14
Reflective and reflexive practice cycle, 105
Reflective practice, 102–111, 131
Reflective principals, 104
Relationships, 150
Relevance, 150
Resources adequacy, 40
Respect for diversity, 15
Respect for others, 15
Risk-taking, 234

SAT. *See* Scholastic Aptitude Tests (SAT)
Scholastic Aptitude Tests (SAT), 123
School calendar, 212–213
School culture, 224–225
School curriculum, 166
School leadership, 226–227, 234–235
School management assessment, 91–93

School organization assessment, 88–89
Schools, high performing, 230
Schools to Watch criteria, 28–34
Schools, traditional, 121–122
School success, factors affecting, 184
School, successful, 223, 225, 231–232
School's vision and mission, 240–241
School year, 250
Science, Technology, Engineering and Math (STEM), 212
SDT. *See* Self-Determination theory (SDT)
"Seat time", 252
Secondary education reform, 204, 209, 212, 215, 262
Self-Determination theory (SDT), 6
Self efficacy, 6, 44, 54, 86
Self–esteem, 80
Shared decision making, 60
Shared experiences, 109
Shared vision, practice of, 240
Sharing of knowledge, 37
Single-sex classrooms, 189, 190
Small-group learning. *See* Cooperative group work
Social cognitive theory, 47
Social equity in schools, 31–32
Social networks, 143
Social persuasion. *See* Verbal persuasion
Social reality, 79
"Soft" skills, 197, 207. *See also* Foundational skills
Spirit of responsibility, 113
Sputnik, 156
Stakeholder involvement assessment, 93–94
State proficiency tests, 213
STEM. *See* Science, Technology, Engineering and Math (STEM)
STEM Learning Studios, 189
Stiggins, Rick, 174, 177
Structures, 53

Student academic deficiencies, 218, 220, 222
Student academic growth, 230, 244
Student achievement, 230
Student assessment, 173, 174–177, 199
Student-centered strategy. *See* Learning-centered strategy
Student education plans, 245
Student learning, 182–184
Student projects, 170
Student relationships and structures, 60
Students curiosity, 205–206
StudentsFirst national movement, 270
Student writing tests, 199
Success, foundation for, 246
Success skills, 251
Summative assessment, 173
Summer "boost" programs, 251
Summer advantage program, 251
"Summer learning loss", 250–251
Summer programs, 251
"Summer slide". *See* "Summer learning loss"
Surveys on American Teacher, 186
Sustainability, 113, 118
Sustainable practice, 77
Sustaining cultures, 114

Teacher
    compensation, 264–265
    dispositions, 80
    efficacy, 43
    empowerment, 44, 55, 61–62
    evaluation, 254–255
    leadership, 56–57, 131
    preparedness, 259–260
    attrition rates, 221
    self-efficacy, 135
    ideas for beginning, 166

teaming, 54
turnover, 221, 222
Teaching, effective planning for, 161
Teaching, indicators of excellent, 81
"Team above self", 62–63
Team creation, 62
Technological skills for teaching, 82
Technology disposition measurement, 82–83
Technology integration, 169
3Rs, 250
Tracking, 54
Traditional professional learning, 59
Turnaround model, 86
21st century, core subjects in, 149
21st century curriculum, 137–138
21st century school, 125, 132, 133
21st century skills, 149
21st century teachers, 121, 125–133

Value-added assessment model, 23, 25–28
Value-added experience model, 25–28
Value-added experiences, 98, 100
Value-added model, 80, 127. *See also* Accountability model
Value-added outcomes, 99, 100
Value-added theory, 97
Verbal persuasion, 48–49
Vicarious experiences, 46, 47
Vision, 39
Visionary educator, 127. *See also* 21st century teachers

Workforce training programs, 152
Writing standards, 154–155

About the Authors

John D. Balls, B.A., M.S., M.B.A., M.A., is a former executive of a Fortune 100 company and a retired educator. He was a teacher, a chairperson of school leadership team and has served as a high school principal in an Early College, an innovative program partially funded by the Bill and Melinda Gates Foundation. He currently is a business partner in a chain of restaurants. He is the co-author of a book on e-business, enterprise resource planning (ERP) and transforming the business enterprise. He has been a guest speaker at a number of business and education forums on the topics of organizational & operational design, change management and high performance teams. He lives in Charlotte, North Carolina with his wife, Greta.

A. Douglas Eury, B.S., M.Ed., Ed.S., Ed.D., is the Dean for the School of Education at Gardner-Webb University in Boiling Springs, NC. He also serves as the director of doctoral studies as well as director for the Center for Innovative Leadership Development. His experience includes 33 years of service as a public school educator in the state of North Carolina. He spent 17 years as a classroom teacher and coach; the remainder of his tenure consisted of administrative experience at the secondary level. He lives in Shelby, North Carolina with his wife, Janet.

Jane C. King, B.S., M.S., Ed.S., Ed.D., provides instructional balance to this team of authors. Her lifelong career in education encompasses teaching, supervising, administration, as well as her own personal learning. Her passion for excellence in teaching and learning follows her throughout her career. She has taught students at all levels of education which gives her a unique view of student needs. In addition, she has taught learning disabled students and she has spent time as a Director of Exceptional Children's Programs for a local public school district. She has held positions as teacher, principal, director and associate superintendent in public schools. Dr. King has a passion for quality teaching and learning and has spent the past years working as an assistant professor at Gardner-Webb University and as an instructional coach in early college high schools. She has a great love for learning and for those who are involved in the process. Helping teachers and administrators know and understand quality curriculum and instruction provides focus for her most recent work. She lives in Kings Mountain, NC with her husband, Jerry.

PEARSON — ALWAYS LEARNING

John D. Balls • A. Douglas Eury • Jane C. King

Rethink, Rebuild, Rebound:
A Framework for Shared Responsibility and Accountability in Education

Workbook

Cover Art: Courtesy of Photodisc/Getty Images

Copyright © 2012 by Pearson Learning Solutions

All rights reserved.

Permission in writing must be obtained from the publisher before any part of this work may be reproduced or transmitted in any form or by any means, electronic or mechanical, including photocopying and recording, or by any information storage or retrieval system.

All trademarks, service marks, registered trademarks, and registered service marks are the property of their respective owners and are used herein for identification purposes only.

Pearson Learning Solutions, 501 Boylston Street, Suite 900, Boston, MA 02116
A Pearson Education Company
www.pearsoned.com

Printed in the United States of America

2 3 4 5 6 7 8 9 10 V0ZN 17 16 15 14 13 12

000200010271666607

MT

ISBN 10: 1-256-73864-6
ISBN 13: 978-1-256-73864-0

In loving memory of my dear sister, Carroll.

John D. Balls
May 24, 2012

Table of Contents

Acknowledgments xi

Foreword xiii

Introduction xv

Section l: Value-Added Mindset/Experiences 1

Section ll: 21st Century Skills 53

Section lll: Education Reforms 71

Section IV: Capstone Scenario 99

Appendices 103

Table of Contents

Acknowledgments xi

Foreword xiii

Introduction xv

Section I: Value-Added Mindset/Experiences 1

Chapter 1 Value-Added Assessment Model: Assessments to Measure Individual and Collective Efficacy **3**

Domain1 – Disposition 5

Domain 2 – Professional Experiences 7

Domain 3 – Structure 9

Domain 4 – Shared Decisions 11

Domain 5 – Assessment Skills 13

Chapter 2 Impacting the Learning Culture with the Value-Added Model **15**

Implemantation Instruments (Phase One) 15

Facilatation of 3 Experiences (Phase Two) 16

Individual and Collective Efficacy Instruments 17

Individual and Collective Efficacy Instruments by Category 17

Chapter 3 Four Keys to School Success **21**

Academic Excellence 21

Developmental Responsiveness 22

Social Equity 23

Organizational Structures 24

Chapter 4 Shared Decision-Making **27**
    What Are the Premises and Goals of Shared Decision Making? 27
    How Is the Principal's Role Change in SDM? 27
    What Factors Are Important for SDM's Successful Implementation? 27
    Which Issues Should SDM Groups Focus on? 28

Chapter 5 Structures that Support Self- Efficacy and Collective Efficacy **29**

Chapter 6 Formative Assessment and Reflective Practice **31**

Chapter 7 Growth Plans **33**

Chapter 8 Planning and Goal Setting **35**

Chapter 9 Empowerment and Efficacy Training **37**

Chapter 10 Transformational Leadership **39**

Chapter 11 Scenario Activities **41**
    Scenario 1: Focus on Learning Communities 41
    Scenario 2: Focus on Learning Cultures and Sustaining Cultures 43
    Scenario 3: Dispositions (Passion to Perform) 45
    Scenario 4: Teacher Efficacy 47
    Scenario 5: Empowerment 49
    Scenario 6: Leadership through Cultural Development 51

Section II: 21st Century Skills 53

Chapter 12 Who are the Teachers in the 21st Century? **55**

Chapter 13 Who are the 21st Century Learners and What is the Teaching-Learning Environment? **57**

Chapter 14 Critical Attributes of 21ˢᵗ Century Learning **59**

    Critical Attributes of 21st Century Education   61

    Multiple Literacies for 21st Century   62

Chapter 15 How Do We Teach? **63**

Chapter 16 Are Students Learning? **65**

Chapter 17 Section II Master Scenario: School Planning for the 21ˢᵗ Century **67**

    Student Knowledge and Skills   67

    Education and Support Systems   67

    Education Leadership   68

    Policymaking   68

    Parents   68

    Partnering   68

    Continuous Improvement   68

Section III: Education Reforms 71

Chapter 18 Needs Assessment **73**

    Needs Assessment Surveys   73

    Needs Assessment Summary   75

Chapter 19 Prioritization **83**

Chapter 20 Implementation Approaches....Excellence in Execution **87**

Chapter 21 Quality Assurance....Results/Expectations Attainment **91**

    Exhibit 3: PDCA Continuous Cycle   91

Chapter 22 Section III Master Scenario **97**

Section IV: Capstone Scenario   99

Chapter 23   Capstone Scenario   **101**

   Indicators of Learning   101

Appendices 103

Appendix A: Action Research Guide   **105**
Appendix B: Benefits of Action Research   **117**
Appendix C: Reporting the Findings of Action Research   **121**
Appendix D: Characterictics of High-Performing Organizations   **125**
Appendix E: Benefits of Empowerment   **129**
Appendix F: Identifying Barriers to Empowerment   **133**
Appendix G: Checklist for Leading Organizational Transformation   **137**
Appendix H: Critical Attributes of 21st Century Education   **141**
Appendix I: Multiple Literaries for the 21st Century   **145**
Appendix J: Needs Assessment Checklist   **149**
Appendix K: Needs Assessment Summary   **153**
Appendix L: Benefits/Cost Analysis   **157**

About the Authors   **161**

Acknowledgments

Without the support of many people from various backgrounds who have dedicated their lives to education this book would not have made it to press. The enthusiasm and commitment to purpose of all those who contributed during the research phase of the book was incredible. We are grateful to the many contributors for their time and insights in helping to make this book relevant to the critical national dialogue on education reform. We thank them all for their encouragement and invaluable assistance.

We especially want to thank several people who offered their assistance and support to make this book a reality. First and foremost, we want to thank our spouses, Greta, Janet, and Jerry who picked up the slack on the home front when we were researching and writing the book. Their support and countless words of encouragement were instrumental in making this book a reality.

A special thank you to the excellent faculty at Stanly Early College in Albemarle, North Carolina who have demonstrated that a passion for excellence, a willingness to take risks and a commitment to continuous improvement leads to academic excellence by the students they so ably educate. They serve as an inspiration for all of us. We want to recognize the North Carolina New Schools Project (NSP) for the pioneering work they have done in education reform. As authors we have benefited from the leadership, guidance and "can do" spirit exhibited by the NSP professionals.

We are grateful for all the contributions and feedback we received from the graduate level students at Gardner-Webb University. Their insight and reflections on their experiences in education were most helpful.

Finally, we owe a debt of gratitude to the "can do" team at Pearson who demonstrated time and again their commitment to excellence and customer satisfaction. We want to thank Michlene Daoud Healy, Bill Clements and Meg Tiedemann for their patience, responsiveness and their overall outstanding support.

Foreword

"As a fulltime graduate student in the late 1970s, I had the pleasure of organizing a regional meeting of the University Council of Educational Administrators. Approximately 50 doctoral students attended. One of the presenters asked how many of the doctoral students wanted to move directly into an assistant professorship and how many wanted to be practitioners. I remember that only three of us indicated that we wanted to be practitioners. At that time, these results surprised me since I entered the doctoral program so that I could apply my training as an administrator in a local school district.

After 30 plus years as a superintendent, I can say that my doctoral training provided a solid foundation for my work as a practitioner. Unfortunately, I had no idea of the time commitment and the inability to personally engage in research (and sometimes not enough time to read it!!). However, I have been able to create a small research staff in my current district and forged some partnerships with local research universities who have supplied doctoral candidates to work on projects for a modest stipend.

I share this bit of personal history to commend the work of three practitioners---John Balls, Doug Eury, and Jane King—who have reflected on their careers and assembled a great book, ***Rethink, Rebuild, Rebound: A Framework for Shared Responsibility and Accountability in Education***. This workbook, along with the accompanying text, provides practitioners with concrete activities to use with staff to help 'fuel and ignite' the passion for the work we all undertake every day. . . . .helping all students realize their potential. This passion is contagious—it is the same passion that leads athletic teams to championships—it allows us to respect and appreciate and listen to our co-workers, so that we are willing to confront what we don't know and feel comfortable sharing what we do, and finally—this passion flows from teachers to their students.

Several years ago, our staff was looking for a consultant that could help each school as well as the whole district become a learning organization. A web search uncovered the Society of Organizational Leadership Education Partnership—SoL Ed for short. SoL Ed is part of a larger organization—The Society of Organizational Learning (SoL)—which consults with Fortune 500 companies all over the world. SoL is directed by Peter Senge at MIT whose name and first book, *The Fifth Discipline*, is associated with systems thinking (refer to page 240 in ***Rethink, Rebuild, Rebound*** 2nd Edition text). SoL Ed began conducting summer 'gatherings' of school districts in 2007.

A small group of central office administrators, principals, and one school board member attended the second gathering. The group came back inspired to cultivate their personal aspirations and help develop common aspirations for their school or department. For the next three years, I attended the SoL Ed Gathering. In 2011, Peter Senge partnered with Michael Fullen to focus on sustaining changes in schools that produce desired outcomes. Senge focused on personal development and Fullen on organizational development.

Conceptually, last year's attendees embraced the work of Senge and Fullen, but putting these ideas into practice is difficult work. The activities provided by **Balls, Eury and King** in their workbook, operationalize much of Senge's work on developing a shared vision and working together to achieve it. Clearly, activities dealing with igniting teacher passion and dispositions, teacher efficacy, personal commitment, leadership training and assessment are about developing personal and organizational aspirations. This workbook contains activities/scenarios that reinforce the development, integration, and sustainability of professional learning communities. These activities/scenarios connect directly to Fullen's work on organizational change in pursuit of achieving outcomes. Not only teachers, but also administrators, must work in professional learning communities in schools and between schools to share successful strategies and adjust instructional approaches and practices.

No Child Left Behind helped all school districts publicly confront achievement gaps. Unfortunately, the methodology of adequate yearly progress unfairly labeled schools as 'failing'. Identifying many schools as failing over the past decade and the incessant ranking of U.S. students on international assessments have fueled political rhetoric to the point that we frequently hear public schools referred to as 'failed government schools'.

At this critical juncture, public school educators cannot be defensive. We must communicate the limitations of current multiple choice assessments and promote the constructed response assessments that will accompany the Common Core. These authentic, challenging assessments will define what rigorous student work means and produce students who can think and solve problems.

In other words, Balls, Eury, and King would say, 'we must ***Rethink, Rebuild, Rebound***'. Their workbook arrives at the perfect time. The diverse scenarios simulate real challenges we as educators confront daily. The scenarios provide the user the opportunity to practice applying the foundational principles as outlined in their text, ***Rethink, Rebuild, Rebound: A Framework for Shared Responsibility and Accountability***. Implementing these strategies in schools and administrative offices will help us immensely to restore faith and pride in our public schools."

Respectfully,

Don L. Martin, Ed. D
Superintendent
Winston-Salem/Forsyth County Schools, NC
State Superintendent of the Year, 2011

Introduction

"Knowing is not enough, we must apply. Willing is not enough, we must do."
Johann von Goethe

Oftentimes we are exposed to a thoughtful treatise on a topic we are passionate about but are not sure how to apply what we have learned or in what context/situation would the applied learning be most useful. In the companion text, **Rethink, Rebuild, Rebound: A Framework for Shared Responsibility and Accountability in Education** (published by Pearson Learning Solutions, 2011) the authors have set forth a comprehensive framework for addressing the challenges we face in education today along with the processes to rebuild this vital institution of K-12 education culminating in a rebound to be again the best in the world.

This workbook provides for the reader a brief synopsis of the detailed discussion in the aforementioned text followed by a series of scenarios intended to provoke thought and provide an opportunity to apply the learning from the text.

Included in each section, which is generally aligned with the textbook beginning with Section II in the text, are overarching scenarios which will encapsulate all the key points in the section. While some of the scenarios focus on principals/administrators it can apply to department chairpersons, lead teachers or teachers as well. The emphasis is on leadership and what actions would you take as a school leader or as a leader in your classroom.

The first section explores the concept of teacher value-added as it relates to learning cultures, empowerment, learning communities, dispositions, leadership, teacher efficacy and sustainability. The next section addresses the skills that teachers will need in order to equip their students with the wherewithal to be successful in their pursuit of higher education and/or to be career ready in the 21st century. The third section looks at school-wide reform initiatives from a needs assessment to developing and prioritizing key initiatives while ensuring quality and integrity throughout. The workbook concludes with a capstone scenario (Section IV) which the authors proffer as a summative exercise drawing on the learning from the entire workbook and text.

We hope and trust this workbook will be the genesis (or a stimulus if already underway) of a series of actions by the reader, faculty, school administration, parents, community-at-large (including the businesses) starting with discussion and debate and culminating in an aligned plan to get us back to greatness in education. We owe it to our children and all generations to follow. Now is the time for action and we offer this workbook along with our text as a blueprint to get the ball rolling.

Section I: Value Added Mindset/ Experiences

Chapter 1

Value-Added Assessment Model: Assessments to Measure Individual and Collective Efficacy

Resource: <u>Rethink, Rebuild, Rebound</u> text by Balls, Eury, and King

Value-added models for student achievement use growth modeling to identify effective teachers, schools, and techniques. This new focus is changing the way in which teachers are assessed, potentially resulting in differentiated pay scales. Most reforms based on this method are focused on obtaining a predetermined goal, such as higher student scores. The authors of this workbook acknowledge that this is a valuable approach, but propose a different view i.e., value-added models on page 25 of text.

The Value-Added Assessment Model focuses on creating a self-sustaining learning culture through assessment of teachers in five domains. The goal of this model is to impact more than student scores. It should encourage a cultural transformation to maximize the performance of the organization as a whole. Below are 5 assessment surveys to assist in the growth monitoring of k-12 teachers. These instruments may be used as written or adjusted to align with agreed upon operational definitions of the five domains.

Assessment Surveys

Each survey has 10 questions. The educator's answer to each survey question is weighted according to this scale:

- Definitely = 5 points
- Somewhat = 3 points
- Not at All = 0 points

Teachers can receive a total of 50 points per survey with 250 points possible for all 5 surveys. The teacher's overall score will indicate his/her efficacy in each domain as well as overall. Individual teacher scores will be averaged together to determine collective efficacy of the organization. The goal is to continually raise the scores over time.

Assessments should be given in the Fall and Spring of each year. This will allow for growth monitoring over the course of the school year. Fall surveys serve as a baseline and provide data for administration to create a growth plan and training opportunities for the year. Spring surveys will show the year's growth and provide comparative data for the upcoming Fall.

Domain 1 focuses on dispositions. This domain assesses how one's personal value system can affect performance and commitment to organizational goals. With this assessment, educators can understand the importance of sharing personal experiences within the content they teach.

Domain 2 focuses on professional experiences. This domain assesses how an educator's professional experiences can affect their abilities through organized activities and personal habits.

Domain 3 focuses on structure. This domain assesses the degree to which professional learning communities are present within the school. Teachers should be experiencing organizational structures that allow for collaborative planning and the maintenance of professional relationships.

Domain 4 focuses on shared decisions. This domain assesses the degree to which teachers are involved in decision making. Teachers should have opportunities for productive interaction and empowerment. They should have common routines and common language for learning. With this data the school administration can make sure teachers have the opportunity to interact with one another in order to create a positive school culture.

Domain 5 focuses on assessment skills. This domain assesses an educator's level of skill in regard to assessment and evaluation. The focus should be on formative assessment. Understanding how individual teachers use assessment can help administrators determine if teachers are reflecting on their practice.

SO WHAT: It is not important to get high scores on the assessments of the domains, but rather use the responses as prompts for discussion and reflection. Without consensus by the organization on what constitutes or defines the domains, it will be difficult to garner strength from the exercise. In addition, it is important to determine (by the organization's members) the dependent variables desired in the assessment or any measure of change. The text makes such suggestions as student performance (actual or meeting predictive growth), teacher working conditions perceptions, student perceptions of classroom and school culture, classroom observation rubrics, or aggregate scores of groups. Again, <u>change and the degree of change are important, not the scores themselves.</u> It might also serve well to set upper and lower limits for acceptable domain scores in order to more narrowly focus on group needs.

Domain 1 – Dispositions

Do you provide direct experience within the content you are teaching?	Definitely	Somewhat	Not at All
Do you use resources from your community? Ex. community history or interactions within the community through discussions.	Definitely	Somewhat	Not at All
In your lessons do you allow your students to participate in collaborative learning?	Definitely	Somewhat	Not at All
From the lessons you teach, learning is personal and self-directed.	Definitely	Somewhat	Not at All
Your personal self is shown throughout your teaching by using a combination of formal and informal experiences.	Definitely	Somewhat	Not at All
You have a deep understanding of the content you teach.	Definitely	Somewhat	Not at All
Your lessons include modeling how you think about or understand content.	Definitely	Somewhat	Not at All
Personal relevance is shown throughout the lessons you are teaching.	Definitely	Somewhat	Not at All
You take your students on extraordinary journeys of discovery, whether of the mind, spirit or body.	Definitely	Somewhat	Not at All
You have a positive attitude towards sustaining learning.	Definitely	Somewhat	Not at All

Domain 2 – Professional Experiences

You evaluate each child's progress regularly using information obtained from ongoing classroom interaction.	Definitely	Somewhat	Not at All
You provide value in-depth information to parents, administrators, and other policy makers.	Definitely	Somewhat	Not at All
You use student portfolios to illustrate their efforts, progress, and achievements throughout the year.	Definitely	Somewhat	Not at All
You understand that each child in your classroom can express what they know and can do in many ways.	Definitely	Somewhat	Not at All
You collaborate with other teachers within your grade level to enhance your own professional skills.	Definitely	Somewhat	Not at All
You contribute to meaningful curriculum planning in order to design appropriate interventions for your students.	Definitely	Somewhat	Not at All
You actively engage students by using reflection strategies during instruction.	Definitely	Somewhat	Not at All
You respond to student questions by providing explanations of student reasoning.	Definitely	Somewhat	Not at All
Your lessons include well-integrated instructional strategies that are tailored to address a variety of specific student needs.	Definitely	Somewhat	Not at All

You provide feedback to your students by referencing the content and language objectives they are trying to meet.	Definitely	Somewhat	Not at All

Domain 3 – Structure

PLC team members demonstrate a collective effort to improve the school.	Definitely	Somewhat	Not at All
The team works diligently to define issues and make representative decisions.	Definitely	Somewhat	Not at All
As a PLC team member you would be willing to observe other schools within the county.	Definitely	Somewhat	Not at All
The PLC team creates strategies that benefit student learning.	Definitely	Somewhat	Not at All
Team members are provided time during the contractual day and school year to meet as a team.	Definitely	Somewhat	Not at All
PLC team has identified a SMART goal that is aligned with our school goals.	Definitely	Somewhat	Not at All
PLC team generates and submits products to school administration that are related to student learning.	Definitely	Somewhat	Not at All
PLC team uses relevant data to promote continuous improvement.	Definitely	Somewhat	Not at All

| The PLC team provides evidence of how the students are achieving goals. | Definitely | Somewhat | Not at All |

Domain 4 – Shared Decisions

You interact with your grade level on a weekly basis to evaluate student performance.	Definitely	Somewhat	Not at All
You get involved in activities that support your school.	Definitely	Somewhat	Not at All
You are willing to discuss opportunities for staff development with school administration.	Definitely	Somewhat	Not at All
You believe that good school based decision-making has a direct effect on student achievement.	Definitely	Somewhat	Not at All
You collaborate with others to discuss school policies.	Definitely	Somewhat	Not at All
You work with others to implement effective instruction.	Definitely	Somewhat	Not at All
You establish respectful and productive relationships with parents and other members of the community.	Definitely	Somewhat	Not at All
You are willing to conduct a needs assessment within your school.	Definitely	Somewhat	Not at All
You feel appreciated at your school.	Definitely	Somewhat	Not at All

Your school acts as a school learning community.	Definitely	Somewhat	Not at All

Domain 5 – Assessment Skills

You use formal methods of assessment to plan instruction.	Definitely	Somewhat	Not at All
You use research as a source for active reflection.	Definitely	Somewhat	Not at All
You analyze student performance using multiple sources of data to modify plans and instructional techniques that promote desired learning outcomes.	Definitely	Somewhat	Not at All
You accurately document and report assessment to parents.	Definitely	Somewhat	Not at All
You use audio or video recordings of you teaching a lesson.	Definitely	Somewhat	Not at All
On a daily basis you reflect on your educational practices.	Definitely	Somewhat	Not at All
You know when and how to use assessment based on student needs.	Definitely	Somewhat	Not at All
You use informal classroom assessments.	Definitely	Somewhat	Not at All
You use ongoing assessments to monitor progress.	Definitely	Somewhat	Not at All
You use anecdotal records as an assessment tool.	Definitely	Somewhat	Not at All

Chapter 2

Impacting the Learning Culture with the Value-Added Model

What is being measured? The quality of being successful (effective) as it relates to the ability of the individual and the total organization based on the implications found in the data generated by the domain assessments.

Indicators of multiple student outcomes: graduation rate, student promotional rate, student proficiency rate, and post-secondary indicators. These are basic sample indicators. It is important that the members of the organization agree upon the criteria or context of what indicates effectiveness of the individual and organization.

How do we measure? Needs assessment matched to proven strategies in areas of individual/collective growth.

What affects individual/collective student growth? The ability and instructional delivery skills of the teacher facilitating student learning related to the ability of the instructor to perform at the highest possible level.

Implementation Instrument (Phase One)

1. Data that provide disposition for individual/collective performance based on commitment to organizational goals (Disposition).

2. Data that provide assessment of individual professional experiences that are proven to impact the individual's ability through organized activities and personal habits (Professional Experience).

3. Data that examine the organizational structure that each individual/collective group experience on a routine basis, focus the degree of PLC that may or may not be present (Structure)

4. Data that would measure degree of shared decision-making opportunities to contribute to the development of productive **interactions**, **routines**, and **common language of learning**-key factors for cultural health (Shared Decision).

5. Data to determine level of skill in planning, implementing and evaluating formative assessments (Assessment Skills). It is important to keep in mind the need to

model best practices, to assess the impact of implemented lessons, and to examine most effetive sequencing.

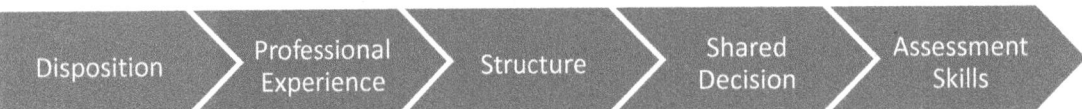

This graphic is not a continuum, but rather a representation that implies the connection of the five domains. Keep in mind, the goal of the assessment is to assess individual and collective efficacy and use the findings to develop individual and group experiences that may impact the measures at another administration of the instrument.

Facilitation of 3 experiences (Phase Two)

STEPS:

1. Growth Plan for individual/school population as identified in the data from a needs assessment on some measure of efficacy. Be sure to include benchmark measure and desired measure for the next administration of the instrument.

2. Involve staff in multiple action research projects that target identified needs in previous assessments that are specific to either grade level or subject level. The key is to develop specific implementations to address identified needs and include a method of evaluating the impact of the intervention. Refer to pages in Appendix A as a guide to action research.

3. Implement training in areas of empowerment and efficacy. It cannot be over stressed that empowerment and efficacy building are not aimed at changing

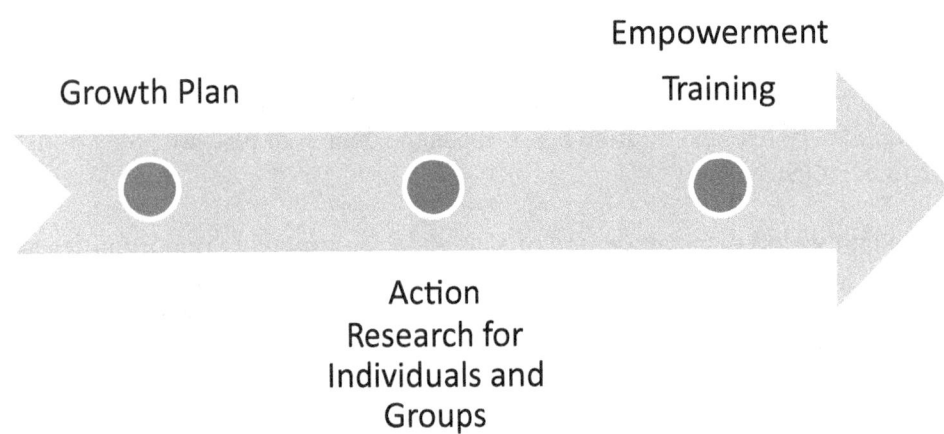

processes as much as they are aimed at changing mindsets. Empowerment is as much an attitude as it is an action. Leaders cannot empower people, rather they build an attitude of empowerment that contributes to the level of efficacy.

Individual and Collective Efficacy Instruments

The instruments above are associated with the five prescribed domains of self and collective efficacy. There are alternative approaches to individual and collective efficacy. Below is an example.

Individual Efficacy

Teacher efficacy has been defined as, "The extent to which the teacher believes he or she has the capacity to affect student performance," or as "teachers' belief or conviction that they can influence how well students learn," (*Review of Educational Research*, Summer 1998, Vol.68, p. 202).

Collective Efficacy

"Collective efficacy is the shared perceptions of teachers in a school that the efforts of the faculty as a whole will have positive effects on students," (http://www.waynekhoy.com/collective_efficacy.html). According to Bandura, and the Social Cognitive Theory, collective teacher efficacy is an important school property. Therefore, collective teacher efficacy explains the different effects that different schools have on student success, and we must understand and tend to this property in order to maintain it!

Individual and Collective Efficacy Instrument by Category

Parent/Teacher Communication

1. I know parental involvement is important to have a successful school.

    Strongly Agree   Agree   Neutral   Disagree   Strongly Disagree

2. I believe every family has some strengths that can be utilized to increase student success in school.

    Strongly Agree   Agree   Neutral   Disagree   Strongly Disagree

3. I believe parental involvement can help me be more effective with my students.

   Strongly Agree   Agree   Neutral   Disagree   Strongly Disagree

4. I look forward to having a conference with each of my students' parents at least once a year.

   Extremely Important   Important   Neutral   Somewhat Important   Not At All

5. I recognize contacting parents about their children's problems or failures is beneficial.

   Extremely Important   Important   Neutral   Somewhat Important   Not At All

6. I recognize contacting parents when their children do something well or improve is beneficial.

   Extremely Important   Important   Neutral   Somewhat Important   Not At All

7. I must tell parents about the skills their children must learn in each subject taught.

   Extremely Important   Important   Neutral   Somewhat Important   Not At All

8. I believe in sending home monthly newsletters, posting e-newsletters, or hosting parent nights to tell them what their children have been doing and learning in school.

   Extremely Important   Important   Neutral   Somewhat Important   Not At All

9. I trust in providing parents with specific learning activities for them to work on with their children.

   Extremely Important   Important   Neutral   Somewhat Important   Not At All

10. I strive to keep an active classroom blog for student and parent access.

    Extremely Important   Important   Neutral   Somewhat Important   Not At All

Teaching Experience and Method

1. Teachers are well prepared to teach the subjects they are assigned to teach.

    Strongly Agree   Agree   Neutral   Disagree   Strongly Disagree

2. Teachers in this school are experienced in a range of methods of teaching.

    Strongly Agree   Agree   Neutral   Disagree   Strongly Disagree

3. Teachers in this school are able to get through to difficult students.

    Strongly Agree   Agree   Neutral   Disagree   Strongly Disagree

4. Teachers here need more professional development in how to deal with these types of student.

    Strongly Agree   Agree   Neutral   Disagree   Strongly Disagree

Supplies and Technology

1. The lack of instructional supplies and/or materials makes teaching and engaging students difficult.

    Strongly Agree   Agree   Neutral   Disagree   Strongly Disagree

2. Using more technology (Smart board, Document Camera, I Touches, etc…) on a weekly basis has proven to be engaging for my students and successful in producing 21st century lessons.

    Strongly Agree   Agree   Neutral   Disagree   Strongly Disagree

3. More professional development is needed in order to utilize the technology in our school in the most effective and educational way.

    Strongly Agree   Agree   Neutral   Disagree   Strongly Disagree

Maintenance of Our Campus

1. Our campus is clean, orderly, organized, and attractive.

   Strongly Agree   Agree   Neutral   Disagree   Strongly Disagree

2. Involving students and staff in a monthly school maintenance day would increase the ownership of maintaining our school grounds.

   Strongly Agree   Agree   Neutral   Disagree   Strongly Disagree

3. A clean, orderly, organized, attractive school leads to positive student/ staff interaction and more student comfort and success.

   Strongly Agree   Agree   Neutral   Disagree   Strongly Disagree

Collaboration

1. All teachers are responsible for student learning.

   Strongly Agree   Agree   Neutral   Disagree   Strongly Disagree

2. All teachers must teach across the curriculum to spotlight Math and Language Arts skills necessary for success on state testing.

   Strongly Agree   Agree   Neutral   Disagree   Strongly Disagree

3. Collaborating across subject areas and grade levels is essential to uphold good teaching methods and innovative ideas.

   Strongly Agree   Agree   Neutral   Disagree   Strongly Disagree

Chapter 3

Four Keys to School Success

The following material on keys to school success is repeated from pages 28 through 34 in the text **Rethink, Rebuild Rebound: A Framework for Shared Responsibility and Accountability in Education.** As a workbook exercise, consider these bullets as checklist of identifiable characteristics or administer as a Likert scale survey for organizational reflection.

Academic Excellence:

High-performing schools are academically excellent. They challenge all students to use their minds well.

1. All students are expected to meet high academic standards. Teachers supply students with exemplars of high quality work that meets the performance standard. Students revise their work based on feedback until they meet or exceed the performance standard.

2. Curriculum, instruction, and assessment are aligned with high standards. They provide a coherent vision for what students should know and be able to do. The curriculum is rigorous and non-repetitive; it moves forward substantially as students progress through the middle grades.

3. The curriculum emphasizes deep understanding of important concepts, development of essential skills, and the ability to apply what one has learned to real-world problems. By making connections across the disciplines, the curriculum helps reinforce important concepts.

4. Instructional strategies include a variety of challenging and engaging activities that are clearly related to the concepts and skills being taught.

5. Teachers use a variety of methods to assess student performance (e.g., exhibitions, projects, performance tasks) and maintain a collection of student work. Students learn how to assess their own and others' work against the performance standards.

6. The school provides students time to meet rigorous academic standards. Flexible scheduling enables students to engage in extended projects, hands-on experiences, and

inquiry-based learning. Most class time is devoted to learning and applying knowledge or skills rather than classroom management and discipline.

7. Students have the supports they need to meet rigorous academic standards. They have multiple opportunities to succeed and extra help as needed.

8. The adults in the school have opportunities to plan, select, and engage in professional development aligned with nationally recognized standards. They have regular opportunities to work with their colleagues to deepen their knowledge and improve their practice. They collaborate in making decisions about rigorous curriculum and effective instructional methods. They discuss student work as a means of enhancing their own practice.

Developmental Responsiveness

High-performing schools are sensitive to the unique developmental challenges of early adolescence.

1. The school creates a personalized environment that supports each student's intellectual, ethical, social, and physical development. The school groups adults and students in small learning communities characterized by stable, close, and mutually respectful relationships.

2. The school provides access to comprehensive services to foster healthy physical, social, emotional, and intellectual development.

3. Teachers use a wide variety of instructional strategies to foster curiosity, exploration, creativity, and the development of social skills.

4. The curriculum is both socially significant and relevant to the personal interests of young adolescents.

5. Teachers make connections across disciplines to help reinforce important concepts and address real-world problems.

6. The school provides multiple opportunities for students to explore a rich variety of topics and interests in order to develop their identity, discover and demonstrate their own competence, and plan for their future.

7. Students have opportunities for voice—posing questions, reflecting on experiences, developing rubrics, and participating in decisions.

8. The school develops alliances with families to enhance and support the well-being of their children. It involves families as partners in their children's education, keeping them informed, involving them in their children's learning, and assuring participation in decision-making.

9. The school provides students with opportunities to develop citizenship skills, uses the community as a classroom, and engages the community in providing resources and support.

10. The school provides age-appropriate co-curricular activities.

Social Equity

High-performing schools are socially equitable, democratic, and fair. They provide every student with high-quality teachers, resources, learning opportunities, and supports. They keep positive options open for all students.

1. Faculty and administrators expect high-quality work from all students and are committed to helping each student produce it. Evidence of this commitment includes tutoring, mentoring, special adaptations, and other supports.

2. Students may use many and varied approaches to achieve and demonstrate competence and mastery of standards.

3. The school continually adapts curriculum, instruction, assessment, and scheduling to meet its students' diverse and changing needs.

4. All students have equal access to valued knowledge in all school classes and activities.

5. Students have on-going opportunities to learn about and appreciate their own and others' cultures. The school values knowledge from the diverse cultures represented in the school and our nation.

6. Each child's voice is heard, acknowledged, and respected.

7. The school welcomes and encourages the active participation of all its families.

8. The school's reward system demonstrates that it values diversity, civility, service, and democratic citizenship.

9. The faculty is culturally and linguistically diverse.

10. The school's suspension rate is low and in proportion to the student population.

Organizational Structures

High-performing schools are learning organizations that establish norms, structures, and organizational arrangements to support and sustain their trajectory toward excellence.

1. A shared vision of what a high-performing school is and does drives every facet of school change. Shared and sustained leadership propels the school forward and preserves its institutional memory and purpose.

2. Someone in the school has the responsibility and authority to hold the school-improvement enterprise together, including day-to-day know-how, coordination, strategic planning, and communication.

3. The school is a community of practice in which learning, experimentation, and reflection are the norm. Expectations of continuous improvement permeate the school. The school devotes resources to ensure that teachers have time and opportunity to reflect on their classroom practice and learn from one another. At school everyone's job is to learn.

4. The school devotes resources to content-rich professional development, which is connected to reaching and sustaining the school vision. Professional development is intensive, of high quality, and ongoing.

5. The school is not an island unto itself. It draws upon others' experience, research, and wisdom; it enters into relationships such as networks and community partnerships that benefit students' and teachers' development and learning.

6. The school holds itself accountable for its students' success rather than blaming others for its shortcomings. The school collects, analyzes, and uses data as a basis for making decisions. The school grapples with school-generated evaluation data to identify areas for more extensive and intensive improvement. It delineates benchmarks, and insists upon evidence and results. The school intentionally and explicitly reconsiders its vision and practices when data call them into question.

7. Key people possess and cultivate the collective will to persevere and overcome barriers, believing it is their business to produce increased achievement and enhanced development for all students.

8. The school works with colleges and universities to recruit, prepare, and mentor novice and experienced teachers. It insists on having teachers who promote young adolescents' intellectual, social, emotional, physical, and ethical growth. It recruits a faculty that is culturally and linguistically diverse.

9. The school includes families and community members in setting and supporting the school's trajectory toward high performance. The school informs families and community members about its goals for students and students' responsibility for meeting them. It engages all stakeholders in ongoing and reflective conversation, consensus building, and decision making about governance to promote school improvement.

TEAM EXERCISE: Below is a graphic representation of the four keys to school success. In groups, prepare a more detailed graphic that expands the relationship of the four keys.

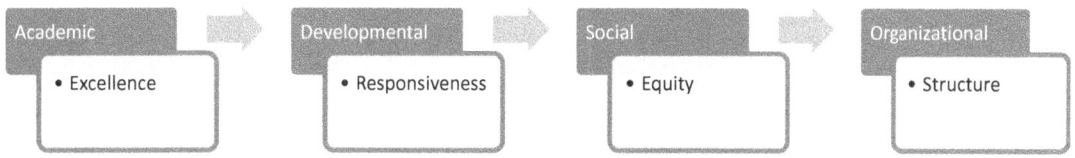

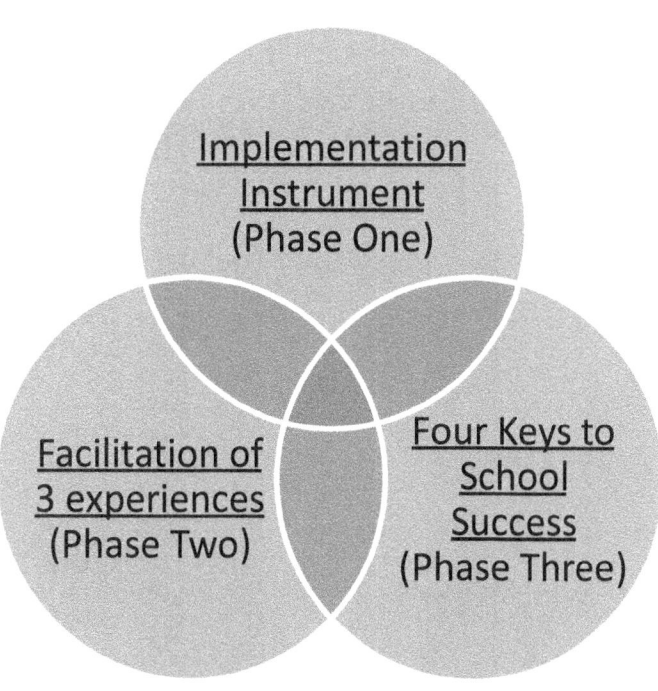

Establishing healthy collaborative relationships, consistent routines and implementing a common language of learning will effectively impact student learning.

TEAM EXERCISE: In groups, as determined by your facilitator, explain and defend the graphic above as it relates to individual and collective efficacy as well as organizational transformation. What is the impact on relationships, routines and a common language of learning? HINT: Can learning occur within the processes? Reference the checklist on high-performing organizations in Appendix D to add depth to your graphic representation and narrative.

Chapter 4

Shared Decision-Making

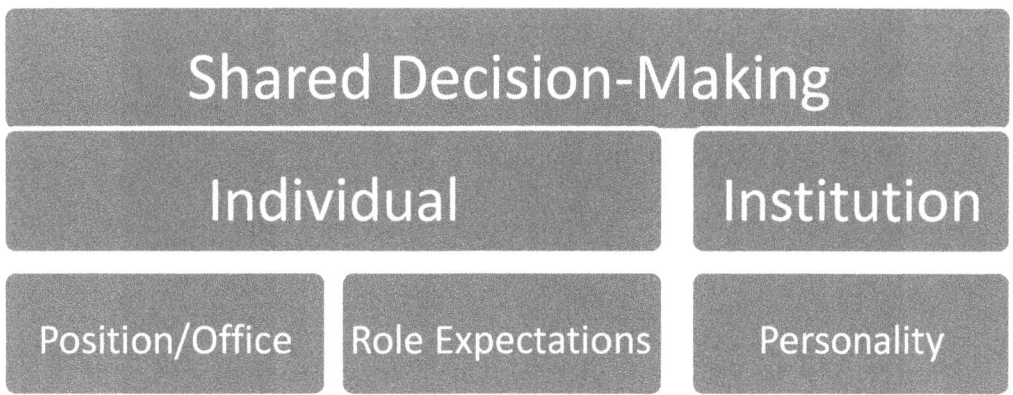

What Are the Premises and Goals of Shared Decision Making (SDM)?

It involves fundamental changes in the way schools are managed, and alterations in the roles and relationships of everyone in the school community. SDM is a *process* of making educational decisions in a collaborative manner at the school level. This process is an ongoing one.

How Is the Principal's Role Changed in SDM?

School Leadership (Principal) becomes "part of a team of decision makers" and will likely make decisions on issues outside the scope of the SDM group or committees. The principal plays a critical role in establishing and maintaining SDM.

What Factors Are Important for SDM's Successful Implementation?

Agree on specifics at the outset. There is no single "right" way to do SDM; it depends on what you want from it. Many schools develop one decision-making team or council; others use several groups or committees.

Be clear about procedures, roles, and expectations. Lack of clarity leads to lack of progress with SDM. Staff needs to understand what steps and procedures are to be followed before decisions are made.

Give everyone a chance to get involved. Volunteer positions or task forces give people the opportunity to participate as much or as little as they want.

Build trust and support. Don't push solutions on the group or override decisions delegated to SDM teams. Lack of hierarchical support can also lead to failure.

Which Issues Should SDM Groups Focus on?

Pick a single, uncomplicated issue, then slowly build on the number and complexity of issues. Knowledge-thoroughly investigate alternatives, disseminate this information to others, and analyze consequences before making decisions.

TEAM EXERCISE: As a group, review chapters 6 and 7 from the text and create flow chart and action plan for implementing a new curriculum program. Assume that the organization has not practiced shared decision-making as a rule meaning your plan should include identifying those most affected, needed information, preparation to make the decisions, desired data, necessary conversation topics, and means of accountability. It would be appropriate to discuss the model on page 66 of the text. In Appendix F is a list of barriers to empowerment that may enhance your action plan. The rating scale in Appendix E may also provide some insight as to the needs to be addressed in the action plan.

Chapter 5

Structures that Support Self-Efficacy and Collective Efficacy

Structures:

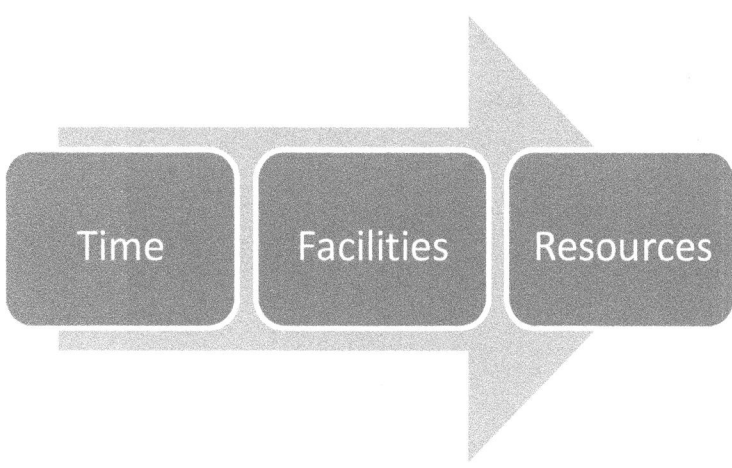

Time-provide students' high quality instruction by allowing teachers planning time and time to meet with peers for modeling and sharing best practices.

Facilities-Using facilities within the school structure to maximize student learning and teacher learning.

Resources-provide quality materials, resources, and technology for teachers in order to facilitate student engagement and high quality education.

INDIVIDUAL OR GROUP EXERCISE: Using discussions from the text, create an opinion paper on the impact of using time, facilities, and resources to impact dispositions toward learning and overall learning effectiveness.

Chapter 6

Formative Assessment and Reflective Practice

INDIVIDUAL OR TEAM EXERCISE: Create a checklist of behaviors and/or activities that encourage teachers to think critically about their performance. Use chapters 12, 17, 18, and 19 in the text as a reference for your considerations for behaviors or actions. Reference the list of benefits of action research in Appendix B as they may relate to reflective practice.

Chapter 7

Growth Plans

INDIVIDUAL EXERCISE: With the five domains identified in the efficacy model on page 25 of the text, create an individual and organizational growth plan based simply on how you perceive yourself and organization in relationship to dispositions, professional experience, organizational structures, shared decision-making opportunities and reflective practice. You will need to use your understanding of the five domains as they are discussed in chapter three. Keep in mind that this exercise is only a reflection and a subjective assessment on your part. Using instruments to measure the level of existence for each domain would be a more scientific approach to this exercise. The purpose now is to get you to apply the domains to a real environment.

Chapter 8

Planning and Goal Setting

Keys to creating Meaningful goals:

- have substance and meaning for the teacher;
- stretch current thinking and practice;
- can be achieved and, therefore, don't lead to frustration; and
- have deadlines that help to ensure that the goal is attained
- A common technique for writing goals is to think about SMART goals.
- **S**—specific and contextual
  M—meaningful measures
  A—achievable within the resources
  R—realistic
  T—time targeted
- Action Words for Developing SMART goals:

  - Apply
  - Attend
  - Contribute
  - Discuss
  - Enroll
  - Conduct
  - Implement
  - Integrate
  - Investigate
  - Join
  - Maintain
  - Mentor
  - Organize
  - Participate
  - Pilot
  - Publish
  - Read
  - Serve
  - Share

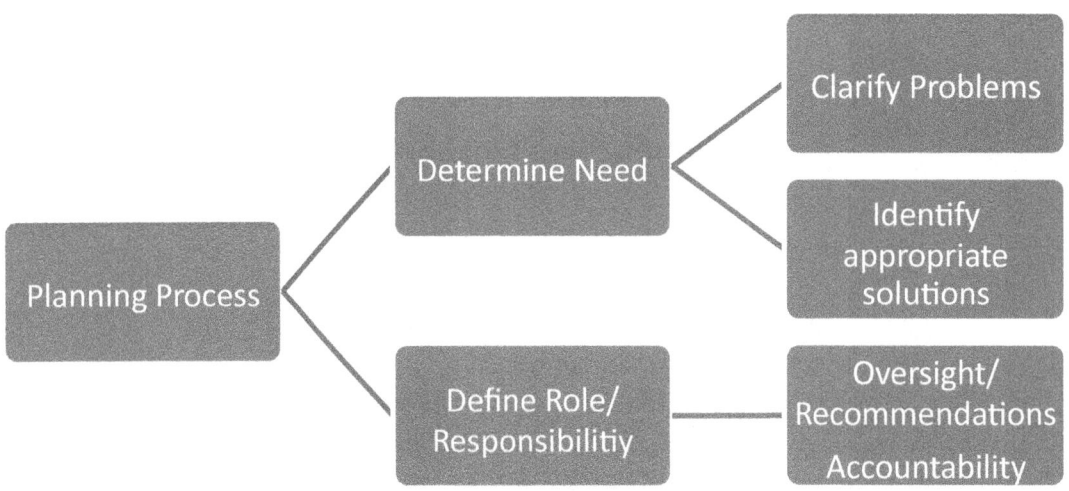

TEAM EXERCISE: Using the growth plan from chapter __7__ on page 33 of this workbook, reflect on how well you have incorporated SMART goal principles. As a team you will be examining each other's individual plan from page 33.

S—specific and contextual

M—meaningful measures

A—achievable within the resources

R—realistic

T—time targeted

Chapter 9

Empowerment and Efficacy Training

Empowerment Training for Staff:

- Purpose is to stimulate dialogue among stakeholders of the teaching profession
- What constitutes the knowledge, skills and competencies that teachers need to assume leadership roles in their schools, districts, and the profession.
- Model standards are often used in the development of curriculum, professional development, and standards for such entities as school districts, states, professional organizations and institutions of higher education.
- These standards are designed to encourage professional discussion of what constitutes the full range of competencies that teacher leaders possess
- This form of leadership can be distinguished from, but work in tandem with, formal administrative leadership roles to support good teaching and promote student learning.
- Role of Principal to inspire others toward collaboration and interdependence as they work toward a purpose to which they are deeply committed. The transformational leader delegates and surrenders power over people and events in order to achieve power over accomplishments and goal achievement.

TEAM EXERCISE: Using principles of empowerment and efficacy discussed in the text, create a training outline that includes agenda items/topics, necessary resources, bibliographical support, and measurable goals for the training.

Chapter 10

Transformational Leadership

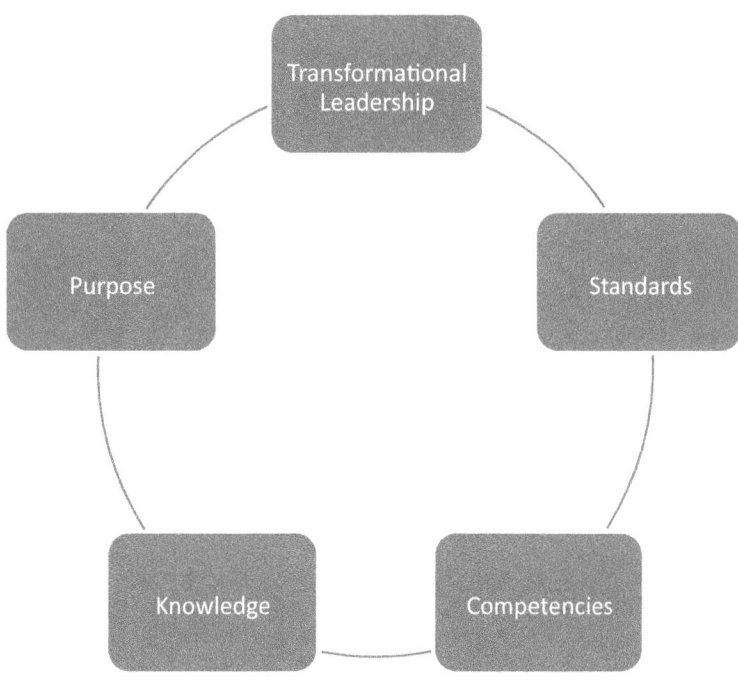

TEAM EXERCISE: As a team, designated by your facilitator, create a more detailed graphic or one similar to a "spicynode" format, that addresses the role of the organizational leadership in creating levels of collective efficacy that would support organizational transformation. Reference checklist in Appendix G for ideas on keys to transforming organizations.

Chapter 11

Scenario Activities

Scenario 1:

Focus on Learning Communities

Sunnyside Elementary is a Title I school with grades K-5. Three years ago, the principal of this school was removed after a District investigation due to complaints to the School Board from parents and teachers. The complaining teachers and parents believed that the principal was not leading the school in practices that were conducive to high levels of learning. Teachers were also complaining that this principal's expectations were not reasonable and that evaluation procedures were not consistent.

Upon the removal of this principal, you were asked to become principal at Sunnyside. You have now been at the school for three years. You have been given the task of creating a cohesive organizational unit for this school and improving the morale of the remaining staff members and families.

Under the former principal's regime, the staff members of Sunnyside were required to form a school-wide PLC, grade-level PLCs, and committees for hospitality, literacy, math, science, social studies, School Improvement Plans, data collection, etc. The staff members were weary of the many meetings (several per week) that were required of them. You discovered that they were no longer engaged in the learning that could come from PLCs and that the committees were no longer functioning in a sound capacity. To gain their trust and demonstrate that you understand their frustrations, you discontinued many of the nonessential committees and limited meetings to boost morale.

Now, three years later, you find your staff departmentalized – vertical articulation is a thing of the past and teachers within the same grade level plan together but do not necessarily have the same vision for learning. The morale amongst your staff has definitely improved and you feel that you have gained their trust. You will be retiring at the end of this year but would like to improve the learning culture of your school.

Discussion Questions:

1. How would you reintroduce vertical articulation and the concept of PLCs?

2. How do you encourage teachers to work together with one shared vision for the school?

3. How do you ensure that the positive changes your school makes are sustained after you are gone?

Scenario 2:

Focus on Learning Cultures and Sustaining Cultures

As principal you are responsible for evaluating the efficacy of your school in regard to individual teachers and as a collective whole. Like other districts, your district has an evaluation system that monitors teachers. The evaluation for first-year teachers and teachers who are new to the district is much more detailed than that for continuing teachers. In fact, the evaluation for continuing teachers consists of the teachers (or the principal) selecting individual and/or grade level goals. They are evaluated on how well they accomplish their goals.

You have overheard teachers in your school and throughout your district talk about the district's evaluation system – stating that it doesn't truly measure the skills that make teachers successful. To a certain degree, you believe that they are correct. Monitoring goals for the year certainly doesn't tell you which teachers are participating in ongoing professional development, collaborative learning, or other key factors of successful teachers.

You know that you must continue the district required evaluation system but you feel that you need an additional system of evaluation for the teachers at your school to determine their areas of need. This new system should measure essential elements such as professional development, empowerment, disposition, etc. You would like to use a system that would be measurable and would encourage growth in several areas.

In order to sustain growth, you know your staff members must believe in the new evaluation system and see it for what it is – a measurement of growth, not a demoralizing process in which they will be reprimanded for their areas of need.

Discussion Questions:

1. What essential elements should be a part of your new evaluation system?

2. How would you get staff members to support your new evaluation system?

3. How will the new evaluation system be used?

Scenario 3:

Dispositions (Passion to Perform)

You are the principal of an elementary school with grades K-5. At the end of last school year, three of your teachers did not renew their contracts – one transferred schools and the other two retired. You assemble a hiring panel which includes yourself, the assistant principal, and teachers from the grade levels with vacancies. After several weeks of interviews, you hire three first-year teachers.

The school year is now several months along and you are very pleased with your new hires. In fact, having them around has made you consider the dispositions of your returning staff members. The passion for teaching displayed by the first-year teachers is infectious and has reinvigorated many teachers within the school. The problem is the fresh enthusiasm of these teachers has truly made you notice the lack of passion in some of your seasoned teachers.

About 1/3 of your current staff members have been teaching for at least 20 years. Some of them have retained the passion for teaching that drew them to this profession while many are just going through the motions, waiting for retirement. While this is not uncommon in many schools, it has become more prevalent to you this year. You find that you have the same core group of teachers participating in the extracurricular fundraisers and events sponsored by the school. These are the same teachers volunteering to be active in the School Improvement Council, PTO, hospitality committee, etc.

You recognize that a teacher's lack of passion outside of the classroom most likely correlates with a lack of passion inside the classroom. You watch the students assigned to these teachers and find that they are less engaged in the learning process than their peers. You know that you need to do something to reignite these teachers' passion to perform.

Discussion Questions:

1. How can you change the dispositions of those teachers who have lost their passion to perform?

2. How can you ensure that all students receive equal classroom environments/atmospheres?

3. What can be done to encourage additional teachers to participate in school committees and events?

Scenario 4:

Teacher Efficacy

You are the principal of a PreK-4th grade school in an inner city. The assistant principal is on personal leave and you must prepare a workshop on teacher efficacy next month. The curriculum coordinator of the county has provided you with various research materials but you must determine the appropriate articles for your school. From your educational experience you believe that teacher efficacy can promote gains in the classroom.

As you prepare for the workshop you attend several grade level meetings to determine how your staff responds to the term "teacher efficacy." In brief, you learn that a teacher's level of confidence about ability to promote learning can depend on past experiences or on school climate. After your discussion, you realize that four beginning teachers want to impact their sense of efficacy. You allow those teachers to observe other teachers within the district that are using a variety of particularly effective practices. During a grade level discussion with your career status teachers you believe that more feedback and collaboration would be beneficial. You encourage these teachers to meet during grade level planning to discuss highlights of effective teaching behaviors while providing constructive and specific suggestions to improve.

From your discussions and observations over the last week, you believe that your school needs a workshop on teacher efficacy using these sub points: setting high goals and ways to try new strategies. Through your reading you learn that you can create a survey for your staff and discuss this data during the workshop.

The survey data found the participating teachers felt themselves to be more effective after the experience and that they had implemented "subtle but powerful" changes in their teaching styles and use of instructional strategies. In order to promote teacher efficacy at your school you must listen to your teachers and model high levels of efficacy.

Discussion Questions:

1. How can you help the career status teachers develop a sense of efficacy?

2. How can you lead in ways that promote mastery experiences for your beginning teaches?

3. You believe that teachers within your school can make a difference. How can you develop a sense of efficacy for the entire school?

Scenario 5:

Empowerment

You are the principal of a new school who is using the concept of empowerment for the school's vision. You have been told by the district elementary coordinator that you must design a model to improve learning and student performance at your school. You must first determine your schools specific needs. In order to determine these needs the elementary coordinator has developed a panel of teachers who will meet with you twice a month.

The school has been up and running for three months now and your panel has met regularly. During the monthly meetings, the team has realized that in order to promote empowerment the school must demonstrate engagement and autonomy. The team believes that the school should undertake a united effort to meet achievement standards and prepare students to participate in democracy. If the school demonstrates autonomy the team believes that effective programs can be created. For example, administrators, teachers, support staff, students, parents, and community members will have a voice that is heard where decisions are more likely to be successful and to produce the best education for children.

You and the panel of teachers share the vision of empowerment at the next staff meeting. The discussion begins with how empowerment can improve student achievement and the belief that critical decisions affecting instruction should be made at the school level by those most closely involved with the children. Several teachers stop the presentation to share their thoughts. Overall, the teachers do not want more added to their plate. You and the panel of teachers try to calm them down but that does not work. After 45 minutes of discussion the staff realizes that their involvement is crucial and the administration team will support them during this process.

Directly involving teachers, in particular, in making the critical decisions that affect the success of their students in the classroom energizes not only teachers but also students, parents, and the business community to make a commitment to the school. Empowerment provides an opportunity for schools to benefit from the expertise available in the corporate world and for businesses to customize their involvement in the process of public education.

Discussion Questions:

1. What type of assessments can you create or use to improve empowerment at your school?

2. How can you make fast decisions concerning what is best for your students?

3. How can you devote more time to your teachers in order to create empowerment?

Scenario 6:

Leadership through Cultural Development

School culture topics have been very hot throughout your school's district this year. Several administrators have created numerous training sessions on cultural leadership at the last two principal meetings. Your school's goal is to promote leadership through cultural development. You believe that the school's inextricably linked to classroom culture. With this in mind, you begin assessing your existing culture.

Through your assessments you find collaborative and collegial relationships between staff members. People share ideas, problems and solutions in order to build a better school. As a principal you want to start shaping culture through your interactions. You begin to spend time touring the school, talking with parents during morning duty, and inviting community members to PTO in order to communicate the school's values. When you interact with staff members or students you reinforce the culture. When you step into classrooms, you discuss student learning, and curriculum and instruction. Your goal is to make every interaction involve reinforcing the core values of the school.

It's critically important to be able to understand the school culture and shape it in everything that you do.

Discussion Questions:

1. How can you create more professional development and staff reflection to promote leadership through cultural development?

2. How can you develop emerging leaders within your school?

3. How could this principal improve cultural leadership during classroom observations?

Section II: 21st Century Skills

Chapter 12

Who are the Teachers in the 21st Century?

The Takeaways in this chapter begin to define the teachers of the 21st century. They are no longer the "sage on the stage" but a "guide by the side" who orchestrate student learning in a technology rich environment. Teachers adapt, communicate, learn, create vision, lead, model, collaborate, and take risks. They are no longer dispensers of knowledge who spend their day in front of a classroom of students sitting in rows and in single desks as the baby boomers did. Generation X (also known as the 13th Generation and the Baby Busters) is the generation generally defined as those born after the baby boom ended. The term generally includes people born during all or part of the 1960s: According to Strauss-Howe generational theory, 1961 is the starting point, though other sources, including the U.S. Census Bureau, consider it to have started in the mid-1960s. It ends in late 1970s to early 1980s, usually not later than 1981 or 1982. The term has also been used in different times and places for a number of different subcultures or countercultures since the 1950s. Descriptions of the generations help teachers understand themselves and their students.

Generation Y, the Millennial Generation (or Millennials), Generation Next, Net Generation, Echo Boomers, describes the generation following Generation X. As there are no precise dates for when the Millennial generation starts and ends, commentators have used birth dates ranging somewhere from the mid-1970s to the early 2000s (decade). Experts differ on the start date of Generation Y. William Strauss and Neil Howe use the start year as 1982, and end years around the turn of the millennium, while others use start years that are earlier or later than 1982, and end years that in the mid to 1993.

One segment of this age-group has often been called the "eighties babies" generation, in reference to the fact that they were born between January 1, 1980 and December 31, 1989.

Generation Z, also known as Generation I, or Internet Generation, and Generation Text, and the "Digital Natives" by Marc Prensky and is the following generation. The earliest birth is generally dated in the early 1990s.

Scenario 1:

Background:

Study the characteristics of the 21st century teacher found in Chapter 14 of the text, **Rethink, Rebuild, Rebound**. Work with a group of peers (PLC, grade/subject level team or other group) to identify the characteristics of the 21st century teacher. Use the chart in chapter 14 as a springboard. Google the Khan Academy and watch Salman Khan a thttp://www.khanacademy.org/video/salman-khan-talk-at-ted-2011--from-ted-com?playlist=Khan+Academy-Related+Talks+and+Interviews.

Response:

In your group, choose one of the following activities to demonstrate your findings:

- Each group member will take a phone shot/video of innovative teaching taking place in the school. By using a selected technological presentation tool found at technologies 2.0, develop a presentation on your group's collective understanding of a 21st century teacher. Be sure you are able to support your presentation with researched facts.
- The group will work with a small group of students in your school/classroom to develop a student's view of a 21st century teacher. With permission from administration, ask students to take phone shots/camera shots/video of teaching scenarios they consider 21st century. (Students should get permission from the teacher to take shots before doing so.) Work with students to develop a Museum Box or Spicynodes presentation to bring back to the group. Ask students to use researched data in their presentation.
- In your group develop a poem, rap, song, or other performance presentation to demonstrate/inform your group about 21st century teaching.

Reflections:

1. Think about the results of your group's activity and make a list of 21st century strategies you see in your school.

2. Beside each item on your list answer the question "why?" Why is this a 21st century skill?

3. If you only have a few 21st century strategies being used, determine how you can begin to focus on more powerful teaching using 21st century tools and strategies.

Chapter 13

Who are the 21st Century Learners and What is the Teaching-Learning Environment?

Generation AO, the Always-On Generation (or Gen AO), was first used by Elon University professor Janna Quitney Anderson in 2012 to describe people born between the early 2000s and the 2020s whose lives have been influenced since their early childhood by connectivity afforded by easy access to people and the world's knowledge through the Internet. A survey of 1,000 experts she and Lee Rainie conducted for the Pew Research Center Internet & American Life Project found that the generation brought up from childhood with a continuous connection to each other and to information will be nimble, quick-acting multi-taskers who count on the Internet as their external brain; the experts also predicted Gen AO will exhibit a thirst for instant gratification and quick fixes, a loss of patience and a lack of deep-thinking ability.

Scenario 1:

Background:

Reread page 137 in the text to get a reminder of the responsibility of educators in America's classrooms today.

Response:

With your group, work together as a team to complete one of the following activities:

- You have been given the responsibility to design a new classroom/school for the 21st century. Using research, words, visuals, and design, create a picture of the 21st century classroom or school environment. Your design should reflect your thoughts and dreams regarding the possibilities for learning environments.
- Reread the top of page 136 in the text. It is easy to see the importance of technology in the lives of students. Yet, we persist in not allowing cell phones in classrooms and in blocking YouTube in schools. As teacher leaders in your group, design a classroom that is technologically updated for use with student learners in the 21st century. Create a visual presentation to display the technologies your group would use with explanations of how they would be used and why you chose them. Be sure to demonstrate how they can act as resources in the teaching/learning process.

- The 21st century environment describes the teacher as coach and facilitator. How does that description change the idea of a "model teacher" of the 1980's? Develop a visual/graphic organizer that explains how a 21st century teacher's responsibilities in coaching and facilitating would work.

Reflections:

1. What are the major environmental changes you would make in the current teaching/learning process? Why?

2. How has this activity created a new mind map for you in the teaching/learning process for your students?

3. What do you need to change to promote a 21st century environment for students and for yourself?

Chapter 14

Critical Attributes of 21st Century Learning

Teachers and students teach and learn differently than former generations. New teachers will be constantly connected and yearn for connectivity in the classroom for themselves and their students. The learning environment must be prepared for them. Students must work together collaboratively as their teachers are required to do.

Scenario 1:

Background:

Review the two Critical Attributes designs (see below & also in Appendices H & I) with this activity.

Response:

Define each attribute in relation to use in your school. The definition of each attribute should be as your school identifies it. Then research the attribute and discover if your meaning was accurate according to 21st Century Learning. Bring back to the PLC or other team and discuss your findings. Assign the following activities to team members to study and bring back a report that will enhance teacher/student understanding of the critical attributes:

1. Discuss and demonstrate multi-media presentation tools other than Power Point. Invite an outside resource (Instructional Technologist) to demonstrate new technologies and strategies for teaching (Web 2.0). Choose a technology application that will enhance student learning and discuss/present it to your study group. Help them see and understand the teaching and learning in the year 2030. (technologies and multi-media)

2. Go to http://www.nationalgeographic.com/xpeditions/lessons/10/g35/ and look at the sample K-12 lesson plans on Globalization. Use the plan to integrate globalization issues into social studies or another subject. Develop a plan for each level at your school and share it with others. (Globalization)

3. Go to http://www.edzone.net/~mwestern/ATA/lessons.html and review the simple plan to integrate subjects into all courses. This site is one of many that can be

found on the internet. Use this valuable tool to discern integrated units for your school/classroom. Make specific plans to integrate subjects in your classroom, especially areas of the curriculum that are hard for students to understand.

4. Project-based learning is a clear way to insure student learning in the 21st century. Students are required to work in teams and solve problems. How does your classroom handle this today? Do students work in teams on problems? What are the challenges to this process? How do you meet the challenges as a professional educator? If you study this website http://www.edutopia.org/project-based-learning-introduction-video and watch the Edutopia videos, you will clearly see the benefits of project-based learning. What do you think? Where would you start?

5. Ecoliteracy is a term educators are using in 21st century learning to define how students can learn to protect the environment. By beginning with the student in this century, changes can be made in current and future practices that will affect the balance of nature on the planet. A website that offers interesting teaching and learning projects is http://www.ecoliteracy.org/teach. Go to the website and read philosophical grounding. In your PLC or team, list the pros and cons of this approach. Why do we need to include this concept in our literacy foundation? (Refer to Multiple Literacies for the 21st Century that follows and also included in Appendix I)

Reflections:

1. Study the multiple literacies chart and describe how you are working to implement your choice in your classroom.

2. Describe a project-based learning activity that you can design with your PLC. What will the critical factors be?

3. How will you integrate 21st century technologies in your teaching/learning process? What are the challenges?

Critical Attributes of 21st Century Education

Technologies & Multimedia

Globalization
Global Classrooms

Student-Centered

21st Century Skills

Relevant, Rigorous and Real World

Integrated and Interdisciplinary

Multiple Literacies for the 21st Century

The Arts and Creativity

Financial Literacy
Project Based &
Research-Driven

Ecoliteracy

Media Literacy

Cyberliteracy

Social/Emotional Literacies

Physical Fitness and Health Literacies

Globalization & Multicultural Literacy

Chapter 15

How Do We Teach?

A critical part of this chapter is on lesson planning. Weekly planning with peers of the same subject or grade level offers a boost to lesson development. Assigning responsibilities for planning offers assistance and provides collaboration. This is not easy because all teachers have their favorite way to teach and/or strategies that they use. It becomes important to work together and secure the best ideas of all teachers and share them with each other. In this test driven environment, teachers become suspicious of using another's strategies. Trusting and learning from peers becomes a critical part of the teaching/learning process. As peers, teachers have much to learn from each other. Try out the following activity to see if it can strengthen your plans.

Scenario 1:

Background:

One of the easiest and best ways to check your teaching is through peer observations. You and another teacher can work together to determine what and how you need to teach youngsters and volunteer to observe lessons in each other's room to determine effectiveness. This takes a trusting and professional relationship in order for the students to benefit.

Response:

During a two week period, conduct peer observations with a partner. Establish a time to meet with the partner and outline your lesson. What strategies are you using that you would like your partner to observe you teaching. Outline your lesson for your peer observer and ask him/her to observe you for 30-45 minutes and note what you are actually doing at a minimum of every 3-5 minutes. Be clear with your partner on strategies you are trying to utilize or improve. Perhaps you are going to use Bloom's Revised Taxonomy in your questioning or you are going to use collaborative work groups for the first time. Working with a peer and then swapping roles can provide informed feedback and improve teaching and student learning. Develop a sheet for observation in order to be sure your observation focuses on the strategy you want observed.

Reflections:

1. What did you learn from the peer observations?

2. What would make your observations better?

3. How did the observations affect your teaching/learning?

Chapter 16

Are Students Learning?

Using Rick Stiggins' thoughts about students on a winning streak and students on a losing streak, how do you as a professional visualize the students in your classroom? School? Knowing and understanding student perceptions (dispositions) about themselves contributes to the teaching/learning process in the classroom. The second session of the chapter touches on assessment, in particular, grading. Teachers must ensure mastery learning and help students by consistently using assessment for learning. By developing rubrics for grading the 21st century teacher prepares students for the specific work to be done. Rubrics allow students to know and understand expectations for learning within the educational environment.

Scenario 1:

Background:

How do we instill self-efficacy and motivation in our students? Rick Stiggins gives us a chart on pp. 174–177 in the text that helps us better see how our students stay on winning streaks or losing streaks. Take your class roll and take each student through the Stiggins model on pp. 174–176 in the text.

Response:

1. List your students as ones on a winning streak or a losing streak. What can you do to differentiate instruction and provide opportunities for the students to be winners? List one specific way you can make a difference with each student. Share with your PLC or teaching group.

2. Study rubric development at http://www.uwstout.edu/soe/profdev/rubrics.cfm. Decide on a rubric you need to make for a classroom activity or project. As you design this rubric for your task, be certain the sections are graduated and each one holds specific, understandable information/tasks that students understand. Ask you peers to review and give you feedback on your work. Try the rubric with your class.

Reflections:

1. What have you learned about your students that may lead you to help them become winners?

2. What are a few things you can do for all students in your classroom to keep them on a winning streak?

3. How can rubrics improve student understanding and assist you with your grading process?

Chapter 17

Section II Master Scenario: School Planning for the 21st Century

In order to prepare yourself and your students for the 21st century, you must consider the status of your school in the preparation process. You will need to know who is prepared for the 21st century. You know or suspect that your school needs support in this effort. Where do you start? How do you establish needs? You have reviewed the test scores and you have some areas of concern. It appears that one subject area (mathematics) is weaker in fifth and sixth grades. Teachers have complaints about the lack of learning motivation by students. Parents are not sure all teachers are teaching for learning. As a leader in the school, where do you begin? How can you determine your school's readiness for the 21st century? We have found an excellent resource to help you determine the status of your school. Follow the next steps to determine the needs of your school in the following areas:

Student Knowledge and Skills to include the following:

Core Subjects

21st Century Themes

Learning and Information Skills

Information, Media and Technology Skills

Life and Career Skills

Education and Support Systems to include the following:

Curricula

Instruction

Assessment

Learning Environments

Professional Development

Education Leadership to include the following:

Administrators and Teachers Leaders

Educators

Policymaking to include the following:

Policymakers

Parents to include the following:

Access to Student Information

Participation in school-based planning

Partnering to include the following:

Business

Community

Higher Education

Vendors

Continuous Improvement to include the following:

State/District/School

  Developed a consensus around a vision and goals for student mastery

  District documents reflect 21st century practices

Go on line and read The MILE GUIDE as a professional learning community (PLC) activity at http://www.p21.org/documents/MILE_Guide_091101.pdf

Also review how to use the MILE GUIDE found at http://science.nsta.org/enewsletter/2004-06/P21_MILE_Guide.pdf

Use the following questions to stimulate discussion in your PLC:

A. *How do we know the implications of Core subjects? What are the Core subjects? How do we access them?*
B. *Describe the learning skills we instill in our students. Are there learning skills/strategies that we know work with our students?*
C. *Do we use 21st Century tools to develop learning skills? What are the 21st Century Skills we use?*
D. *How do we teach and learn in a 21st Century context? Describe the student learning environment at your school.*
E. *Are we teaching 21st Century content to the students? What is 21st Century content?*
F. *Discuss 21st Century Assessments that measure Core subjects and 21st Century Skills. List assessments used in your school/classroom. How do they assess for learning?*

Review the Mile Guide Quiz self assessment tool found at http://www.p21.org/mileguide/

Take the MILE Assessment in your school.

Go to the section in the MILE Guide that starts with *Using the MILE Guide*.

Follow the steps:

- *Use* the self-assessment results to generate a shared vision for future progress.
- *Develop* a comprehensive, aligned plan of action.
- *Implement* your plan. The plan can also add information to other plans your district might require of you. Make sure the MILE Guide aligns with other planning required of your school/district.
- *Institute* a cyclical review of the MILE Guide self-assessment process to track progress and revise your strategic plan as needed.
- *Communicate* progress to all participants and stakeholders.

Use this information to lead your school to 21st century teaching and learning. Students will be the winners!

Section III: Education Reforms

Chapter 18

Needs Assessment

Fundamental to reforming any institution is the need to assess current strengths and areas for growth. This assessment would include identifying vulnerabilities, barriers to achieving excellence and capabilities to execute on a recovery/reform plan. A needs assessment is simply a systematic process of gaining pertinent information. It involves, generally, a comprehensive review of a department, location or an entire organization. Oftentimes, it starts with completing an inventory of operations and assessing the value and the level of performance of each element (i.e., process, policy, program and people). This can take the form of a survey (refer to Exhibit 1 below which is an extract from an online version) or a checklist. There exist several high quality survey tools that can be employed to meet one's needs without having to re-invent one for your use. A sample of an inventory review and needs assessment checklist can be found in Appendix J. These are tailored to the type of institution being assessed (e.g., schools, businesses, hospitals, not-for-profit agencies, etc.)

Needs assessments can run the gamut from a formal, all-encompassing initiative to one that is focused on a narrow area with informal and limited data collection. Depending upon the criticality of the matter the scope and extensiveness will vary. In this workbook, we will focus on a broad/comprehensive approach to a needs assessment. For implementation purposes, it is easier to begin by focusing on a more extensive approach to a needs assessment and scaling back than the reverse.

Needs Assessment Survey

Key Attibutes	Strongly Disagree	Disagree	Neutral	Agree	Strongly Agree
1. The school has goals that support the district vision.					
2. The school has adequate resources to achieve its goal.					

3. School leaders are flexible in dealing with change and are willing to experiment.					
4. School leaders practice and promote equity and excellence for all staff and students					
5. School leaders model the behaviors expected of staff and students.					
6. School leaders cultivate community support for the school and its vision.					
7. Every student is expected to achieve at a high level.					

Exhibit 1: Characteristics of a Successful Schools survey. The entire survey can be found at http://dpi.wi.gov/sig/improvement/surveyguide.html.

There are a number of sequential steps in completing a needs assessment. They are

1. **Identify and clarify the purpose of the needs assessment and what/who is the target area.** This includes asking questions such as what do you know, why are you doing the needs assessment, what will you do with the information, what will you be measuring and how will you measure it, who will be responsible for each of the steps in the process?

2. **Decide how the needs assessment will be conducted.**

3. **Decide on what needs assessment tool you will use to gather information (take inventory).**

4. **Gather the data/take the inventory.**

5. **Analyze & prioritize the data.**

6. **Implement a plan of action based on the results.** Identify short and long term goals and initiatives, allocate resources, set timelines including key milestones, and appoint leaders who are responsible for each initiative.

These steps could take the form of a checklist. Skipping any step in this process will increase the risk and potentially jeopardize success.

Using the results of the inventory (survey and/or checklist), a level of importance (LOI) is placed on each item. The LOI is a rating that is tied directly to the organization's goals and objectives (which should be a reflection of its mission). The LOI rating can be numeric (1 to 5) or a descriptor such as high, medium or low. The purpose is to help evaluate the significance of each of the inventoried items in your needs assessment in order to maximize the utilization of resources. The exhibit below depicts, for illustrative purposes, a needs assessment summary template (blank form can be found in Appendix K);

Needs Assessment Summary

Identified Needs	School Improvement Plan Linkage	Impact on Goals (H,M,L)	Overall LOI (1-5 highest)
After school tutoring program	Section 1, Goal 1: Student Achievement	High	5
Expand representation of School Improvement Team	Section 4, Goal 2: School Improvement Team	Medium	4
Secure add'l copier	Section 2, Goal1: Efficiency	Low/medium	2

Exhibit 2: Illustrative Needs Assessment Summary template

In the authors' textbook, **Rethink, Rebuild, Rebound: A Framework for Shared Responsibility and Accountability in Education**, more information on this topic can be found in Sections II, III, and IV to supplement the key points outlined in this chapter.

Let's put to work what we have learned. Using information from the authors' text and this chapter and forms from the Appendix (or forms you have used in the past) prepare responses to the scenarios below some of which are subsets of a more comprehensive needs assessment.

Scenario 1:

Background:

You have recently been appointed to be the principal of an elementary school in your district. Prior to this assignment you were a teacher in a neighboring elementary school and had been there for several years. Even though this was your 1st administrative position you had been lead teacher in your former school and a member of its school improvement team.

The school you will be leading has a reputation for academic excellence and has exceeded its student achievement goals for the past few years. The school district has reassigned 100 students from another school (not your former one) to your school which will represent a 15% increase in student enrollment. You will be allotted 4 new teachers. You have had a meeting during the summer with your school improvement team and they have listed a number of requests for your consideration.

Response:

1. What actions will you take and explain why?

2. What are the benefits of doing a Needs Assessment as soon as possible?

3. What are the risks and/or drawbacks, if any? Explain.

4. What will be the barriers to instituting a Needs Assessment? Explain

5. Prepare a Needs Assessment Inventory Survey (using the Needs Assessment Checklist form in Appendix J) and base the survey on your **real** experience/assessment in the school you are currently at.

6. Prepare a Needs Assessment Summary (blank form in Appendix K) using the survey information from the previous response.

Scenario 2:

Background:

You have been appointed to be Exceptional Children's (EC) Director for the district. There are a number of requests for additional resources as well as concerns regarding the inability of some of the schools to meet the growing needs of the EC program.

Response:

1. What steps will you take? Explain.

2. How would a Needs Assessment benefit the program? Please be specific.

3. Assuming you have decided to do a Needs Assessment, list 10 key attributes you would include in your Needs Assessment survey. Explain why you chose these ten.

Scenario 3:

Background:

You are an education consultant. You have been called in by a local school board to assess what needs to be done to meet the challenges facing its school system. The superintendent has recently retired.

Response:

1. What will be your initial actions/steps? Explain.

Reflection:

1. What is the value of a needs assessment?

2. In your opinion, how often should one be done?

3. Have you participated in one? If so, how did you feel about the process and were you satisfied with the outcome?

4   What have you learned from these exercises and how will you apply the learning in your school?

Chapter 19

Prioritization

With the needs assessment completed now we turn our attention to prioritizing those needs given that we operate in an environment of limited resources (i.e., time, money and personnel). There are several approaches to employ in rank ordering your needs list. You can do it according to how much time it will take to satisfy the need i.e., those that can be satisfied in a short period of time are ranked higher than the longer term needs' solutions. You can do the ranking by identifying the most critical needs first regardless of time, resources required or benefit. The approach we will use it this workbook will be the benefit/cost analysis. Those needs which produce the highest benefit/cost ratio (i.e., more return on the dollar) will be ranked at the top. This will require a calculation of how much benefit will be attained and at what cost. This exercise is not meant to be an exact science but a good faith effort to quantify the benefits (e.g., cost/process improvements through efficiency measures, cost avoidance, increased revenues/funding, etc). That said, there will probably be benefits that will be difficult to quantify such as improved employee morale (the key here is to try to minimize these by making an earnest effort to place a value on as many benefits as possible). It is important to capture those and incorporate them into the overall evaluation. On the cost side of the ratio, you will need to identify all actions necessary to satisfy the need. Some examples might be additional personnel, more equipment, training expense, additional supplies, etc. Each carries a price tag which needs to be quantified. Again, there might be costs that do not lend themselves to quantification. A good faith effort to minimize those and list them as part of your analysis is essential. Finally, the element of risk must be addressed. What is the risk involved in implementing a change to address/satisfy the need? Simply assessing the likely risk and placing a numeric indicator (1 to 3, 3 being the highest risk) next to the benefit/cost ratio for that particular need will enable the decision- maker(s) to project the probability of success. There are a number of forms one can use in preparing a benefit/cost analysis. We have included in Appendix L a simple, straight-forward one for your use. The purpose here is not to make this a high level math or finance exercise but an attempt to capture and quantify the key determinates in satisfying the need.

Let's put to work what we have learned. Using information from the authors' text and this chapter along with the forms from the Appendix (or forms you have used in the past) prepare responses to the scenarios below some of which are subsets of a more comprehensive needs assessment.

Scenario 1:

Background:

As the principal of a local elementary school you have completed your needs assessment and are prepared to prioritize the needs using the benefit/cost approach outlined above. In a call from the superintendent this morning, you have been asked to present your prioritized needs assessment to the Board of Education next week.

Response:

1. Using the needs assessment from Chapter _18_ above (Scenario 1, responses to questions 5 & 6) and the benefit/cost analysis form in Appendix L develop a prioritize needs assessment you will present to the Board.

2. What will be the key points you will make in your presentation with respect to the approach you used in prioritizing the school's needs?

   _____
   _____
   _____
   _____
   _____
   _____
   _____
   _____
   _____
   _____

3. What are the advantages of using a benefit/cost analysis approach to prioritizing needs?

   _____
   _____
   _____
   _____
   _____

4. What, if any, drawbacks do you see to this approach?

_____
_____
_____
_____
_____

Reflection:

1. What is the value of prioritizing the needs assessment?

_____
_____
_____
_____
_____
_____
_____
_____

2. How does the benefit/cost analysis approach help in making decisions on where to spend your precious resources?

_____
_____
_____
_____
_____
_____
_____
_____

3. How would you answer the question, "why not just vote on what to do first, second, third, etc."?

_____
_____
_____
_____
_____

4. What has been your experience in prioritizing a list of needs?

_____
_____
_____
_____
_____
_____
_____
_____

Chapter 20

Implementation Approaches…..Excellence in Execution

As postulated in our book, <u>Rethink, Rebuild, Rebound: A Framework for Shared Responsibility and Accountability in Education</u>, excellence in execution is the bridge that connects planning to achieving desired results. We will look at several steps (components) in what constitutes best practices as it relates to developing an implementation plan. It must be stated that **communications** is critical to the success of any implementation plan. It is the "glue" that holds together the plan. That said, the steps to follow in preparing an implementation plan are:

1. **Prepare** the organization. Identify and communicate to those affected (& the key constituencies) the what, when, why, who and how. Understanding the need for the project (change), the expected results, the timeline and how processes/procedures will be affected is essential.

2. **Coordinate** with other organizations that will be affected (e.g., working with the transportation department on changing your school's start and ending times).

3. **Develop** and deliver training to all affected personnel. Depending on the nature and size of the "to be implemented" project, the training could be delivered in multiple sessions leading up to the "cutover".

4. **Implement** the "solution(s)". Again, if the solution is a complex, comprehensive change to current procedures/processes or adding a new process(es)/procedure(s) than it may be appropriate and prudent to appoint a project/implementation leader. Oftentimes, if more than 1 process is involved and the project will take more than a few days to implement a project leader is warranted.

5. **Update** data systems/metrics (if appropriate).

6. **Perform** final verification (go/no go) decision based on the organization's readiness.

7. **Implement** "solution(s)".

8. **Monitor** implementation. This is the quality assurance step. There are 5 components that comprise this activity. They are 1) measure performance, 2) compare to project expectations, 3) analyze root causes of variance from expectations,

4) Determine course correction(s), and 5) document and communicate changes to all those affected by the project.

Mindful of these steps, let's put in practice what we have learned. Below are scenarios that will draw upon your experiences and the knowledge you have acquired. Using the textbook (Rethink, Rebuild, Rebound) and the information in this workbook prepare your responses to each scenario.

Scenario 1:

Background:

You are and have been the principal of a local elementary for the past 3 years. Your school has struggled academically in recent years. Your school's performance in terms of student proficiency has declined significantly in each of the past 4 years. You have completed a needs assessment and have prioritized those needs. The analysis has identified that your greatest need is to improve literacy. You have commissioned a team comprised of several of your teachers along with representation from the Central Office and a representative from another school in your district that has produced outstanding results in this area for a number of years. The team has recommended you adopt a new approach to teaching reading in the early grades. The new program is significant change from what the school is currently doing. You are supportive of the recommendation and believe if implemented properly it will produce the results you and your faculty are seeking. However, you are concerned given that your faculty is very experienced (average teaching experience is 10 years and the majority of the faculty has been at the school for 8 years) that the change will be very disruptive and not well received.

Response:

1. Prepare an outline of an implementation plan by addressing how you would approach the key steps outlined above.

2. With respect to communications, describe below what actions you would take to introduce the team's recommendation to your entire faculty and what actions would you take to address your concern regarding acceptance of change.

_____
_____
_____
_____
_____

3. One of your teachers approached you after your faculty meeting where the recommendations were reviewed and said, "why do we have to change what we are doing now, it will only make for a chaotic situation and our students will suffer?" How would you respond?

Reflection:

1. What skills does one need to be an implementation leader?

2. What has been your experience in adopting change?

3. Based on your personal experiences and observing others, what are the greatest barriers to making change?

4. What strategies can a principal/leader employ to overcome these barriers?

Chapter 21

Quality Assurance….Results/Expectations Attainment

Quality assurance (QA) is the process of verifying or determining whether the program implemented meets or exceeds the expectations/objectives that were established. Quality assurance is a process-driven approach with specific steps to help define and attain goals. This process considers design, development, implementation, and assessment.

There are many tools in use today throughout industry and government that provide quality assurance. One of the more famous tools used to determine quality assurance was developed by Dr. W. Edwards Deming. It is represented by a cycle and consists of four steps: *Plan, Do, Check,* and *Act* (or PDCA).

The four quality assurance steps within the PDCA model stand for:

- **Plan:** Establish objectives and processes required to deliver the desired results.
- **Do:** Implement the process developed.
- **Check:** Monitor and evaluate the implemented process by testing the results against the predetermined objectives
- **Act:** Apply actions necessary for improvement if the results require changes. Repeat the cycle.

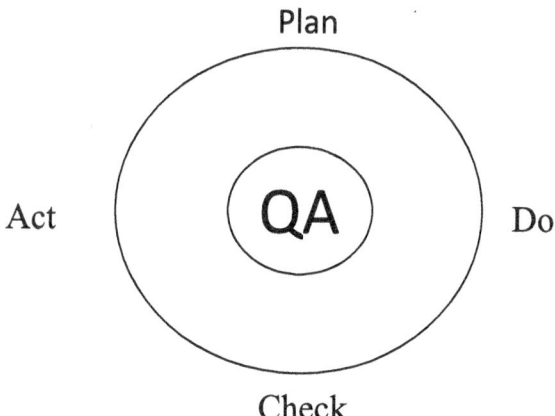

Exhibit 3: PDCA Continuous Cycle

PDCA is an effective method for monitoring quality assurance because it analyzes existing conditions and methods used to assure objectives/expectations are met and, if not, what adjustments need to be made. The goal is to ensure that excellence is inherent in every component of the process. Quality assurance also helps determine whether the steps used to meet the program objectives are appropriate for the time and conditions. In addition, if the PDCA cycle is repeated throughout the lifetime of the project/program, it helps improve internal organizational (e.g., school) efficiency.

Let's look at each step in the cycle in more detail.

Planning involves developing objectives based on the needs of the organization. A needs assessment provides input to the planning process. Plans should be specific, realistic, resourced and time-bound. Organizations generally have both a near term (up to 12 months) and a longer term (12 months & longer) set of plans. The objectives which drive the plans should be specific, measurable, achievable, realistic and timely.

Doing is the implementation of the plan. As noted in the previous chapter it is comprised of 8 steps from preparing the organization to monitoring the implementation. Continuous communication to all stakeholders is vital to the success of the execution of the program/project. Not to suggest it isn't important in the other 3 steps but to emphasize the criticality of maintaining "alignment" as project tasks are being performed and completed.

Checking is the process of comparing what you planned to do versus what you did. It is the equivalent of the measuring stick. Did we accomplish what we set out to do? The comparative analysis is both a qualitative and quantitative exercise. It results in identifying the variances.

Acting is the process of developing and implementing actions to close the variances identified in the Checking step. These actions must be specific and timely. Depending on the complexity of the "fixes" the actions may be first tested (piloted) prior to full scale implementation.

This is a cycle so the entire process (PDCA) is repeated over and over again.

More information on PDCA can be found in the text, **Rethink, Rebuild, Rebound: A Framework for Shared Responsibility and Accountability in Education.**

Now, let's apply what we have learned here as well as draw on our own experiences to respond to the scenario on the next page.

Scenario 1:

Background:

You are principal of a middle school and have developed a plan with your faculty to implement a new student behavioral management program. The faculty fully endorses it and is enthusiastic about the prospects of its success. However, the parents while informed and knowledgeable about the program are concerned about the mixed results it has produced in other districts. You are convinced that it was implementation issues in those schools that did not experience success with the program. You will be the 1st school in your district to implement this program and your superintendent views it as a pilot initiative.

Response:

1. Identify below the key aspects of a quality assurance plan using the PDCA model.

2. In which step(s) in PDCA will you address the parents concern with respect to mixed results in other districts and your belief it was due to implementation issues? How will you assure the parents, using the PDCA model approach, that this initiative will be different and will produce desired results?

Reflection:

1. Have you used a quality assurance model before? If so, which one was it and what was your experience?

2. What is your impression of the PDCA model? What do you see as the key advantages/benefits of the model?

3. How and where could you use it in your current assignment?

In concluding Section III on Education Reform we hope this section provides you, along with the companion text, an approach for your consideration in instituting reform from start to finish. There are no silver bullets/easy solutions only "heavy lifting". However, reform is at the heart of continuous improvement and is the antidote for sustained mediocre or poor performance whether that be in industry, education or any other segment of our society. It provides the foundation for developing and sustaining high performance organizations.

In wrapping up this section, below is a scenario which encapsulates the key messages/learning from these chapters. Let's role play.

Chapter 22

Section III Master Scenario

Background:

You have been appointed principal of a new high school which will open in September. Given that it is February, you have approximately 7 months to develop and execute a plan ensuring a smooth opening of the school. There are 2 other high schools in your district and the new school will start with 9th, 10th and 11th graders in its 1st year. Construction is well underway however there is concern that it may not be fully operational by the start of the new school year in September.

Response:

1. Using your real experiences or hypothetical data develop a <u>prioritized</u> needs assessment (using the templates in the Appendix K), an implementation plan and the PDCA quality assurance approach that you will present to your superintendent and the school board.

2. Identify the key points of your presentation to your superintendent and the school board.

Reflection:

1. Can you spend too much time planning and, if so, what risks do you run in doing so?

_____
_____
_____

Section IV: Capstone Scenario

Chapter 23

Capstone Scenario

Indicators of learning

You have recently been appointed principal of a large urban high school with 150 staff members. Standardized test scores indicate good, but not great indicators of learning. As you begin to talk with staff members, you get the feeling that they are satisfied with current performance and this is reflected in state-wide working condition's survey data. You are charged as the leader to continue to make progress with respect to improved performance.

Response:

1. In priority order, what are your considerations as you begin this job?

2. Prepare a prioritized list of activities (based on your needs assessment) with possible timelines.

3. What are the theoretical contexts of the problem at hand especially compared to a low performing or struggling school?

4. Discuss potential organizational structures that may assist in shifting or improving collective efficacy.

5. What are the benefits and risks associated with your actions?

APPENDICES

APPENDIX A
Action Research Guide

Steps in Action Research

Phase II of the Value-Added model suggests a full action research project that may be completed by individuals or groups. This document contains the principles found in planning, conducting and reporting action research. It would prove beneficial to the process to share the findings of the action research. Degree of formal writing rests with the facilitator.

The Action Research Project

Introduction

By identifying a problem, designing a solution strategy that will result in positive change and analyzing the results, you will be taking an active leadership role in the improvement of a situation in your work setting. This guide is designed to lead you through the process in a step-by-step format to ensure your success in all phases of your research project.

Action Research Defined

Action research as defined by Sapp is "a practical experience in systematic problem solving designed to result in positive change" (1994). It differs somewhat from the traditional approach to research. Rather than focusing on issues and questions of a broad or theoretical nature, this method (also known as classroom inquiry or teacher research) requires the researcher to identify and document the existence of a problem in his/her own setting. Based on a scholarly review of current literature, the researcher must then propose and implement a plan to solve or improve the problem. Finally, the researcher develops a system to evaluate the effectiveness of his/her solution. Calhoun, Neal and D'Arcangelo (1994) suggest that action research is really a five-part process:

1. Select a focus (what is the problem?)

2. Collect data (how can you prove a problem exists and what does the literature say about the problem?)

3. Organize the data (what is the most effective method for presenting your findings?)

4. Analyze and interpret the data (what are some possible causes of the problem?)

5. Take action (what can be done to improve the problem?)

Troen and Boles (1996) encourage teacher researchers to "tackle issues you can do something about, limit the scope of your topic and choose a topic that is important to you and your students" (p. 20).

Writing the Problem Statement

Perhaps the most important step in the process is clearly stating the problem. Avoid beginning this process by developing research questions. Historically, students new to the research process have no idea why they should even be asking one. Some typical questions have been, "What have researchers found out about dyslexia?" or "Who are the most notable experts in the field of drug and alcohol awareness?" Too large in scope or irrelevant to their own setting, these questions often result in a frustrating, lengthy discussion between student and faculty.

Problems should also be more than a program evaluation. In action research, you should think critically about your own setting and write down 1–3 problems that you feel currently exist. A statement like, "It is not known what effect Silent Sustained Reading (SSR) has on students' test scores" does not necessarily mean a problem exists. After a study of this nature is conducted and results analyzed, the findings will be that the program has a positive effect, a negative effect or no effect at all. In this case, a student is merely wondering if a problem does exist. Results can be reported, but change is not necessarily made. *Action* is the key word in action research: what can be done to change the current situation? A better statement might be "Students who practice SSR for one hour a day exhibit low reading scores." If this problem can be documented, the student can then recommend an alternate plan which, if implemented, might improve the reading scores. This is the process schools and businesses currently engage in through school improvement teams or continuous improvement committees. Rarely do busy professionals take the time to study something that is not a documented problem. Herein lies the difference between action research and traditional research.

You should also choose a problem you have the ability to impact within the context of this study. For example, one student may feel his/her school building is too small to house the current student population; if his/her solution strategy involves the construction of a new school building, it is probably a problem that cannot be solved within the scope of his/her study. You should address problems which:

1. Directly impact your students, co-workers, or campus;

2. Can be improved within a realistic time frame (3–4 months); and

3. You, personally, have the ability to impact.

Solutions should not be mentioned in the problem statement:

1. Appropriate problem statement: Some students in bilingual classrooms are failing district-reading tests.

2. Inappropriate problem statement/solution mentioned: Pull-out programs are not meeting the needs of bilingual students.

In the second example, "pull-out programs" are really a statement about a solution strategy, effective or not. It may be a cause; it may be part of another solution. *The problem statement should address only the problem.* As a researcher, you should look only at observable, measurable conditions that actually document the existence of a problem.

The Planning Phase

Before you begin writing, you should think about the relationship of the various proposal components to one another. Developing a matrix or completing a fishbone-type analysis is critical. You will then have an idea of how the parts relate to one another, in order to design a solution (method) that directly addresses the causes. Clearly illustrate the fact that the problem is the opposite of the goal, the documented evidence is the opposite of the anticipated outcomes, and solutions directly address causes. For example, if some of the documented causes of low test scores are poor study habits, lack of parent involvement, or inferior teaching methods and a student proposes a new school lunch program as a solution, he/she has missed the point. By using a matrix format, you will easily understand the component relationships.

Chapter 1: Introduction

1. Problem statement

2. Purpose

3. Description of the community

4. Description of the work setting

5. Writer's role

Chapter II: Study of the Problem

1. Problem description
2. Problem documentation
3. Literature review
4. Causative analysis

Chapter III: Outcomes and Evaluation

1. Goals and expectations
2. Expected outcomes
3. Measurement of outcomes
4. Analysis of results

Chapter IV: Solution Strategy

1. Statement of problem
2. Discussion

Description of Selected Solutions

The outline must also include hard data that supports your problem and must include solution strategies gleaned from your literature review. You should review a significant number of sources prior to completing your outline, but you may add other sources as you proceed through the implementation and report phases of the project. To demonstrate your application of referencing as described in the *Publication Manual of the American Psychological Association (APA Guide)*, include a complete reference at the end of your outline. Include citations to the literature in the literature review sections of the outline. The next section in this guide provides specific information on what to include in each section of the outline/proposal. Remember that the outline is written in the third person, future tense. When your research advisor has critiqued and approved the outline, you will receive credit, and you may begin writing the research proposal.

Writing the Formal Proposal

Following is a summary of the Research Proposal: Chapters I, II, III, and IV.

Note: The proposal is written in the third person, future tense; it is a plan of action you intend to take. You should not mention specific people, schools, cities, states, etc.

Chapter I: Introduction

1. Problem Statement (subheading: 1–3 sentences)

    When writing the problem statement, be sure to satisfy the following requirements:

    a. The problem statement should begin with: "The problem is . . ."
    b. The problem statement should be clear.
    c. The problem(s) addressed should be more than program evaluation. In action research, you should think critically about your own setting and write down 1–3 problems that you feel currently exist. Action is the key word in action research: what can be done to change the current situation? If the problem can be documented, you can then recommend an alternate plan that, if implemented, might solve the problem.
    d. Select a problem(s) you have the ability to influence within the context of the study.
    e. Address problems that directly impact your students, co-workers, or campus and can be improved within a realistic time frame (3–6 months).
    f. Address problems you have the ability to personally influence.

2. Purpose (subheading: 1–2 paragraphs)

    This is a statement of what the student expects to accomplish and gives direction to the study. The section should begin, "The purpose of this study is . . ."

3. Description of the Community (subheading: 1–3 pages)

    In this section, you should "give the reader an understanding of your setting by describing geographic references, the community size, the socio-economic situation, and any other relevant information that places the work setting in context" (Sapp, 1994, p. 13).

4. Description of Work Setting (subheading: 1–3 pages)

    This section provides the reader with specific information about the actual setting in which the study will take place. Items of importance may include basic demographics, mission statements, faculty make-up, and any other factors unique to their environment.

5. Writer's Role (subheading: 1–2 pages)

In this section, describe your primary role in the setting, length of employment, additional responsibilities, membership on campus teams or committees, and any other relevant factors deemed important. In doing so, clearly document your ability to actually impact the problem (Sapp, 1994).

Chapter II: Study of the Problem

1. Problem Description (subheading: 1–2 pages)

Beginning with a restatement of the problem, go into greater detail in this section by specifically describing the problem in your setting, including "... difficulties being encountered, the population affected and the reasons why the problem has not been solved" (Sapp, 1994, p.15).

2. Problem Documentation (subheading: 2–4 pages)

In this section, you must clearly prove a problem actually exists. Too often, educators define problems evidenced by little more than "gut feelings" or "intuition." Research requires more concrete proof. Documentation may include test scores, grades, needs assessments, surveys, structured observation, and record/archive review. You are encouraged to present these findings using tables and figures (descriptive statistics) along with narrative explanations.

3. Literature Review (subheading: 8–12 pages)

A literature review should summarize all important research relevant to the problem, demonstrating a current understanding of the topic. Articles from professional publications should be within the last two to three years. In short, this section should be a synthesis of the bibliographic research, which specifically relates to the problem in your setting. Avoid discussing solutions in this section and pay more attention to the problem and purpose sections of the literature.

4. Causative Analysis (subheading: 2–4 pages)

In the final section of the chapter, analyze the documentation collected from your setting, as well as evidence gleaned from the literature, and then brainstorm all possible causes of the problem. There may be one or several. A complete description, including details specifically pinpointing the cause(s), is appropriate. It should be emphasized that, although you may finally propose a solution strategy which addresses only one or two of the causes, in this section all possible causes should be considered. In Chapter III, you will select an area you feel you have the greatest probability of influencing and formulate a solution strategy targeting one or two specific causes (Sapp, 1994).

Chapter III: Outcomes and Evaluation

1. Goals and Expectations (subheading: 1–2 paragraphs)

   This section should reflect the purpose of the study; it is, essentially, the opposite of your problem statement. In 1–2 paragraphs, describe what the situation will look like after a successful intervention plan has been implemented. The section should start out with a statement like "The goal of this study is . . ." It may be taken directly from the planning matrix and should not make reference to the solutions.

2. Expected Outcomes (subheading: 2–4 paragraphs)

   Present specific outcomes that include the change expected at the end of the implementation phase, stated in observable, measurable terms. Refer to the planning matrix. These outcomes should relate specifically to the documentation you provided that the problem exists in your setting. Number each outcome and present each in list form.

3. Measurement of Outcomes (subheading: 1–2 pages)

   Include a section that describes how you plan to measure each projected outcome. Be specific about particular instruments and methods you will use. This information is intended to aid another researcher interested in replicating your study. **Note: If you include copies of tests, questionnaires, or other instruments you did not create, be sure to include full bibliographic information. If you design your own instruments, they must be approved by your research advisor prior to implementation.**

4. Analysis of Results (subheading: 2–4 paragraphs)

   Describe your plan for analyzing results. How will you present your findings? Will you use particular statistical tests (this may include descriptive and/or inferential statistics), charts or graphs? How will you determine if your solution strategy was effective? If it was not, can you give reasons why? This section is your plan for analyzing results; you will revise this section with your actual results for the final report. You should answer questions like "How will I know if the implemented plan has impacted the problem? How will I present results to the reader?" (Sapp, 1994, p. 23).

Chapter IV: Solution Strategy

1. Statement of Problem (subheading: 1–3 sentences)

   Re-state the problem in 1–3 sentences.

2. Discussion (subheading: 3–5 pages)

   In Chapter II, you reviewed the literature for problems similar to the one in your setting. This section is also a review of the literature, specifically related to solutions or methods. In this chapter, you will include citations from the literature that specifically support the selection of your solution strategy.

3. Selected Solutions/Calendar Plan (subheading: 6–10 pages)

   This is a detailed description of the plan that you could implement in order to improve the problem in your current setting. It should be very specific and detailed so that another researcher could read this section and duplicate the method with few questions. (Compare this section to a recipe or cookbook plan.) For example, do not say, "Teachers will receive training on methods to modify assignments for diverse learners." Rather, give the reader specific information and training guidelines on how you will accomplish this, with step-by-step instructions to easily replicate the process. Include copies of specific material needed in an appendix. Remember, you cannot be too specific in this section.

   Include a week-by-week, operational calendar plan that could be used for the implementation phase, as well as specific directions on how each component could be implemented. Remember to tell the reader when to begin, who will be involved, at what points specific aspects of the solution should occur, how long various components of the plan should be applied and how often and when results should be evaluated. Present the plan as Month One, Week One, Week Two, etc. A plan must be written for each week on implementation; avoid phrases like "Repeat Week 4." (Sapp, 1994, p. 27).

Chapter V: Results

1. Results (subheading: 1–2 pages)

   Begin Chapter V with a brief re-statement of the problem and goal. Next, present your "anticipated" results, using the Expected Outcomes section of Chapter III as a guide. Present each outcome and state whether or not it was achieved. Remember, outcomes were either met or not; avoid saying, "This outcome was almost or nearly met." Use the following format for each outcome (Note: Results will be "fabricated" for students who have not actually conducted the implementation.)

   a. State the expected outcome
   b. State whether or not it was met
   c. Discuss the results, briefly

2. Discussion (subheading: 2–4 pages)

   After presenting the facts, discuss your analysis of the results in terms of your research. You may reference the literature here, as appropriate. If outcomes were not met, what might be some of the causes? If outcomes were met, what are the implications? Discuss any unanticipated events that could have occurred, as well. Conclude with a summary.

3. Recommendations (subheading: 1–2 pages)

   What recommendations do you have for other researchers interested in replicating your study? What recommendations do you have for use of your solutions in your setting? Number your recommendations, providing a brief rationale for each.

4. Plans for Dissemination (2–4 paragraphs)

   Describe your plan for disseminating the results of your study. Could you present your findings to a parent group, the school board, or your faculty? If you did implement the study, could you try to publish your research in a professional magazine or journal? If so, which one?

Other Parts of the Final Report

1. Title, Title Page and Table of Contents:

2. Abstract: An abstract must be included in the final report. It should be a single-spaced, single-page summary of your action research project. Include three

paragraphs: the problem addressed, along with the major goals; the solution strategy applied; and a brief summary of results. Note the required format and use of descriptors.

3. Appendices: Forms, questionnaires, assessment instruments, and similar original documents should be appended to the report rather than included as part of the text. Every appendix must be referred to in the body of the report. Title each appendix, assign it a letter, and continue sequential pagination.

References

American Psychological Association. (2001). *Publication manual of the American psychological association* (5th ed.). Washington, DC: Author.

Creswell, J. W. (2005). *Educational research: Planning, conducting, and evaluating quantitative and qualitative research* (2nd ed.). Upper Saddle River, NJ: Pearson.

McMillan, J. H., & Schumacher, S. (2006). *Research in education: Evidence-based inquiry* (6th ed.). Boston: Pearson.

Sapp, M. (1994). *Practicum guide for the problem-solving experience.* Ft. Lauderdale, FL: Nova Southeastern University.

Troen, V. and Boles, K. (1996, August). Teachers, take charge! *Creative classroom,* (pp.20–29).

APPENDIX B
Benefits of Action Research

Benefits of Action Research

1) Leads to best practices in the work environment

2) Justifies one's actions

3) Promotes interventions for a problematic situation

4) Leads to continual improvements

5) Fosters reflective practice

6) Generates further research

7) Brings merit to a profession

8) Fosters collaboration with others in the field

APPENDIX C
Reporting the Findings of Action Research

Reporting Findings from Action Research

Communicating research findings

- There are many ways an action research project may be used to benefit students, school districts, and the educational community.
    - Often, results are used to leverage additional funding through grants, foundations, or private funding agencies.
    - Researchers share the information gleaned from their projects with the educational community by presenting to local groups, and to state and national conferences.
    - Results of research studies have been used to initiate changes through legislative bodies.
    - Many researchers publish their findings in a variety of publications, such as magazines, journals, newsletters, and media releases.
    - The results of research projects have been of interest to the general public and led to changes in local, state, and national organizations.
    - A few researchers establish their businesses based on the development of new procedures, processes, or products.
- Various methods for communicating results: Depends on the audience and purpose for dissemination
    - Brochures or posters
    - Conference presentations
    - Executive summaries
    - Media appearances
    - Memos
    - News releases
    - Personal discussions
    - Popular articles
    - Press conferences
    - Public meetings
    - Staff workshops
    - Technical professional papers and reports
- Potential stakeholders or audiences
    - There are a variety of potential audiences that may be interested in the results of action research.

- Be aware of a variety of perspectives when disseminating your findings.
- It is important to know and use optimal methods of communication to educate, contribute to, or enhance best practices.
- It is important to clarify which format would be most appropriate for a specific audience; writing style, tone, vocabulary, and technical format must be adjusted for each audience or stakeholder.
  - Advisory committees
  - Community groups
  - Funding agencies
  - Media
  - Political bodies
  - Potential clients
  - Professional organizations
  - Program administrators
  - Program service providers

APPENDIX D
Characteristics of High-Performing Organizations

Characteristics of High-Performing Organizations
(checklist or items for survey instrument)

_____ The work is challenging to all members of the organizations.

_____ The experiences provide opportunities for learning and growth.

_____ Workers have control over the factors that will lead to high performance.

_____ Continuous improvement is a common and shared belief by all workers.

_____ Relationships are positive and provide inspiration to all learners in the organization.

_____ Workers share a feeling of contribution to the outcomes of the organization and this feeling is supported by measurable data.

_____ Top level leadership supports the high performing quest.

_____ Motivation and/or reward are more intrinsic than extrinsic.

_____ Measurable results are shared and used to drive daily work habits.

_____ A common language of learning is shared, but more importantly demonstrated by all.

_____ Performance critiques are desired, not resented.

_____ Action research is a common practice of continuous improvement.

_____ Reflective practices are observable.

APPENDIX E

Benefits of Empowerment

Benefits of Empowerment

(On a scale from 1 to 10 (strongest), rate your organization. Use the assessment as basis of conversation as to the level of empowerment in the organization).

_____ Provides opportunities to surpass expected growth or expected outcomes.

_____ Expands level of interdependency thus allowing the expansion of organizational knowledge about itself and its business.

_____ Provides greatest impact on knowledge, skills and dispositions of each member of the organization.

_____ Enhances the likelihood of critical thinking, creativity and much needed innovation.

_____ Provides the most effective means of building organizational trust.

_____ Ensures alignment of organizational critical needs and potential contributions.

_____ Impacts leadership in that management becomes a support rather than a control.

APPENDIX F
Identifying Barriers to Empowerment

Identifying Barriers to Empowerment
(Checklist for Reflection)

_____ The organization has fixed methods and procedures that are inflexible.

_____ The organization lacks necessary resources to complete the tasks effectively.

_____ The organization lacks an adequate professional development program.

_____ The professional development program is not properly aligned with desired outcomes.

_____ The culture of the organization is one that penalizes and discourages rather than encourages risk taking.

_____ There is a lack of alignment in goals and priorities especially across the system.

_____ Desired direction is vague and lacks support.

_____ Staffing is not adequate and not aligned to determined needs.

_____ Structures do not allow for conversations and dialogue about learning.

_____ Incentives create more competition than collaboration.

_____ There is not a full environment of trust among the learners at all levels.

_____ Individuals in the organization do not want the responsibilities and/or the accountability associated with empowerment.

_____ Individuals in the organization lack integrity and honesty.

_____ Individuals have a misconception of what indicates a culture of empowerment.

_____ Roles and responsibilities are poorly defined in the organization.

_____ Personal gain is valued more than organizational growth.

_____ The work ethic is more of survival than excelling.

_____ Experience is low and impacts the ability to assign responsibilities.

_____ Quality is seen as the word of the day and not one of continuous improvement.

_____ Data from a 360-degree information gathering is rarely used.

_____ Members of the organization are not self-directing by nature.

_____ Leaders in the organization do not seek out and utilize talents of the individuals.

_____ Leaders do not understand the components of effectiveness.

_____ Leaders are not nurturing by nature.

_____ Win-win agreements are not practiced in the organization.

_____ There is a lack of systematic operations in the organization.

_____ Policies and procedures do not support a value of collaboration.

APPENDIX G
Checklist for Leading Organizational Transformation

Checklist for Leading the Transformation of an Organization

_____ Study and become an expert in future trends.

_____ Study and become an expert in systems operations and analyses.

_____ Read current research in the field of learning cultures.

_____ Gains skills in a leadership style that foster cultural growth.

_____ Expand your personal and professional experiences.

_____ Understand change and its consequences as well as its benefits.

_____ Be emphatic about building competencies in your employees.

_____ Create, contribute and develop strong support networks for dealing with issues.

_____ Set personal mastery as a priority.

_____ Accept and promote self-efficacy and collective efficacy.

_____ Align professional development with current needs and anticipated future needs.

_____ Remember that you have a responsibility to those in your organization to practice behaviors that support the cultural development of all stakeholders.

_____ Demonstrate a continuous passion for performance.

APPENDIX H
Critical Attributes of 21st Century Education

Critical Attributes of 21st Century Education

- Lifelong Learning
- Globalization Global Classrooms
- 21st Century Skills
- Rigorous and Real World
- Adapting to and Creating Constant Personal and Social Change
- Student-Centered
- Technologies & Multimedia
- Integrated and Interdisciplinary

APPENDIX I
Multiple Literacies for the 21st Century

Multiple Literacies for the 21st Century

The Arts and Creativity

Financial Literacy
Project Based &
Research-Driven

Ecoliteracy

Media Literacy

Cyberliteracy

Social/Emotional Literacies

Physical Fitness and
Health Literacies

Globalization &
Multicultural
Literacy

APPENDIX J
Needs Assessment Checklist

Needs Assessment Checklist

1. ____ Define the purpose of the needs assessment (What)

2. ____ Develop timeline with milestones (When)

3. ____ Identify the population (Who)

4. ____ Determine what data you need to collect/analyze

5. ____ Design a survey instrument (How)

6. ____ Communicate initiative to targeted population

7. ____ Distribute survey/collect data

8. ____ Analyze data and perform benefit/cost analysis

9. ____ Develop strategies to address prioritized needs

10. ____ Develop implementation plan(s) for strategies

11. ____ Establish a Quality Assurance process (PDCA)

APPENDIX K
Needs Assessment Summary

Needs Assessment Summary

Identified Needs	School Improvement Plan Linkage	Impact on Goals (H, M, L)	Overall LOI (1–5 highest)

APPENDIX L
Benefit/Cost Analysis

Benefit/Cost Analysis

Benefits:

Benefit/ Quantified	Year 1	Year 2	Year 3	Total
Total Cumulative: Present Value*:				

Costs:

Cost/Quantified	Year 1	Year 2	Year 3	Total
Total Cumulative: Present Value*:				

- Formula for calculating Present Value (PV) equals Future Value divided by $(1 + i)^n$, where i is the interest rate and n is the timeframe of the project analysis.

- **Total Benefits (Present Value) –Total Costs (Present Value) = Net Present Value**

About the Authors

John D. Balls, B.A., M.S., M.B.A., M.A.,

is a former executive of a Fortune 100 company and a retired educator. He was a teacher, a chairperson of school leadership team and has served as a high school principal in an Early College, an innovative program partially funded by the Bill and Melinda Gates Foundation. He currently is a business partner in a chain of restaurants. He is the co-author of a book on e-business, enterprise resource planning (ERP) and transforming the business enterprise, *E-Business and ERP*. He also co-authored a textbook on education reform, *Rethink, Rebuild, Rebound: A Framework for Shared Responsibility and Accountability in Education*. He has been a guest speaker at a number of business and education forums on the topics of organizational & operational design, change management and high performance teams. He lives in Charlotte, North Carolina with his wife, Greta.

A. Douglas Eury, B.S., M.Ed., Ed.S., Ed.D.,

is the Dean for the School of Education at Gardner-Webb University in Boiling Springs, NC. He also serves as the director of doctoral studies as well as director for the Center for Innovative Leadership Development. His experience includes 33 years of service as a public school educator in the state of North Carolina. He spent 17 years as a classroom teacher and coach; the remainder of his tenure consisted of administrative experience at the secondary level. He also co-authored a textbook on education reform, *Rethink, Rebuild, Rebound: A Framework for Shared Responsibility and Accountability in Education*. He lives in Shelby, North Carolina with his wife, Janet.

Jane C. King, B.S., M.S., Ed.S., Ed.D.,

provides instructional balance to this team of authors. Her lifelong career in education encompasses teaching, supervising, administration, as well as her own personal learning. Her passion for excellence in teaching and learning follows her throughout her career. She has taught students at all levels of education which gives her a unique view of student needs. In addition, she has taught learning disabled students and she has spent time as a Director of Exceptional Children's Programs for a local public school district. She has held positions as teacher, principal, director and associate superintendent in public schools. Dr. King has a passion for quality teaching and learning and has spent the past years working as an assistant professor at Gardner-Webb University and as an instructional coach in early college high schools. She has a great love for learning and for those who are involved in the process. Helping teachers and administrators know and understand quality curriculum and instruction provides focus for her most recent work. She also co-authored a textbook on education reform, *Rethink, Rebuild, Rebound: A Framework for Shared Responsibility and Accountability in Education*. She lives in Kings Mountain, NC with her husband, Jerry.